Writers and Miners

Writers and Miners

Activism and Imagery in America

David C. Duke

The University Press of Kentucky

Publication of this volume was made possible in part by financial assistance from The West Virginia Humanities Council, a state program of the National Endowment for the Humanities.

West Virginia Humanities Council

Scholarly publisher for the Commonwealth,
serving Bellarmine University, Berea College, Centre
College of Kentucky, Eastern Kentucky University,
The Filson Historical Society, Georgetown College,
Kentucky Historical Society, Kentucky State University,
Morehead State University, Murray State University,
Northern Kentucky University, Transylvania University,
University of Kentucky, University of Louisville,
and Western Kentucky University.

Editorial and Sales Offices: The University Press of Kentucky
663 South Limestone Street, Lexington, Kentucky 40508-4008

06 05 04 03 02 5 4 3 2 1

Library of Congress Cataloging-in-Publication Data

Duke, David C.
Writers and miners : activism and imagery in America / David C. Duke.
p. cm.
Includes bibliographical references (p.) and index.
ISBN 0-8131-2237-6 (cloth : alk. paper)
1. American literature—History and criticism. 2. Coal miners in literature. 3. Coal mines and mining in literature. 4. Mines and mineral resources in literature. I. Title.
PS173.C63 D85 2002
810.9'352622—dc21
2002009426

This book is printed on acid-free recycled paper meeting
the requirements of the American National Standard
for Permanence in Paper for Printed Library Materials.

Manufactured in the United States of America.

As always, for Rainey and Nathan with love
and Stuart Thomas and Donna Spindel,
who have taught all of us the meaning of courage

This is as strange a maze as e'er men trod;
And there is in this business more than nature
Was ever conduct of: some oracle
Must rectify our knowledge

–William Shakespeare, *The Tempest*

Contents

Acknowledgments

A number of colleagues provided me with generous assistance in completing this book. Although all cannot be mentioned, a special few must be recognized. Steve and Maria Carmen Riddel, Dan Holbrook, Lenney Deutsch, Bill Palmer, Terry Dennis, Barbara Smith, Ron Lewis, Shirley Lumpkin, Betsy Nordeen, Michael Galgano, and Marat Moore have taken time from their busy careers to help on numerous occasions. I am extremely fortunate that David Cobb, who is young enough to be a son but editorially wise enough to be a father, has been my editor at the University Press of Kentucky. His creativity and patience are remarkable. My dear friend Donna Spindel has read and reread the manuscript far too many times, and I hope she realizes how deeply I appreciate her support and assistance. Finally, if my son Nathan has always been willing to share his love and knowledge of films with me during the course of this project, my wife Rainey has provided so many different kinds of assistance that I scarcely know where to begin. She has given so generously of her analytical, editorial, and interpretive abilities while meeting the demands of her own career in the English Department at Marshall University that there is simply no way for me to acknowledge her contributions. Whereas the assistance of these friends and colleagues has immeasurably improved this book, I alone must bear the responsibility for its shortcomings.

Introduction

Coal mining as an industry and way of life today is a far cry from its heyday early in the twentieth century. Deserted tipples, rusting equipment, and abandoned mining communities are sharp reminders of a bygone era. The once-powerful United Mine Workers of America is a scaled-down version of its former self; the name of its president is scarcely known beyond the country's mining regions. Strikes against the A.T. Massey Coal Group and the Pittston Coal Company still make national news, but they pale in comparison to the strikes of the Lewis era in the 1940s and 1950s. Young men from Ohio, Indiana, Illinois, Pennsylvania, and West Virginia who earlier would have sought union jobs in mines close to home now look for other kinds of work; well over 30 percent of the bituminous coal produced in the country is now dug in nonunion mines in the West. Ironically, as the coal mining industry in America is significantly shrinking in size, images of the mining life still loom large in popular culture.

Take for example John Grisham's 1991 best-selling novel, *The Firm,* in which the main character, Mitchell Y. McDeere, is from a coal mining family. On page one Grisham writes that McDeere "had the brains, the ambition, the good looks. And he was hungry; with his background, he had to be." Except for a brief early mention that McDeere's father had been killed in a coal mine and a later passage describing how coal dust had altered his brother's complexion, there is no other mention of mining in the novel. This is not surprising. By associating his character with coal in a single sentence, Grisham created the desired impression. Life in the mines was hard, no one in his right mind would want to pursue it, and those who managed to escape were therefore highly motivated to succeed. The image is not entirely negative, for McDeere was fifth in his graduating class at Harvard, and he certainly managed, despite his background, to rise to the top. His harsh beginnings apparently complemented his intelligence and provided him with a drive, cunning, determination, and intensity that helped outwit the competition.[1]

Elmore Leonard in his two most recent novels, *Pronto* and *Riding the Rap,* also turned to the Kentucky coalfields as the birthplace for major characters. Federal Marshal Raylan Givens is a modern-day Wild West prototype with his Stetson, cowboy boots, courteous demeanor, and sharpshooting skills. He is a very awkward fit in Italy, where the first of the novels takes place, and later amidst the glitz of south Florida, but his courage, persistence, and acute sense of right and wrong soon seem more important than his odd appearance. Like a Hemingway hero, Givens constantly shows grace under pressure, a quality that, he explains to a young punk intent on killing him, grew out of his own young life in Harlan County, Kentucky. "I've worked deep mines, wildcat mines, I've worked for strip operators, and I've sat out over a year on strike and seen company gun thugs shoot up the houses of miners that spoke out," he informs the startled hoodlum. "They killed an uncle of mine was living with us, my mother's brother, and they killed a friend of mine I played football with in high school," he continues. "This was in a coal camp town called Evarts in Harlan County, Kentucky, near to twenty years ago. You understand what I'm saying? Even before I entered the Marshals Service and trained to be a dead shot, I'd seen people kill one another and learned to be ready in case I saw a bad situation coming toward me."[2] Bad situations were inevitable in Givens's world, but mobsters in Florida and Italy were no worse than the gun thugs he knew while growing up in Eastern Kentucky. Like McDeere, his coal mining past had helped prepare him for the present.

The ability to face danger was not the only important lesson that Givens had learned growing up in the coalfields. In *Riding the Rap,* he stops himself from breaking into a house without a warrant when he remembers how gun thugs, searching for his uncle, had pushed his mother aside and entered the family's house despite her rebuke: "You don't walk into a person's home 'less you're invited. Even you people must believe that. You have homes don't you? Wives and mothers keeping house?"[3] It was also his mother who refused to allow Givens to work for a strip miner in the area and who finally decided to leave Harlan County altogether. After her brother was shot and killed during a strike and her husband died from black lung, she simply said "That's enough" and moved the family to Detroit, where Givens went to college and became a Marshal.[4]

Grisham and Leonard juxtaposed the negative and positive modes of mining life to develop their characters. McDeere and Givens grew up in coal mining regions surrounded by hardships and dangers, but they had supportive families who nurtured their morality and encouraged levelheadedness. These qualities enabled each character to prevail in a Hobbesian world without totally becoming a part of it. References to class violence, harsh working conditions, black lung, death in the mines, strikes, and the vulnerability of life in a company town were all intended to support the Givens family's abrupt and final departure from Kentucky. Grisham and Leonard made doubly sure that, just as Thomas Wolfe could not go home, there was no turning back for McDeere or Givens. They had not grown up in just any mining community, but in Harlan County, Kentucky. Harlan County in the popular mind is as closely tied to ugly industrial violence as are urban areas to drug-related violence today. In the early 1950s Robert E. Lee Prewitt escapes from a coal mining background in Harlan County into the peacetime army in James Jones's *From Here to Eternity.* "Why the hell do you think I got in the Army? Because I didnt want to sweat my heart and pride out in a goddam coalmine all my life."[5] Little had changed by the 1990s, and who would disagree that McDeere and Givens must press on in their own worlds rather than return to the ones they had left behind.

My own initial interest in coal miners and mining also had a great deal to do with images. Unlike McDeere and Givens, however, my early life in middle Tennessee was untouched by mining lore, though I was subject to my father's view of miners. His favorite film was *How Green Was My Valley* (1941), based on the best-selling novel by Richard Llewellyn, but his enjoyment of the saga of a Welsh mining family was offset by his intense dislike for John L. Lewis and the United Mine Workers. He also believed that the annual thumping of the Vanderbilt football team by the University of Tennessee was accomplished only because Tennessee had "a gang of coal miners playing for them." My own limited image of miners and mining families was primarily shaped by reading Emile Zola's *Germinal.* In the 1970s I moved to West Virginia, where I had a colleague and friend who had grown up in the southern West Virginia coalfields. From her I learned that her father often came home from the night shift so energized that, after making sure that his eleven children were all safely tucked in their beds, he checked their homework and school papers before going to sleep. Big John Sizemore was proud of where he lived and what he did, pleased that some of his sons followed him into the mine. Although he lacked the engineering skills to capture management's attention, as a foreman he loved to bring blueprints of the mine home and pore over them to design better ways of getting coal to the surface.[6] This was not my image of a coal miner and his family; nor was it an image in the popular mind.

I turned to this project not to enlarge my understanding of miners and the mining community but to sort out those images of the mining life so firmly fixed in our culture today. Since the late–nineteenth century, writers and intellectuals have interacted with and written about coal mining, miners, and the people of coal mining communities; and the majority of these writers, whether as activists or authors, have viewed mining people as "the other," as objects waiting to be defined rather than subjects capable of defining themselves. Tzvetan Todorov and Edward Said both show that writers and intellectuals not only use "the other" to define themselves but also to limit the subjectivity of groups different from them.[7] Postcolonial and feminist critics also argue how western intellectuals, both male and female, assume much like Jean Paul Sartre that "there is always some way of understanding an idiot, a child, a primitive man or a foreigner *if one has sufficient information.*"[8] This approach suggests the psychological transparency of the writer/intellectual, allowing him or her to speak for another person or group without acknowledging his or her own cultural assumptions.[9] Most writers in this study invoke just such an essentialist agenda while claiming to describe, act for, or speak for mining people. Just as Robert F. Berkhofer shows how the idea of the American Indian was created by Caucasians, and Chandra Mohanty suggests that well-meaning western feminists view women in other parts of the world as "ourselves undressed," many of the writers and intellectuals in this study envision mining people as ourselves with dirty faces, "others" who would rather be more like us.[10]

Given the limitations of our own perspectives, encounters with different individuals or groups involve varying degrees of domestication and appropriation. In the extreme, "the other" becomes an object of our creation; there is little equality in encounters between us and them. "The other" lacks a voice, and monological description rather than dialogical discourse is the result. Todorov describes nondialogical cultural encounters in the Americas during the sixteenth century: "Spanish authors speak well of the Indians, but with very few exceptions they do not speak to the Indians. Now, it is only speaking to the other (not giving orders but engaging in a dialogue) that I can acknowledge him as subject, comparable to what I am myself."[11]

The work of Todorov and Said applies in different but pertinent ways to encounters between American writers and coal miners. The "otherness" of class, race, ethnicity, professionalism, location, and culture often served as barriers between writers and the people they were trying to help or creatively engage. Many of the writers who wrote about miners admired the people they were working with or writing about; they especially praised their courage, work ethic, and endurance. But even in the glow of their admiration, the writers had a tendency to speak about rather than to the mining community. According to Abdul R. JanMohamed, in a postcolonial analogy, if the European "assumes that he and the Other are essentially identical, then he would tend to ignore the significant divergences and to judge the Other according to his own cultural values. If, on the other hand, he assumes that the Other is irremediably different, then he would have little incentive to adopt the viewpoint of that alterity: he would again tend to turn to the security of his own cultural perspective."[12] Like non-western people, mining folk become marionettes whose lives tell us more about the puppeteer than the puppet. The underground workplace with its images of dirt, darkness, and danger is so overwhelming that the job rather than the person becomes the defining motif. Said described a similar phenomenon when he wrote that "an Oriental man was first an Oriental and only second a man."[13] Miners too become one-dimensional social types defined by what they do rather than who they are. They are firstly miners and secondly human beings.

When writers assume a gloomy mining life, they fail to see how their craft shapes their activism and imaginative ambitions. All writers, especially those who hope to make a living through their work, always look for new themes to explore or new inspirations for their famished muses. American writers in particular search for copy through "the cult of experience" or by sifting through the raw materials of everyday life.[14] David S. Reynolds argues that the literary giants of the American Renaissance—Melville, Poe, Whitman, Hawthorne, Emerson, Thoreau, and Dickinson—found much of their inspiration through the popular writing and culture of their era.[15] Eric J. Leed suggests travel as a source of literary inspiration.[16] Robert Penn Warren believed that most writers store their observations and experiences in a kind of mental warehouse that they draw on unexpectedly in unpredictable ways.[17] John Dos Passos, for example, described how his trip to Harlan County helped him to write not only about Glen Spottswood's activities there but also about his relationship with the Communist Party. "I wouldn't have known about conditions in Harlan County or what was behind either Defense Committee if I hadn't been through those experiences," he explained. "I wouldn't have known how to describe them. Of course, I think you always have to have a little seed of personal experience, although it's often a very small seed, to produce the real verisimilitude, which is what you are looking for."[18] Finally, in a recent issue of the *New York Times Book Review,* Mary Gordon offers a definition of the novel that is similar to that of Dos Passos: "The novel—all prose fiction for that matter—is the love child of two deeply incompatible parents. It has journalism for a father, poetry for a mother."[19] Here then is a reference to a widespread belief—one not unique to the writers who ventured into the coalfields—that one can find the great work amidst the turmoil of the great cause.

Activists usually bring a personal and political agenda with them to the causes that they serve; writer/activists are no exception. Their personal agenda is often related to their craft, and more often than not they intend to create while helping others. Even among the most committed writer/activists, these ideological and artistic intentions can create artificial barriers of "otherness" between the helpers and those being helped. Any attempt to explore the interaction between writers and miners is, in effect, an effort to analyze the political and creative tensions of a cultural encounter that focuses on two entirely different ways of life.

Through their conceptual and creative work, Stephen Crane and Jack Reese exemplify these two ways of life and define the perimeters of this study. The two symbolize the differences between those who stereotyped miners and those who did not. They also signify another major difference as well. Ironically, most writer/activists as well as most of those whose creative impulses take center stage actually never entered a mine. Crane and Reese did. *McClures'* magazine commissioned Crane and an artist friend, Corwin Linson, to visit a coal mine in Scranton, Pennsylvania, in June 1894. Crane was to use his considerable talents to write about the experience. Reese needed no special commission to enter a mine. He dug coal for a living.

Crane's article "In the Depths of a Coal Mine" was published in *McClures'* in 1894 and later carried by a number of newspapers. The extent to which Crane's manuscript was edited is unclear, but Linson believed that *McClures'* editorial staff deleted material offensive to business interests.[20] Crane hoped to describe an experience both eerie and intriguing. The finished product reads like a tone poem suggesting entry into Plato's cave. Crane's images of the descent into the earth imply the uncanny rather than the fantastic.[21] Mining work is transformed by his flair for the dramatic into a "forbidding and mystic calling." Riding an elevator into the mine, Crane muses, he "might as well have been tumbling among the stars." At the bottom he finds "an inscrutable darkness," a "tangible loneliness." As the first miners he sees "turned their heads to regard our tramping party, their eye-balls and teeth shone white as bleached bones. It was like the grinning of two skulls there in the shadows." Crane could be "confronting terrible specters" instead of working people.[22]

He sees another group of miners who happen to be stretched out on the ground resting. As they "up-reared" to stare at him, Crane was reminded of a resurrection, not of Christians but of figures with "ghoul-like movements, mysterious figures robed in enormous shadows." Like Jules Verne's undersea setting in *Twenty Thousand Leagues Under the Sea,* this dark environment was a different and multifarious world where, unbelievably, fungus could grow "white as a druid's beard."[23]

Once underground, Crane quickly loses all sense of time, direction, and distance. He finds himself in a battle zone. The titans have regained control of the earth. The miners are mere mortals engaging in ceaseless combat with nature. They "have carried the war into places where nature has the strength of a million giants. Sometimes their enemy becomes exasperated and snuffs out ten, twenty, thirty lives."[24]

The breaker boys in this surreal environment are both a "wonder and a terror," more like "New York gamins" or "imps" than working-class boys.

Their dreams of the future intrigued and puzzled Crane. "And before them always is the hope of one day getting to be door-boys, down in the mines and, later, mule boys. And yet later laborers and helpers. Finally when they have grown to be great big men they may become miners, real miners," he emphasizes, "and go down and get 'squeezed,' or perhaps escape to a shattered old man's estate with a mere 'miner's asthma.' They are very ambitious."[25] Crane pities the breaker boys and writes with condescension of their limited aspirations. His article reflects the difficulty that many writers have had in dealing with the coal mining experience. From their middle-class perspectives no worker should spend a lifetime digging coal. The breaker boys knew no better. How else could Crane explain their limited aspirations? How else could they and anyone else committed to mining coal for a living be viewed in any way except as "the other"?

For writer Jack Reese, who supported himself with a shovel rather than a pen, the distance between the world of his imagination and the world in which he lived was shorter than it was for Crane. Toward the end of his life he wrote about his work as a coal miner in what might be called a nonfictional novel, *Grubbing the Bowels of the Earth.* Reese tells the reader that he uses fictionalized names and "added some fiction to make it more interesting." His stories and recollections of life in the coalfields of southwestern Pennsylvania during the early and mid–twentieth century are neither exceptional nor particularly heroic. He is content to describe the work, the lack of job security, his commitment to the United Mine Workers, his thoughts on what it meant to be a miner's wife, and other related topics. Reese was adamant that he liked his work and had no regrets. "Why did I choose the life of a miner? I like to grub the soil, I like to see things grow. I like to see people succeed and reap the profits of their work honestly," he explained. "When my uncle took me in the mine when I was twelve years old I realized this was the kind of work I wanted to do." Reese's ambitions are different from those envisioned by Crane, and, as his novel suggests, he was capable of interpreting his own life's experiences.[26]

All of the writers in this study, professional and nonprofessional, were engaging in a discourse about popular perceptions of coal mining and the mining life. For reasons that will never be fully understood, these writers were willing to put their views before the public. Here they differed not only from most of their fellow human beings but also from the uniquely anarchistic character, Arkady Volchak, in Bruce Chatwin's *The Songlines.* An Australian citizen of Cossack origins, Volchak is infatuated with the idea of the Dreamtimes in which the first inhabitants of the country engage in walk-abouts to link past to present. Chatwin and Volchak both want to understand Dreamtimes, but their interests differ in one important way. As an author, Chatwin wants to learn for creativity's sake, but Volchak "began to take note of everything he saw or heard, not for publication but to satisfy his own curiosity."[27] Most of us are like Volchak. We explore our world because we are curious. The subjects of this study, like Chatwin, are different. A few became directly involved in the affairs of the mining community, but all wrote about coal mining and miners. In this way they added an important dimension to a way of life that continues to repel as strongly as it attracts.

Chapter 1

Idiosyncratic Activism while Assisting "The Other"

In the late summer of 1889 two men of different background, class, and age found themselves in Spring Valley, a small, largely immigrant coal town on the banks of the Illinois River. John Mitchell, a nineteen-year-old itinerant coal miner of Welsh ancestry, had just returned from several years of wandering and working throughout the mining West. He had gotten a job in one of the local mines in 1888 but, along with the other miners, lost it when the Spring Valley Coal Company locked out its workers to drive down their wages. That same summer a forty-two-year-old patrician journalist/reformer perpetually in search of copy, Henry Demarest Lloyd, traveled to Spring Valley from Rock Island, Illinois, where he had delivered a Labor Day address to trades unionists. Although these two men did not meet that summer, their lives dramatically intersected thirteen years later in what is still regarded as one of the most important events in American labor history—the 1902 Anthracite Coal Strike. By 1902 Mitchell was the youthful head of the United Mine Workers of America (UMWA) and Lloyd was nearing the end of a career battling the spread of corporate monopoly. Lloyd found not only copy but a cause in Spring Valley, and from then until his death in 1903, he sustained an interest in coal mining and the problems of miners. Still, Lloyd always saw miners as an abstract "other" whose causes seemed dwarfed by his own consuming fear that the nation's fuel and industrial output were falling under the monopolistic control of giant corporations.

Born in 1849, Lloyd grew up with a family of seven in an atmosphere of piety and genteel poverty. His father was an inadequate provider as a Dutch Reform minister and later as a bookseller in New York. Lloyd attended public school in New York City and entered Columbia College in 1862 as a scholarship student. By 1869 he had completed Columbia Law School and passed the New York bar exam at age twenty. After working as a field agent for the American Free Trade League, in 1872, he became the night editor of the *Chi-*

cago Tribune. By the time he left the paper in 1885 he was its chief editorial writer. Shortly after arriving in Chicago, Lloyd married Jessie Bross, the daughter of one of Chicago's elite and quarter owner of the *Tribune.* The Lloyds divided their time between a spacious home in Winnetka, Illinois, a suburb of Chicago, and a summer home in Rhode Island. When he left the *Tribune,* Lloyd never again held a full-time job. Instead he divided his time between writing and supporting the various reforms that interested him.

An eclectic intellectual, Lloyd was familiar with the works of Carlyle, Emerson, the English Utilitarians, Ruskin, Cobban, and the Manchester School of Economists.[1] He believed that the unchecked growth of monopolistic capitalism was an insidious development that put the nation in danger. The trouble was that the American people failed to recognize the dangers all around them. In 1881, he laid the cornerstone for the muckraking era by publishing "The Story of a Great Monopoly" in *Atlantic Monthly,* an article he hoped would awaken his fellow citizens. Thirteen years later in his monumental condemnation of Standard Oil, *Wealth Against Commonwealth,* he argued that Western Civilization itself was in danger of being destroyed from above rather than below because of monopolistic excesses. "Our great money-makers have sprung in one generation into seats of power kings do not know."[2]

Although he is best remembered for his attacks on Standard Oil, Lloyd was interested in challenging all forms of monopoly, including the growing control by the railroads of the bituminous and anthracite coalfields. Since they depended on transportation outlets for their mined coal, the coal corporations were increasingly coming under the control of a relatively small number of railroads. To maximize profits, the railroads limited production. This in turn kept the price of coal artificially high and, in the process, increased the unemployment of miners. To observe this process in operation, Lloyd journeyed to Spring Valley to see for himself the suffering that until then he had only read about.

Lloyd came to Spring Valley with well-formulated ideas about the operating practices of corporate monopolies and, once there, quickly confirmed his suspicions. The Chicago and Northwestern Railway Company controlled three dummy corporations: the Spring Valley Coal Company, the Town Site Company, and the Northwest Fuel Company of St. Paul, all of which dominated the town and its industry. In December 1888 the Spring Valley Coal Company laid off approximately one-third of its workforce without warning. Four months later the remaining miners lost their jobs as well because the company hoped to increase future profits through decreased production. It was a lockout on the part of management or, as Lloyd later claimed, a strike of millionaires against miners. When the mines shut down, so did the company store. The miners then formed a relief committee under the direction of the

National Progressive Union of Miners. Eventually in late August 1889, the director of the Chicago and Northwestern Railway offered to reopen the mines on its own terms. Maintenance work would increase and three miners instead of two would share each working area in the mine. These two changes alone reduced by almost half the pre-lockout wage scale. To make matters worse, the miners were told to sign individual contracts to eliminate collective bargaining. The lockout became a strike when the miners countered with a union contract of their own. Lloyd arrived in Spring Valley shortly after the strike began. He was searching for a story to illustrate the perils of uncontrolled monopoly. Instead he found a cause, but one that envisioned the miners as pawns in a much larger struggle.[3]

Shortly before coming to the mining town he had corresponded with John F. Power, a Roman Catholic priest and supporter of the miners who lived in Spring Valley. The clergyman now provided Lloyd with additional information about the strike as well as introductions into the mining community. It took little urging on Power's part for Lloyd to assume an active role. Soon after arriving, he personally financed provisions for destitute families including medicines, food, and children's shoes.[4] He also tried to raise funds outside the community for the strikers.[5] Lloyd lobbied the National Progressive Union of Miners to take a more active role by inviting its head, John McBride, to visit Spring Valley to lend the strikers moral support.[6] As his familiarity with the strikers increased, he also took depositions from them that documented the company's inhumane treatment of its employees.[7] In mid-October he went to Chicago to lobby the city's newspapers to take a more even-handed approach in reporting the strike, and, as he wrote to Father Power, he believed the visit did some good.[8]

In spite of Lloyd's optimism, neither his nor Power's efforts succeeded. In late October, management offered to increase slightly the miners' wages and to decrease minimally the unpaid maintenance work in the mines. The company also insisted that all future contracts would have to be individually signed, and confirmed its hard-line position by advertising for miners willing to work under these terms. Facing a winter with no income, two weeks later the miners voted to return to work. Lloyd understood and sympathized with the defeated miners, but from his perspective far more had been lost than a strike. "If the business men and other 'middle class' people of Spring Valley have not the wit, and virtue and bravery to see, feel, and say . . . that the miners' cause is their own, and that the miners have been treated throughout with cruelty and duplicity, they will deserve their fate."[9] It would be a fate that Lloyd associated with the growth of corporate monopolies capable of destroying communities much larger than Spring Valley.

Lloyd thought that, unlike the miners and their spokesmen, he saw the larger picture and thus believed that middle-class intellectuals like himself could do more for working people's causes than the workers themselves. Toward the end of the Spring Valley Strike, for example, he was concerned because miners from the surrounding region intended to march on the town to show solidarity with their striking brothers. He wrote to Father Power suggesting that "the miners in Penn., LaSalle should be dissuaded from marching to S.V.., but their attentions and energies should be directed to peaceful means of getting . . . [the] new men to give up work by visiting them, explaining the state of affairs, and promising them support." If Power agreed with him, "telegrams should be sent Scaife, McBride and all other leaders to tell the miners elsewhere to keep away." Lloyd ended the letter by announcing that in a couple of days he intended to come to the very spot that he had just warned the outside miners to avoid. "Do you know of any place near the center where I could get a comfortable bedroom with a fire, where I could work?" he wrote.[10] The work Lloyd had in mind was his book *A Strike of Millionaires against Miners,* which he obviously believed would do more for the miners than they could do for themselves. He would be their voice. Comfortable with the dignity of their suffering, he feared the unity of their anger.

A Strike of Millionaires against Miners (1890), which one critic has called the *Iliad* of the industrial revolution, was published the same year as Jacob Riis' *How the Other Half Lives* and sixteen years before Upton Sinclair's efforts to confront the nation with the problems of immigrant laborers in *The Jungle.*[11] Lloyd provides a straightforward analysis of the lockout and strike. He focuses on the suffering of the miners by noting their inadequate pay, their dangerous working conditions, and the terrible living conditions of their families. He anticipates the works of others by comparing mining to a kind of slavery. In providing this perspective, Lloyd hoped to offset the completely one-sided report of the state's Attorney General.[12] Most important, however, Lloyd issued a warning that he had reiterated throughout his career: "What has been done at Spring Valley is not an extreme case; it has simply been given monopolistic morals."[13] The events at Spring Valley were the tip of the iceberg. What had happened to the miners and their families was tragic, but what was happening to the country through the growth of monopolistic capitalism was worse. For Lloyd, the perfidy of the robber barons rather than the plight of the strikers was still the overriding concern.

In 1902 Lloyd was still emotionally and philosophically prepared to help the working classes as he had done at Spring Valley, but he was out of the country when the 1902 Anthracite Coal Strike began on May 9. There had been trouble in the anthracite fields since the later 1890s, when the United Mine Workers, fresh from its effective campaigns in the bituminous fields in the Midwest, refocused its organizing efforts on the hard coal regions of Pennsylvania.[14] Union campaigns in the East were especially difficult because of the diversity of the workforce and the power of the operators, who had built a coal trust dominated by railroads. An uneasy peace had settled over the anthracite fields since 1900, when the head of the Republican Party, Mark Hanna, intervened in a strike for fear that it would harm President McKinley's reelection campaign. Although the operators refused to recognize the miners' union, they grudgingly awarded their workers a 10 percent wage increase. In reality the settlement produced very little change. Wages were still deplorably low and the miners averaged only about three hundred dollars yearly. Moreover, the operators who paid their workers by the ton had gradually inched up the minimum tonnage to almost thirty-two hundred pounds by charging miners for impurities in the mined coal and by requiring them to fill railroad cars eighteen inches above the edges. Miners also had to pay high prices for powder, had to trade in company stores, pay monthly doctors' fees, and, perhaps most galling of all, work for companies that refused to recognize their union.

The strike of 1902 began when the operators refused to negotiate a new contract. They seemed even more determined not to surrender to pressure as they had done two years earlier. The miners were also better organized; eventually 150,000 answered their union's call to leave their workplaces. This time they demanded a 20 percent increase in wages; strict adherence to the twenty-four-hundred-pound ton; a checkweighman (a representative to insure the coal was fairly weighed) hired by themselves; semi-monthly wage payments; abolition of the company store, doctor's fees, and high powder prices; as well as the recognition of their union. The strike lasted six months as public sympathy increasingly shifted toward the miners. The intransigence of the operators was best symbolized by their spokesman, George F. Baer, who was also president of the Philadelphia and Reading Railroads. Baer arrogantly endorsed the use of the three-thousand-pound ton, of coal and iron police in the coalfields, and he vilified the miners, their leaders, and their union. Baer also added to the folklore of American labor history in his response to a letter admonishing him, on Christian grounds, to bring the strike to an end. He wrote that "the rights and interests of the laboring man will be protected and cared for—not by the labor agitators, but by the Christian men to whom God in His infinite wisdom has given the control of the property interests of the country, and upon the successful management of which so much depends."[15] This kind of blatant arrogance so dismayed President Roosevelt that he created an arbitration commission to try to end the strike. But Roosevelt was also moved by the fear that a continued strike might close industries down, and a long winter lay ahead for the American public. On October 23, the miners went back to work awaiting arbitration. Five months later in March 1903, the commission granted the miners a 10 percent wage increase, shortened their working day, and established a negotiating board to settle future disputes that might arise during the three-year term of the agreement. With no mention of management's formal recognition of the UMWA of America, the settlement was only a partial victory for the miners.

The strike was in its third month when Lloyd returned from a European tour. By early September of 1902, however, he was taking an interest in the ongoing struggle. He believed it to be the start of a huge effort by the financial elite to gain control over hard and soft coal mining areas in the United States. As always, the issue of monopoly sparked his anger; and, as always, he found no indication that the American public understood what was going on.[16] More than anything else it may have been a letter from his old comrade-in-arms of Spring Valley days, Father Power, that finally pulled him toward the striking workers by rekindling memories of their work together thirteen years earlier. "I think I must go to Pa. to see this other great strike of millionaires against miners," he wrote to Power in the middle of September. "You brought up John Mitchell. Will you give me a word of introduction to him?"[17]

Unlike his experience with the Spring Valley Strike, Lloyd would not be the only writer to help the miners in Pennsylvania. One of the many journalists and observers who gathered around the UMWA headquarters in Wilkes-Barre was Walter Weyl, another young writer who would play an active role in the strike, often alongside Lloyd. Weyl's involvement in the strike was circumstantial, since there was nothing in his background to suggest any interest in mining or miners.[18] The son of an immigrant father and American mother, Weyl and his five brothers grew up in Philadelphia where his mother had moved after his father's death. He finished high school at seventeen, won a scholarship to the Wharton School of the University of Pennsylvania, and eventually completed a Ph.D. in economics at the University of Pennsylvania.

For the next five years he traveled widely, worked briefly for the Bureau of Statistics, and conducted several statistical surveys for the United States Bureau of Labor.[19] The 1902 Anthracite Coal Strike would have been a great attraction for a young economist interested in public issues and still trying to focus his interests. Having little knowledge of the mining industry, Weyl possibly became involved in the strike for reasons similar to those that motivated young writers like Ernest Hemingway, E.E. Cummings, and John Dos Passos to find their way to Europe during the early stages of the First World War: for the reasons of both the experience offered and the excitement, it was an event they could not ignore.

Both Lloyd and Weyl intended to use their skills as writers to aid the striking miners. More fully than most of the other activists, they integrated their professional contributions into a worker-controlled organization. They gathered documents, collected testimony from the miners and their families about life and work in the coalfields, wrote statements for the press, and rebutted charges by the owners in ways that were helpful to Mitchell and his staff.[20] The two writers traveled with Mitchell on several occasions and advised him on ways of dealing with the operators, the press, and the public.[21] Throughout the late fall and into early winter of 1902, Weyl and Lloyd were frantically busy helping prepare the union's case before the arbitration commission.

When the hearings finally began, Lloyd and Weyl's primary responsibility was helping to select witnesses who would dramatize the difficulties of mining coal for a living and convince the commission of the need for a general wage increase. On December 3, one of Lloyd's witnesses testified. A miner's wife, she described the difficulty of holding together a family of seven on her husband's salary, which ranged from eighty-one cents to sixteen dollars every two weeks. When Lloyd met with her privately before the hearing, she was far more graphic in describing the family's destitution. She told Lloyd that she never bought more than one pound of meat at a time and boiled potatoes in lard to make them more palatable. In the presence of the commission, however, to Lloyd's dismay, she was far more circumspect, too proud to reveal the depth of her family's suffering. Lloyd had intended for pain rather than pride to come across in the hearing, but the witness, speaking for herself in front of others, obviously had no intention of becoming an object of their pity. In spite of everything, Lloyd still believed that her testimony was effective. In a letter to his wife he mentioned another witness he was convinced would bring a greater sense of drama to the hearing. His assessment proved to be correct. Andrew Chipie was the star witness of the hearing. Twelve-year-old Chipie revealed that after his father's death in a mining accident, the company promised his mother that she would not have to pay any rent. When Chipie went to work as a nine-year-old breaker boy to help his mother provide for four younger siblings, the company deducted his forty cents a day from the back rent that it now claimed his mother had failed to pay. From Lloyd's perspective this villainy outdid any of the events observed at Spring Valley.[22] The day after Chipie's testimony, an engineer who operated the cages in which men were carried in and out of the mines conveyed his own powerful message to the court. He explained that while dozens of lives depended on his alertness, he often had to work sixty hours without a break, in a state of complete exhaustion.[23] The commission and the public also learned why mining was considered among the most dangerous of all industrial jobs. Among the crippled miners who described their work-related injuries was an elderly miner who "at one time or another had been so burned, broken, cut and blinded, that he was literally a wreck."[24]

On February 9, 1903, Lloyd appeared before the commission and read from a fifty-one-page document that in many ways summarized the positions he had taken and the arguments he had been making for years. Lloyd pointed out that strikes like the present one did not have to happen. In future negotiations, he stressed, "rights" rather than "favors" had to be at the center of the bargaining process. Maintaining this level of cooperation would only be possible if the workers were represented in unions of their choice. The American public would welcome this because unions as representative bodies were far more democratic than any political or religious organization, and especially more so than corporate ones. Unions also symbolized a mature workforce since their membership was committed to accepting negotiated agreements. But union workers would also not abide any longer the imperious demands of management; negotiated compromises had to become one of the cornerstones of the new industrial order. Through their democratic bargaining, working people were not just defending their own interests but the rights of all Americans against the growth of corporate monopoly.[25]

Lloyd's testimony before the arbitration commission epitomizes both his and Weyl's activities during the 1902 strike. Neither had much contact with the miners or their families; they focused their energies on the union offices. Lloyd did interview miners in Wilkes-Barre soon after arriving in the coalfields, and he and Weyl met with others while preparing witnesses for the hearings before the arbitration commission.[26] The two writers were not, however, asked to testify because of their knowledge of how miners lived and worked. Instead, they would publicly articulate how the strike encompassed the needs of all working people. Their perspectives and presentation of the issues were better suited to challenging the owners' testimony, winning public support, and publicizing the needs of the union. Others would have to lend support to the miners in a more personal way since the dangers of corporate monopoly remained Lloyd's primary concern.

The strike was something of a turning point in Weyl's life: he benefitted from it far more than Lloyd.[27] From his strike-related activities, he had gained additional confidence as a researcher and as a writer. His first published articles were based on his observing an event in which he was participating. More importantly, Weyl gained valuable practical experience with a social issue that had interested him for some time. While working for the Bureau of Labor Statistics, he had developed an interest in the concerns of labor, but nothing that he had previously done came close in significance to his participation in the 1902 strike. Like the volunteer ambulance drivers in World War I, he had done something meaningful while participating in an extraordinary historical event. For the miners and their families the strike was, at best, a partial victory. But for Walter Weyl, the great strike of 1902 turned out to be an opportunity for personal growth. It allowed him to gain confidence in himself while working for others who, because of the magnitude of the event, remained abstractions in his youthful universe.

Unlike Weyl, Lloyd had participated in two strikes. In declining Mitchell's offer to reimburse him for expenses incurred during the 1902 strike, Lloyd explained that he was happy to have made a contribution. "I have had a very warm feeling for the miners ever since I saw their heroism and suffering at Spring Valley."[28] Despite these feelings, Lloyd, like so many others during the Progressive Era, was never comfortable with change originating from below. When Mitchell was securely in command during the 1902 strike, Lloyd never worried that things might get out of hand. But at Spring Valley he feared what might happen if miners outside the area joined the strike. His immediate concern was that a difficult situation might become explosive. Yet there was another issue as well. He had worked with miners, interviewed them, prepped them for their testimonies before the arbitration commission, and personally identified with the suffering of his "subterranean brothers."[29] But neither the striking miners at Spring Valley or in Pennsylvania nor the American people understood the full extent of their exploitation. In Lloyd's way of thinking, only a handful of intellectuals and reformers like himself fully appreciated the dangers of monopoly. Big business was slowly strangling the life from the Republic. Lloyd saw no signs that the situation was going to improve. It would be a gigantic task to awaken his somnambulant countrymen, especially for a writer; yet this remained his life's goal. His excursions into the mining regions in 1889 and 1902-03 were important parts of this effort to awaken the public. But Lloyd's involvement in the coal strikes was always secondary to what he ultimately hoped to accomplish. The demands of the miners were just, and Lloyd sympathized with them, but he believed their struggle must remain in the hands of the few who understood the larger issues. In maintaining this position, Lloyd was similar to some post–World War II intellectuals who likewise believed, Nobel Prize winner Czeslaw Milosz suggests, that they alone had a "broader understanding" of "historical processes." This belief is "ultimately, a pretext. What they are really after is to push others into the position of objects in order to look upon themselves as subjects."[30] With this unconscious motivation, Lloyd was always more interested in combating millionaires than in helping miners.

Two years after the end of the anthracite strike, the UMWA was again busily organizing. As the union tried to establish itself among the arroyos and bleak mountain landscapes of the Colorado coalfields, it found fewer men than in 1902, encountered more overt violence, and achieved not even the limited success of the Pennsylvania effort. For a short time, events in Colorado attracted as much national attention as had the great anthracite strike.

The Colorado walkout began as a labor dispute and then shifted to open warfare between the strikers and supporters of the mine owners, including the state militia.

When the UMWA traveled to the Colorado coalfields in 1903, Colorado claimed the nation's largest bituminous coal reserves—though the development of that resource was much slower than in the East and Midwest. By the 1870s and 1880s, as railroads reached the West, investors started to find substantial mining possibilities. In 1892, two of the major companies in the area, the Colorado Fuel Company and the Colorado Iron Company, merged to form the largest and most powerful coal and steel enterprise in the West: the Colorado Fuel and Iron Company. This new industrial conglomerate dominated the coalfields in southern Colorado as well as fields in the adjacent states of Wyoming and New Mexico. Eleven years after its founding, John D. Rockefeller acquired 40 percent of its stock. Representatives from the company's board of directors oversaw his investments. Among them was his son, John D. Rockefeller Jr., who, in turn, left the overall management of the company to local officials.[31]

The UMWA first entered the Colorado fields in the summer of 1903. Ten years later, having sustained more failures than successes in their piecemeal organizing efforts, the union announced in July 1913 its intention of organizing all of Colorado's coal miners. Although the miners wanted a 10 percent wage increase, an eight-hour day, a checkweighman, and the abolition of company stores, what they most hoped to win was union recognition. The strike that became known as the Great Coalfield War began on September 23, 1913. It quickly became violent.[32] Within a matter of days miners and mine guards were attacking one another, causing casualties on both sides. The violence quickly escalated into a small-scale war. On October 28, the state's beleaguered governor, Elias Ammons, ordered the National Guard into the strike zone; they were soon engaged in breaking up picket lines, arresting strikers, and deporting strike leaders—including the indomitable Mother Jones. By the end of 1913 there were over nineteen thousand men, women, and children, mostly immigrants, living in the union's tent colonies. The largest of these colonies was located on forty acres of land leased by the union near an important railroad spur at Ludlow. On the morning of April 20, 1914, sporadic fighting between strikers in the tent colony and the National Guard turned into a major battle. By evening it was over, the strikers routed and their tents burning. In addition to the ten men and one child killed in the shooting, two women and eleven children suffocated in one of the cellars dug beneath the strikers' tents to shelter their families from gunfire. The victims had crawled into the pit shortly after the firing began, and they suffocated when the tent above them caught fire. As news of the killing spread through the

Colorado coalfields, enraged miners attacked the National Guard and vandalized mine property along a forty-mile front. President Woodrow Wilson sent federal troops into the area on April 28, and by early May of 1914, the Great Coalfield War was over. For all practical purposes, so too was the strike; federal troops allowed scab miners to enter the mines. With management still refusing to negotiate, Wilson tried to save face by creating an arbitration commission. But this body had no power or importance other than to provide the UMWA with an institutional means of calling off the strike on December 7, 1914. The events since September had been disastrous for the miners: the strike was lost, the operators would not recognize the union, and they continued to exercise complete control of the Colorado coalfields.

The Colorado strike was far more dramatic and tragic than events twelve years earlier in the Pennsylvania coalfields. This helps explain why writers like Max Eastman, John Reed, George Creel, and Upton Sinclair were caught up in the turmoil. Yet they were attracted not so much by the strike itself or even the plight of the striking miners, but by the news of the Ludlow massacre, the increased violence in its aftermath, and Rockefeller's role in the episode. All four writers viewed the events in Colorado the way Lloyd had the 1902 strike, as part of much larger issues, and this understanding—as well as personal needs and ambitions—relegated the miners and their families into pawns caught up in abstract issues that transcended the events at Ludlow.

Eastman, Reed, and Creel arrived in Colorado within ten days of each other. They saw themselves as poets then, although none would be remembered for his verse. All three were political activists as interested in writing about their adventures as in experiencing them. Max Eastman arrived first with fellow socialist Frank Bohn. The pair had traveled together from New York, and they made it to the coalfields the day after the Ludlow tragedy. Born in 1883 in Canandaigua, New York, to parents who were both ordained ministers, Eastman grew up in an intellectually-charged, liberal atmosphere. By 1912 he considered himself a socialist, and that same year he abandoned his work toward a Ph.D. in philosophy at Columbia to become full-time editor of the most joyfully radical magazine of the era, *The Masses.* A year and a half before coming to Colorado, Eastman had observed striking miners in the Kanawha and New River coalfields in West Virginia, and he publicly attacked the Associated Press for failing to carry the strike news on its wire service.[33]

Although John Reed had never had contact with coal miners, it was inevitable that he too would find his way to Colorado upon learning of Ludlow. Born in 1887 in Portland, Oregon, to an upper-middle-class family, he graduated from Harvard and then settled in the Village, determined to be a writer. He was soon caught up in the same intellectual and political ferment that had so excited Eastman, and his participation in a strike by Patterson silk workers in the spring of 1913 hastened his movement towards the Left. That same year he jumped at the opportunity to see a revolution in progress. He went to Mexico, commissioned by *Metropolitan Magazine,* and rode with the Villastas, emerging with a reputation as one of the most promising young journalists in America. Pleased with his work in Mexico, *Metropolitan* then sent him to Colorado in the aftermath of the Ludlow massacre.[34]

Reed and Eastman were friends and had worked together on *The Masses.* As Eastman later recalled, shortly after Reed arrived the two of them "traveled the whole region in search, you might almost say, of a battle. I truly wanted to fight for Mrs. Toner and her babies [they had suffocated under the burning tent], and if necessary against all bourgeois society."[35] Finding no battles to join in this class war, they sought to aid the miners in less dramatic ways. Both made public appearances on behalf of the strikers during their stay in Colorado, but it was through their writing that they hoped to make their most important contribution.[36]

Eastman, as editor of *The Masses,* was in the best position to broadcast his anger. He later recalled, "Our May and June numbers [June and July], with their flame and blood-colored covers by John Sloan, cartoons by Art Young and Charles Winter, a decorated testimonial to '120 soldiers of the National Guard of Colorado for distinguished and heroic service in refusing to obey the command of their superior officer to entrain for Trinidad. . . ,' and my two articles, 'Class War in Colorado,' and 'The Nice Ladies of Trinidad,' were as proletarian-revolutionary as anything that had appeared in the United States."[37] Seething with anger, Eastman found many of the same tactics used earlier against striking miners in West Virginia now employed against their brothers in Colorado. Even though the counterattack by Colorado miners against mine property and the National Guard suggested class warfare, such conflict offered the only hope for the future. Eastman himself, who abhorred violence, would "find joy in going up the valleys to feed his eyesight upon tangles of gigantic machinery and ashes that had been the operating capital of the mines. It is no retribution, it is no remedy, but it proves that the power and the courage of action is here."[38] Eastman's articles were intended to shock, but by publishing them in *The Masses* he was preaching to the converted. His articles scarcely helped the miners, but may have had a therapeutic effect on him. Unable to find a battle in progress, he attacked the enemies of the working class as a writer rather than a soldier and moved on. There were other class-dragons to slay, and, like Lloyd, he saw the striking Colorado miners as part of a much larger struggle.

Reed's article "The Colorado War" differed in tone and approach from the kind of material collected in his first book, *Insurgent Mexico* (1914). In these brilliantly episodic vignettes, the author's persona held center stage even as he captured the color, feeling, and personality of a country in the midst of revolution. When he wrote about Ludlow, the facts themselves seemed far more important than his own activities. Reed hired a socialist labor organizer, Fred Boyd, to help him research the article, which, among other things, required a tedious sifting through numerous government reports.[39] In his Ludlow account, Reed concentrated on narrating what one critic calls "the rhythm of events."[40] His detailed, factual reporting prefigured the style he would use five years later in his masterpiece on the Bolshevik seizure of power, *Ten Days That Shook the World.* When he described the problems American working-class organizations faced, Reed, like Eastman, tried to suggest similarities of events in West Virginia with those in Colorado to verify the national scope of management's union-busting activities. In the future he would praise the radicalism of the Petrograd workers as they fought against the entrenched power of the state, but in Colorado it was the traditional values of the immigrant miners that most interested him. Neither socialists, anarchists, nor syndicalists, they "had come to America eager for the things that the Statue of Liberty in New York harbor seemed to promise them. They came from countries where law is almost divine, and here, they thought was a better law. They wanted to obey the laws."[41] Tragically, the law and the full power of the state had been used against them when they tried to fulfill their dreams by unionizing. Like Lloyd, Reed hoped his readers would recognize that Ludlow was not just another labor-management confrontation but the terrible residue of unchecked corporate might. From this perspective Reed's interest in workers was abstract: it hardly mattered what kind of work they did. The struggle of the miners in Colorado differed little from that of the silk workers in Patterson: most were immigrants, they were oppressed, and their actions were justified. Such abstraction is understandable since neither he nor Eastman were in Colorado long enough to see the miners as anything other than an exploited class whose mistreatment needed to be publicized. Although writing as an avowed anticommunist some years later, Eastman was always more analytical about his participation in the strike than Reed. He recalled one beautiful Sunday afternoon in Colorado in which he thought about his poetry more than the striking miners. In this moment of poetic insight he realized that in spite of his anger over injustice, he remained a spectator in the midst of someone else's battle. He could leave the strike at any time. The miners had to wait it out. For them it was not a matter of making a principled gesture but a genuine life-and-death struggle.[42] They remained just as much "the other" in his memories as they had been while he was in Colorado, and speaking for them was neither to endure nor even understand fully their suffering.

Unlike Eastman and Reed, thirty-seven-year-old George Creel had social and political connections in Colorado. He had worked, among a number of careers, as a muckraking journalist for newspapers in Kansas City and Denver, had written a book of verse, *Quatrains of Christ* (1907), and served as Denver's progressive police commissioner until his removal by the local machine in 1913. That same year he left Denver for New York, where he planned to pursue a career as a writer. Creel later claimed in his autobiography that the telegrams sent to him by Ludlow strike leaders led him back to Denver.[43] His statements to the local press on why he had returned suggest that the strike as well as personal concerns brought him home.[44] In fact, his most immediate concern was not the plight of the miners but the tax burden that Governor Ammons's use of the National Guard was imposing on local citizens.[45]

Far more knowledgeable about the political realities in Denver than either Eastman or Reed, Creel immediately put his experience to work in assisting the miners. He helped convene a mass meeting on Sunday, April 26, in front of the state capital during which he and others in support of the strikers spoke. In his speech Creel pilloried Rockefeller, corrupt state officials, and the destruction of the state's natural resources by greedy capitalists. He then warned the crowd what lay ahead. The people of Colorado and the nation would have to unify like the corporations or be swept into political and economic oblivion. As he neared the end of the speech, he repeated his belief that the crowd was there not just to support the miners but also because they feared for America's future. "If the miners are crushed today it means that Chase [commander of the National Guard] and his murderers will be used to crush you tomorrow."[46] As Creel spoke, State Senator Charles Thomas kept pulling at his trousers and urgently whispering: "George! George! For God's sake, tone it down."[47]

Even though Creel continued to speak over the next few weeks both in and outside of the city, Senator Thomas had little to fear about the former police commissioner's rhetoric. As reported by the press, his speeches were moderate, especially when the audience was white-collar. In fact, the more Creel spoke, the more his message was that of an aspiring politician rather than an aggrieved labor leader. While addressing Denver's City Club, for example, he told his audience of businessmen and professionals that he was not taking sides and that he was tired of the public having to foot the cost of the strike. In mid-May, however, while speaking in San Francisco on the same topic, Creel took a decidedly more pro-labor stand by claiming that "a journey through the coal mine town is like a page out of Hugo." Still in San Francisco a little over a week later, he was once again the conciliatory public official striving to bring the two sides together.[48]

By June 1914, when Creel published his final analysis of the Ludlow strike, "The High Cost of Hate," for *Everybody's,* he had settled comfortably into the role of Progressive reformer rather than labor advocate. Creel's interpretation of the conditions that led to the strike clearly favored the miners.

But his conclusions about what needed to be done to prevent such tragedies leaned toward no particular side. He argued that the rights of society were greater than those of either capital or labor. He avoided confronting the issue of how labor was to resist the many forces aligned against it or of the biased role played by government in the tragedy. Creel's final appeal was to the state's fair-minded citizens. They would insure that Colorado's future would be free of the rapacious few or radical organizations like the Western Federation of Miners and the Industrial Workers of the World. "The Rockefellers and the Haywoods are to be denied alike, and their menacing organizations met and defeated by a social solidarity based upon equal justice."[49] Creel the Progressive politician and Creel the labor sympathizer no longer found a common ground. His position on working people seemed to be as ambiguous as his reasons for returning to Denver in the spring of 1914. Horrified as he was by the Ludlow massacre, he never tried to examine its causes thoroughly. He never strayed very far from his belief that a middle-class public could rein in both labor and capital. Political ambitions rather than moral outrage always tempered Creel's reactions to the events at Ludlow. All those outside middle-class civility, including the miners, were irresponsible "others" incapable of recognizing the compromises necessary to maintain the public good.

Creel had already been in Colorado for several weeks by the time Upton Sinclair appeared in May 1914. At the time of his arrival, this prolific writer and activist had already been indirectly involved in protesting the massacre through his attempts to prove John D. Rockefeller Jr.'s involvement. He had attended a meeting in Carnegie Hall on April 27 at which the wife of a United Mine Workers organizer had detailed the horrors of the massacre as well as the many problems the striking miners still faced.[50] When the morning papers carried little about the meeting, Sinclair was convinced that there was a "conspiracy of silence" about the events in Colorado because of the veneration that the press had for John D. Rockefeller Jr.[51]

Determined that the miners' situation should be fully publicized and believing that Rockefeller was ultimately responsible for the tragedy at Ludlow, Sinclair and his wife went to the Standard Oil offices at 26 Broadway and requested a meeting with the tycoon. When their requests were rejected, the next morning, April 29, Sinclair and five other volunteers, all wearing bunches of funeral crepe, began picketing the Standard Oil offices. The pickets remained silent to symbolize their grief for the dead women and children at Ludlow. The picketing continued until the police told them to walk elsewhere. When they refused, they were arrested. Sinclair and his associates were charged with illegal picketing, were placed in a city prison known as "The Tombs," and then released after several hours.[52] They were to appear the next morning in court. Making the most of his brief incarceration, Sinclair announced to reporters that he had engaged in his own two-day hunger strike. He also read to them a poem, "The Marseillaise in the Tombs," that he had hastily written in prison.[53] Like his "hunger strike," Sinclair directed the poem more toward New York authorities than to those in Colorado.

On Thursday, April 30, Sinclair appeared in court and, after refusing to pay a three-dollar fine, was sentenced to three days in The Tombs. By late Saturday afternoon, May 2, Sinclair was back on the picket line. He had decided to pay the rest of the fine, believing that his presence at the center of the movement was more important than his remaining in jail.[54] As the picketing continued, the miners seemed to have been forgotten. When reporters asked Sinclair about the scope of his activities, he described his stay in jail and a speech attacking Rockefeller he was preparing to deliver in a West End lecture hall.[55] With the press losing interest in the picketing, Sinclair decided to go to Colorado to examine the strike for himself. He also wanted to view events in the coalfields from a novelist's perspective and hoped that he might recapture the public's attention as he had done years earlier with *The Jungle.*[56]

He arrived in Colorado the second week in May as a correspondent for the *Appeal to Reason.*[57] Over the next two weeks he wrote commentaries on the strike that the *Appeal* continued to carry long after his stay in Colorado had ended.[58] He also spoke publicly on behalf of the miners on several occasions.[59]

After only four days in Colorado, Sinclair learned that President Wilson had sent Governor Ammons a telegram expressing his concern that the state's legislature was about to adjourn without attempting a mediated end to the strike. Ammons told Wilson that the legislature had already passed a resolution establishing a committee on mediation. But Sinclair knew that the resolution made no mention of any kind of mediation and that the legislature had adjourned.[60] To make matters worse, the Associated Press had failed to carry any mention of the discrepancy between Ammons's telegram and the legislature's resolution. If in New York the enemy was Rockefeller, in Colorado it was a biased, capitalist press and a devious governor. Yet Sinclair had not completely forgotten the miners. He suggested a tactical maneuver that he believed would lend public drama to their predicament. Sinclair knew Judge Ben Lindsey of the Denver Children's Court. He asked the judge, his wife, and several miners' wives, including Mary Petrucci, whose three children had perished under the tent at Ludlow, to travel to Washington and meet with President Wilson.[61] The delegation stopped at Hull House in Chicago and then traveled on to the nation's capital in early June. Even though the initial activities of the Colorado delegation were covered by the press, John Reed, for one, questioned their overall effectiveness. In a letter to Sinclair he argued that the group had accomplished little in either Washington or New York. "I don't think Judge L & the women managed it very well with the President. As for New York,—they failed badly. The Papers didn't notice them—they got in with socialists and other—ists, so the public never knew they were here."[62]

By the time of Reed's letter, the Sinclairs were living in a rented cottage at Croton-on-Hudson where Upton had begun working on an anthology of social protest, *The Cry For Justice,* and a novel, *King Coal,* based on material gathered while in Colorado. Although the strike was over by December 1914, Sinclair made a final gesture on behalf of the miners in January 1915 when he prepared a statement for John R. Lawson, the most important UMWA official in Colorado during the strike, for presentation to the United States Commission on Industrial Relations.[63] This body was created during the Taft administration in response to a growing concern about industrial disorder and violence. President Wilson appointed the commission's nine-member board, which was headed by Frank P. Walsh, a lawyer with a working-class background. When he testified before the commission on January 29, 1915, Lawson emphasized Rockefeller's ignorance of working conditions in the Colorado coalfields. Reading from a text prepared for him by Sinclair, he said that he had listened in horror as the financier outlined the various philanthropic interests of the Rockefeller Foundation: "Health for China, a refuge for birds, food for the Belgians, pensions for New York widows, university training for the elect" were Rockefeller's attempts to substitute charity for justice. There was never "a thought or a dollar for the many thousands of men, women and children who starved in Colorado, for the widows robbed of husbands, children of their fathers, by law-violating conditions in the mines, or for the glaring illiteracy of the coal camps." Profit, not justice, was Rockefeller's goal in Colorado, and Lawson suggested that there were "thousands of Mr. Rockefeller's ex-employees in Colorado today who wish to God that they were in Belgium to be fed."[64]

Sinclair's active participation in the Colorado strike ended with Lawson's testimony. His interest in the strike had been more enduring and his activism on behalf of the miners more effective than those of any of the other writer/activists. Still, his participation was relatively brief. This was how most of his fellow writers had responded to the Colorado strike. The Ludlow massacre angered them, the Rockefeller name suggested villainy, and they all interrupted busy careers to show solidarity with the miners. But every one of them, perhaps with the exception of Creel, was first and foremost a writer. In fact, by 1918, when the UMWA dedicated a memorial at the site of the Ludlow tent colony, most of these writer/activists were supporting other causes or were immersed in their writing careers. The memory did linger for some. Upton Sinclair, who could never separate the personal from the political, remembered his involvement in the Colorado coalfields as one of the most sensational events of his life. Yet in his understanding of the miners and their strike he never advanced much beyond an egocentric perception of events. He could become enraged when he heard about the massacre at a public lecture, and he did write sympathetically about the miners in *King Coal.* But it was always the protesting, picketing, letter writing, and public attention that most energized his activities as he, like his fellow writers, transferred a miners' strike into his own cause.

The events in Colorado were long since forgotten when, a decade and a half later in February 1932, after over a year of strikes, violence, and unwelcome publicity, a group of prominent citizens of Pineville, Kentucky, banded together to counter the negative image of their county and state. Their main concern was an expected congressional investigation of conditions in the state's mining districts. A committee of these citizens sent telegrams to several members of Congress suggesting that the city of New York and "the nest of communists there" be the starting point of any forthcoming inquiry. "The citizens of Pineville have for six months been pestered to death with Communists disguised as writers from New York whose purpose was to obtain publicity for their doctrines and for books they intended to write."[65] These "communist writers" and not the mine owners, according to Pineville citizens, should be under investigation.

Ironically, the Pineville citizens were half right. Two groups of writers, the Dreiser Committee and the Frank Committee, had indeed visited Harlan and Bell Counties during the fall and winter of 1931 and 1932, and there were a few communists among them. Both groups also supported the communist-dominated National Miners Union, which backed the striking miners but also opposed the UMWA. Most of the writers appreciated the party's efforts to help the striking miners, but most had not gone to Kentucky out of party loyalty. They hoped their presence would generate helpful publicity for the miners. As writers, they also foresaw using their personal experiences in creative and professional ways. Ultimately the citizens of Pineville misdirected their concerns. The two groups that converged on their town were not communists disguised as writers. Instead, they were writers disguised as activists. Moreover, their interest in and activism on behalf of the striking Kentucky miners would prove to be as ephemeral as those of their fellow writers eighteen years earlier in Colorado; the miners remained just as much "the other" in the 1930s as they had in 1913-1914.

The Harlan County coal strike of 1931-32 had been building for a number of years.[66] The Harlan region, comprised of Harlan, Bell, Knox, Breathitt, and Perry Counties, had its first railroad in 1911, and as World War I generated increased demand for coal, it created a boom atmosphere there. In Harlan County alone, the number of active miners grew from 169 in 1911 to 11,920 by 1930. Yet by the 1920s the economic good times were already receding. Except for a brief flourish in 1926 as a result of the British general strike, depressed conditions in the coalfields of Eastern Kentucky reflected a national trend. Overproduction affected the entire industry. By 1930, nearly half the bituminous miners in the country were out of work. The UMWA was as sick as the industry it represented, having lost two-thirds of its members by 1930. As a result, the union no longer had a presence in Kentucky. The Depression severely worsened conditions there. By 1931, Harlan County mines were operating only three days a week on average. Miners often took home as little as four or five dollars for their efforts. Yet it was not the widespread suffering alone that led to a strike. The miners and their families also endured many of the same company-imposed practices that inflamed the anger of Colorado workers a generation earlier. Company stores, payment in scrip, lack of checkweighmen, and nonpayment for essential work around the mining areas were as prevalent in the Kentucky coalfields as they had been in the West. Miners also objected to the absence of union recognition and to the obvious fact that the coal companies controlled county government. When one of the area's largest companies announced a 10 percent wage reduction on February 16, 1931, a spontaneous strike began. This strike, as one historian suggests, not only challenged unsatisfactory working conditions but also served as a "miners' revolt" against the "arbitrary economic, political, and social power" of such Harlan mining companies as Harlan-Wallins Coal Corporation, Black Star, and the Black Mountain Coal Corporation.[67]

In his masterful analysis of the power relationships that dominated the area, John Gaventa has documented how the United Mine Workers at first encouraged and then abandoned the striking miners.[68] In Pineville, Kentucky, on March 1, 1931, over two thousand miners listened to the union's vice-president, Philip Murray, pledge his organization's support of the strike and ensure the return of the UMWA to the Kentucky coalfields. The next day, several firms in Harlan County began dismissing miners who had attended the meeting, and the strike spread. Many of the unemployed miners and their families who had been turned out of their company-owned houses drifted into Evarts, one of the few incorporated towns in the county. As their numbers in the town grew, so too did the resentment against the scabs hired by the companies and the armed guards paid to protect them. On May 5, on the outskirts of the town, a violent clash occurred between armed miners and three carloads of deputies. Three deputies and one miner were killed in what was soon called the "Battle of Evarts." Two days later, National Guardsmen were sent in to maintain order—a decision that turned out to be as arbitrary and one-sided as the imposition of martial law in Colorado.

Even though eleven thousand miners had taken Murray's promise seriously and joined the union, John L. Lewis and the UMWA withdrew their support soon after the strike began. Lewis was concerned about the militancy of the strikers, the legal and relief costs that the union would have to pay, and about the impact on union morale of supporting what was generally perceived to be a lost cause. He declared that the strike was unauthorized and ordered the men back to work in the spring of 1931. Many desperate miners, feeling sold out, turned to the communist-organized National Miners Union, whose agents first entered the region on June 6.[69]

The National Miners Union was the largest affiliate of the Trade Union Unity League. This organization emerged in 1927 as a result of a change in policy in the Soviet Union known as the "third period." Instead of trying to control existing unions by working from within, which had been the tactic until this time, the new strategy called for a more open confrontation with capitalism through the creation of dual unions—communist-organized unions that would attempt to destroy more established, conservative ones like the American Federation of Labor. Organized in September 1928, the NMU was by far the most visible of the three national unions formed under the guidance of the Trade Union Unity League. But the National Miners Union also experienced many more defeats than victories in Illinois, Pennsylvania, and West Virginia. It was not until June 1931 that the first NMU organizers arrived in Harlan County.[70]

By the time the NMU began to focus on Kentucky, the UMWA had already abandoned the striking miners. For all intents and purposes, the strike was over. Yet the Communist Party still hoped to expand its influence among the eastern Kentucky miners. The NMU began setting up soup kitchens to boost morale. It also undertook the legal defense of the miners charged with murders that had resulted from the Battle of Evarts. Despite these efforts, the NMU had no chance for victory. Most of the miners who joined the union were already blacklisted and not in a position to shut down any of the working mines in the area by striking. The NMU found itself, just like the UMWA, supporting an unwinnable strike that put a tremendous drain on its resources. Unlike earlier confrontations in Illinois, West Virginia, and Pennsylvania, however, the Harlan County strike became an important symbol of the decade. This happened in large part because of the two groups of writers who visited the area to dramatize and publicize the situation there.

The first of the two committees of writers to enter Harlan County was headed by Theodore Dreiser and included fellow writers John Dos Passos; Samuel Ornitz; Melvin P. Levy; Lester Cohen; Charles Rumford Walker and his wife, Adelaide; as well as Bruce Crawford, editor of *Crawford's Weekly;* three party members; Dreiser's personal secretary, and his traveling companion, Mary Pergain. Supervised by the party's legal arm, the International Labor Defense, the trip itself was sponsored by an auxiliary organization known as the National Committee for the Defense of Political Prisoners, which had helped defend the Scottsboro Boys in Alabama. Dreiser and Dos Passos had served as officers in an earlier organization, the Emergency Committee for Southern Political Prisoners, from which the National Committee for the Defense of Political Prisoners had emerged.[71]

Dreiser was sixty years old with the most creative portion of his career behind him by the time he went to Harlan County. All of his life he had been infatuated with the concepts of power, individualism, and personalities who stood out in the crowd. At the same time he held a deep intolerance for human suffering, social injustice, and the seemingly unlimited power of corporate America. In 1927 he traveled to Russia. Three years later, in the midst of the Great Depression, he observed widespread suffering on a personal fact-finding trip through America. These experiences surely pushed him to the Left. As early as 1930 he was suggesting the possibility, if not the desirability, of a communist revolution.[72] In 1931, he went so far as to apply for Communist Party membership, only to be turned down apparently because of his unpredictable individualism.[73] Critic Murray Kempton later recalled Dreiser's utter lack of political orthodoxy and noted that when he was closest to the party he continued to write as if it did not exist.[74] Still, Dreiser's name added luster to any event, and in the late spring of 1931 the party suggested that he go to western Pennsylvania to publicize a strike there.[75]

During his two-day visit to the coalfields in western Pennsylvania, Dreiser pursued a predictable round of activities. He interviewed several miners and their wives at his hotel. He visited over fifteen mines where picketing was in progress and interviewed several local officials. He also listed for the press the living and working conditions—starvation wages, exploitation by company stores, poor housing, high rents, and antiunion violence—that he found most deplorable.[76]

Three months later, the party again sought his help and suggested that he organize a subcommittee of members of the National Committee for the Defense of Political Prisoners. The subcommittee would visit Harlan County to show how local officials were totally disregarding the civil rights of the strikers and their families. Fearing that such a group would be intimidated in Kentucky and ignored elsewhere, Dreiser tried to assemble a blue-ribbon group of prominent citizens.[77] Clearly disappointed by the lack of support from prominent men, he joked that he had failed to engage the help of "representative Americans" and instead had to settle for writers.[78]

The group left Pennsylvania Station on Wednesday, November 4, changed trains in Cincinnati the next morning, and arrived at the Continental Hotel in Pineville, Kentucky, that afternoon. The next day the committee would drive to its headquarters at the Lewallen Hotel in Harlan. They would interview miners, operators, and local officials over the weekend and then return to New York on Monday.[79]

Dreiser's activities over the next three and a half days have become part of the folklore of the 1930s. He met Mary Pergain in Cincinnati, and the two spent the night together in the Hotel Continental in Pineville, which would raise a furor before they left town. Someone on the hotel's staff informed local Comstockians that Pergain had entered Dreiser's room that evening; when toothpicks placed against the door demonstrated that she had stayed the night, the uproar began. On the day that the committee departed Kentucky, a Belle County grand jury indicted Dreiser and Pergain for adultery, a misdemeanor under Kentucky law.[80] Earlier, on November 6, before this event became public, Dreiser had engaged in a heated exchange with a local newspaper editor, Herndon Evans, over the question of equity in the region. When the editor turned the questions toward the writer and asked how much of his income he donated to charity, a spluttering Dreiser had to admit that he gave precious little. The issue of Dreiser's philanthropic failings was yet another distraction drawing public attention away from the needs of miners.[81] Finally on November 16, a little over a week after the committee had left Kentucky, a Belle County grand jury indicted the entire Dreiser committee for engaging in criminal syndicalism during their tour of the mining region. If convicted, committee members faced up to twenty-one years in prison.[82] Even though a trial never took place, the publicity surrounding the charges dominated most of the committee members' activities once they arrived back in New York. Like historians of the Von Ranke School, the group had gone to Kentucky to get the facts. These facts would help publicize the plight of the striking miners, but in the process, Dreiser in particular and the group in general had drawn attention more to themselves than to those they sought to assist. The committee had inadvertently set its own agenda, turning the trip to Kentucky and the needs of the striking miners into a kind of subtext as misunderstood as it was neglected.

The itinerary of most committee members, however, differed considerably from the diversionary and self-absorbed activities of their leader. Miners testified at hearings in Pineville and Harlan, where their statements were recorded. They interviewed local officials, visited mining camps, and attended an NMU meeting on Saturday evening. On Sunday they split up. Some ate lunch in an NMU soup kitchen and attended another NMU meeting. Others traveled to Winchester and Mount Sterling, Kentucky, to see if they could help the legal defense of those miners held on murder charges stemming from the Battle of Evarts.[83]

Dos Passos, at least, sensed how the miners' occupation and the remote area where they lived created an image of geographic and class "otherness" that impacted his fellow writers in ways they did not truly fathom. As he and his fellow writers left one of the evening meetings in the darkness, Dos Passos felt a sense of isolation and the same kind of "scary lonesome feeling" he had observed as an ambulance driver during a lull in the fighting on the Western Front. To some extent his uneasiness suggests the discomfort of a city person in a rural environment, a middle-class writer in a mining region. Yet, on another level, perhaps Dos Passos felt something akin to the existential sense of isolation and helplessness that James Agee, the interviewer and outsider, described in *Let Us Praise Famous Men.* As Agee too stood in darkness, he looked in the window of a sharecropping family, sensing that both he and they were inexorably alone, that his longing for companionship and their desperate huddling together were predicaments shared by all human beings.[84] Dos Passos, on his own evening walk, noted how the mountains towered above the "pumpkincolor" lights along the creekbottom. The miners were returning to their homes, the writers to their hotel. Their paths had briefly intersected, but their lives remained as separate and as different as the isolated communities that dotted the terrain of that rugged countryside. Dos Passos, like his fellow writers, acted for the striking miners and not with them, but on a deeply personal level he recognized that both groups shared the basic human condition of loneliness.[85]

More typical of committee members' perspectives was that of screenwriter, novelist, and later one of the Hollywood Ten, Samuel Ornitz, who was more interested in the universality of the issues in Kentucky than in the uniqueness of a specific strike. "I wrote pictures and barnstormed against fascism," he later explained. "I helped organize the Hollywood Anti-Nazi-league. I worked to free the Scottsboro Boys and Mooney. I went to Harlan, Kentucky, to help starving coal miners. . . . Writing didn't interest me. I gave all my time to fighting fascism and war."[86] Even before going to Kentucky, Ornitz had published an article, "Bleeding Bowels in Kentucky," in the October 1931 issue of *New Masses.* The article reveals the limited extent of his commitment. It begins with a series of staccato, one-sentence paragraphs outlining the reasons for the miner's woes. Ornitz then turns his attention to the failures of the "capitalist" oriented UMWA and the need for the more radical NMU. His approach is predictable, if not formalized, until he describes the one event that most captured his imagination—the appearance of a twenty-three-year-old organizer sent by the International Labor Defense to assist the miners. Jesse London Wakefield's introduction to the coalfields was accompanied by violence and intimidation. She survived a car bombing, imprisonment, and death threats. Eventually the parent organization recalled Wakefield to save her life. Ornitz praised her courage and respected her determined opposition to fascism and oppression, which, like his own committed struggle for social justice, transcended time and place. He sympathized with the miners' plight, but in his view they were conflated with Tom Mooney and the Scottsboro Boys as symbols of oppression. Ornitz took no particular interest in the uniqueness of miners' lives or the details of their concerns.[87] He and Jesse Wakefield both believed that they were engaged in a titanic, unending struggle that happened, at the time, to be in Harlan. Though Dreiser later claimed that Ornitz was one of his most valuable assistants on the Harlan trip, Ornitz suffered from the same inability to separate the strike from a larger picture. They, rather than the miners and their families, would determine the causes and effects of the conflicts.[88]

Hoping to direct national attention to events in Harlan County, in February 1932, the committee published *Harlan Miners Speak: Report on Terrorism in the Kentucky Coal Fields.* Underwritten by the National Committee for the Defense of Political Prisoners, the volume was edited and narrated by Dos Passos with an introduction by Dreiser. For the most part this work failed to fulfill its promise. Even the title was misleading. The interviews took place in Belle as well as Harlan Counties, and only a third of the book was actually devoted to interviews with members of mining families. Another third included essays by members of the Dreiser committee or other writers approved by the NCDPP. The last portion of the book is filled with interviews with Harlan County officials, a speech by Sherwood Anderson in which he supports the committee's activities, and excerpts from the Senate testimony of the Frank Committee members describing their failed efforts in Kentucky.

Dreiser's introduction put the strike in a war context. His committee "invaded" a state where public officials and coal operators were "making war" on the miners and spying on the writers. He "found the same line-up of petty officials and business interests on the side of the coal operators and as against the miners as I have discovered in almost every other labor war or controversy that I have had the opportunity to observe. The small town bankers, grocers, and editors and lawyers, the police, the sheriff, if not the government, were all apparently subservient to the money and corporate masters of the area."[89]

While Dreiser focused on the universality of the strike, Dos Passos wrote about its localism. His brief narrative sections describing the committee's activities during the three-day visit are the best written parts of the book.[90] Many of the other essays, however, stereotyped Appalachians and showed the extent to which they remained "the other" from the writer's perspective. In a little more than two pages, Lester Cohen, who was in the apprentice stage of a writing career, used words such as "primitivism," "moonshining," and "feuding" while suggesting that Kentuckians had an "inherent" propensity for violence. Playwright and novelist Melvin Levy went even further in describing barefoot mountain folk who still rode two to a mule. He generalized about the ill-effects of "clan breeding," moonshining, and the ignorance of people who had never read a book or seen a map. He noted the striking contrast between "beautiful, tall miner-mountaineers, with long slender faces and thick blond hair, and the occasional woman, belly distended and ugly, walking barefooted until late November, then with a pair of men's shoes tied about her feet."[91] Cohen and Levy had gone to Kentucky to help, but the "otherness" of their preconceived notions of Appalachian culture got in the way.

No part of the book and no part of the committee's activities better demonstrate the "othering" of the strikers than the way in which they and their families were expected to voice their concerns. The entire process was daunting. The participants first had to brave a gauntlet of townspeople, deputy sheriffs, and public officials to reach the hearing room on the hotel's second floor. Company guards, who carefully scrutinized the witnesses, occupied a nearby room. This public exposure could not have helped the mining families—especially after the writers left the region. The questioning itself was intimidating. Instead of allowing the miners and their wives to speak about what concerned them most, committee members posed leading questions. During the course of the hearings, each person to be questioned was seated at a large table surrounded by strangers. Dreiser's severe visage and the stenographer recording every word surely made the interviewees uneasy. They could not tell their stories or answer questions without well-intentioned interruptions. Instead, these men and women from the coalfields found themselves responding to a flurry of questions in the midst of confusion and fear. Dreiser's initial queries did not encourage lengthy replies. This set a pattern of short, terse responses. By the end, the committee had learned little about the backgrounds, feelings, and expectations of the miners. The committee did learn about wages, working conditions, hours of employment, number of dependent children, standards of living, and problems with local officials. As historian William Stotts suggests, most of the questions guaranteed that the poor would assume the anticipated role of being both "dumb and righteous."[92] Only rarely would a spontaneous remark break through, giving life to the miners' woes. When Dos Passos asked a miner if he believed a greater reward awaited him for his suffering, the miner replied, "I know I ain't never going to get nothing here. My children has got no clothes. The little girl here, she has got no underwear on."[93] More sensitive and reflective about the region and its people than most of the committee members, Dos Passos still saw no problem with the process and later remembered the committee was hearing exactly what it had expected. The trip, from his perspective, was going as planned.[94]

The last part of the book included Sherwood Anderson's speech and the testimony several of the writers gave in Washington. When Dreiser could not attend an NCDPP meeting in New York on December 6, 1931, Anderson spoke in his place. The purpose of the meeting was to protest the continuing ill treatment of the Kentucky miners. In some ways, Anderson's long, rambling talk served as a coda for the trip and the book. Anderson briefly mentioned the miners, but he quickly shifted to the needs of all workers and finally ended by discussing the activist role of writers. While reiterating the need for writers to "line up with the underdogs," he concluded by emphasizing why he had left his Virginia home to speak in New York: "I am here because I think that Mr. Dreiser has got a rotten deal. What he has done has been twisted in some places into something it wasn't at all. I think the press, the pulpit and all of us are to blame. As I said before, I think that if they can take Mr. Dreiser out there to Kentucky and try him in that court for criminal syndicalism then we ought all to begin committing criminal syndicalism as fast as we know how to do it."[95] With unsurprising irony, the miners faded into the background as Dreiser took center stage. Anderson was calling for solidarity, but was it for the workers or the writers?

The book closes with parts of a hearing in Washington on February 12, 1932, organized by Waldo Frank and his own group of writers. These men and women, who included Malcolm Cowley, Edmund Wilson, and Mary Heaton Vorse, followed the Dreiser group to Kentucky in hopes of helping and interviewing the miners. Their trip, however, was cut short by violence. By the time the Frank group reached Pineville in February 1932, many of the local citizens had endured enough from meddling outsiders. Frank and the writers stayed just a few hours.

The Frank Committee, or the Independent Miners' Relief Committee as it was also known, was a mix of men and women most of whom wrote for a living. Benjamin Lieder, for example, was a newsreel cameraman who later fought for the Loyalists and was killed in Spain. Liston Oak was publicity director for the International Labor Defense, John Henry Hammond, a radical-thinking heir to a Vanderbilt fortune, and Elsa Reed, a retired California physician. Although not a committee member at first, Alan Taub, the communist lawyer from New York who represented the International Labor Defense, had joined the group in Pineville. Harold Hickerson, Quincy Howe, and Polly Boynden had each done a bit of writing at one time or another, but scarcely enough to establish a literary career or reputation for themselves.[96] Four committee members—Waldo Frank, Malcolm Cowley, Edmund Wilson, and Mary Heaton Vorse—were well known writers. From their perspective, it was more the cause of the miners rather than the miners themselves that became "the other." The writers believed they understood what the strike symbolized, and the committee developed a plan of action in which the miners were ultimately beneficiaries rather than participants. All four went to

Kentucky with professional goals that undermined their political ones. They wanted to help the miners, but they also hoped to enhance their writing careers.

Within the context of the strike, the Frank Committee's efforts to aid the miners was largely a continuation of what the Dreiser group had tried three months earlier. In his memoirs Frank wrote that Dreiser's report on the impossibility of getting food to the miners led to the organization of the Frank Committee.[97] Malcolm Cowley remembered that Charles Rumford Walker had easily convinced him to participate during a visit to Cowley's *New Republic* office in January 1932. Walker told him that the Dreiser Committee had focused the nation's attention on Kentucky and also forced local officials to abide by the law. This in turn encouraged the miners to go out on strike a second time. "Charlie thought that another such mission might 'open up the situation,'" Cowley recalled, and also "help in raising money for relief, and keep 'the law' from interfering with the distribution of food."[98] Mary Heaton Vorse was not so easily persuaded. She had enough experience with the terrorizing tactics of local officials while covering the textile strike at Gastonia, North Carolina, in the spring of 1929. Vorse would not be drawn into another well-meaning but futile effort to help workers. Apparently it took three nights of intense lobbying by Dos Passos and a telegram from the Walkers to change her mind.[99] Only Edmund Wilson seemed unresponsive to the Dreiser Committee's findings. But Dos Passos and Wilson had been friends for some time. It seems likely that they discussed the strike sometime after Dos Passos returned from the coalfields. In any case, a trip to Kentucky could be a continuation of the fact-finding journey that Wilson had recently made across depression-ridden America for the *New Republic.*[100]

Both the Dreiser and Frank groups worked through the National Committee for the Defense of Political Prisoners. According to Cowley, his group agreed on three relatively simple goals. They planned to distribute several tons of food purchased in Knoxville, Tennessee, to open up channels through which the miners could be supplied on a regular basis, and to determine if local authorities were observing the miners' rights as American citizens.[101] On February 7, most of the group traveled from New York to Knoxville.

Although the exact sequence of events remains unclear, it appears that on February 9, committee members made an excursion to the little Tennessee mining town of La Follette located about thirty miles from Knoxville and ten miles from the Kentucky border. The NMU was engaged there in yet another strike. Members of the committee acclimatized themselves to the coal region and to industrial conflict by visiting miners' homes, interviewing strikers about living and working conditions, and distributing milk to mining families.[102]

Early on the morning of February 10, the committee left Knoxville in rented automobiles and drove into Kentucky through Cumberland Gap. The Frank Committee brought with them several trucks loaded with food, which struggled to get over the steep mountain roads.[103] The general feeling, as Cowley remembered it, was not unlike that of "driving north from a French railhead in 1917 toward the front lines."[104] The situation only worsened when they learned that Harry Simms, a twenty-year-old NMU organizer from New York, had been shot in the abdomen. Simms was walking along the railroad tracks near Bush Creek when two deputy sheriffs riding a railroad handcar attacked him. He and a companion were on their way to meet NMU strikers and lead them back to Pineville to join up with members of the Frank Committee. Simms lay bleeding beside the tracks for several hours before he was taken to a local hospital. He died there the next day.

After losing sight of the heavily loaded food and clothing trucks, several members of the group stayed behind to wait. Others went on to Pineville to meet with a local attorney and the mayor to insure that town officials would not try to stop them as they distributed the food to the miners.[105] Later that day the county attorney gave his permission to distribute the food as long as there was no public speaking. By mid-afternoon, the writers were finally engaged in one of the activities for which they had come. By the time they arrived on the scene, however, two other members of the group who were not aware of the no-speaking policy had already been arrested and taken to jail for addressing the miners.

Back at their hotel that evening, group members discovered that their luggage had been searched. Then they heard a rumor that the local government would charge them with criminal syndicalism. Apparently, local officials had confiscated several pages of the *Daily Worker* in which Frank had wrapped his shoes. The final event of the day was a committee meeting at the hotel. There they decided to buy a truckload of supplies to distribute at Wallins Creek in Harlan County before they left the state. Most of the committee members eventually went to their rooms. Frank, Wilson, and several others stayed up to swap lighthearted stories about their day. Frank was the first of the four to leave but quickly returned with news that a group of men was standing outside the door of his room. Within a short time, deputies arrested the entire committee, took them to the courthouse, and charged them with disorderly conduct in public places. Within thirty minutes, all charges were dropped, and officials told committee members to return to their hotel. An even larger group of citizens including deputies, merchants, and coal operators was waiting for them there. Officials paired committee members two by two and placed each pair in a car with a driver and two deputies. There were thirteen cars in the caravan. The journey ended at Cumberland Gap, where the automobiles were arranged in a semicircle, headlights turned off, and the writers ordered out. In the darkness, Taub and Frank, who had ridden together, were clubbed from behind with a jack handle. Taub's screams possibly saved them. A few seconds later, after the headlights were turned back on, one of the night riders jovially announced that Frank and Taub had been fighting. The vigilantes searched one more time for film in the group's baggage; finding none, they drove off. The very frightened delegation walked about a mile to the little town of Cumberland Gap, rented cars and drove back to their hotel in Knoxville.[106]

It was a battered and tired group that answered reporters' questions the next day and left by train for Washington that evening. Frank, who suffered a nasty scalp wound, was repeatedly photographed with his head swathed in bandages. The group never returned to Kentucky, though various members continued to work for the striking miners. On February 12, 1932, Frank, Oakes, Taub, and Walker met with Senators E.P. Costigan of Colorado, Bronson Cutting of New Mexico, and Marvel M. Logan of Kentucky to inform them of their treatment. Four days later several members of the committee publicly protested in New York, and on February 22, others including Cowley, Wilson, and Vorse spoke at a public meeting in the Star Casino.[107]

While meeting with Senators Costigan, Cutting, and Logan, Cowley tried to explain that the committee was independent and not under the control of any organization like the Communist Party. In doing so, he pointed out that its individual members not only paid their own expenses but that some, like Waldo Frank, had also helped pay others' expenses.[108] Cowley's memory of the trip appears to be accurate, for Frank was among the most committed and enthusiastic of the participating writers.

By the time of the trip to Kentucky Waldo Frank was a relatively successful but not widely read writer. As fascinated with Hispanic culture as he was with his own, in 1926 he had written *Virgin Spain,* which one critic calls a "dramatic tone poem."[109] An inveterate traveler, Frank only briefly discusses the trip to Kentucky in his memoirs. It may be that at the time he went to the coalfields he was far more interested in his writing career than he was in the miners. At the time he was struggling to find the right literary path. His next novel would not focus exclusively on the individual as had his earlier ones. Instead his newest work would unite the individual with his society in symphonic wholeness.[110] Beginning in April 1926, he planned to take a year to write the novel that he had tentatively titled "David Markand: An American History." But early in 1927, he set aside the fifty thousand words he had completed. Unable to write the novel he had hoped for, Frank frequently pushed it aside for other projects, including a lecture tour of Mexico and South America in 1929-30, which he described in *America Hispana* (1931), and a 1931 trip to the Soviet Union.[111]

In his notebooks he wrestled with writer's block, wondering if it were a question of his creative limitations or if he did not know enough about the world. On December 22, 1931, he sensed that it is essentially a matter of turning inward: "What I must find is the focus for the material that I have. There is no use—it is going off the track altogether—to try to scan the country for material for your novel. Scan the country of your mind for the novel." As he reminded himself in the same entry: "You have lived in this country 40 years. Not material enough?" The problem, as he understood it, remained an intensely personal one—"now is the time to know what I really know, & to be what I really am." Even as the Kentucky trip drew closer, there is still no mention of striking miners, but abundant reference to his anguish over the novel not yet written. By mid-January, 1932, his creative obstacles seemed both internal and external.

> I am experiencing fundamental difficulties in focusing my book: a) of feeling, b) of materials. I must not intellectually & apriori plot out a story that is not my stuff. This is crucial. What do I NOT know? for objective treatment:
> —Farm life
> —Factory life
> —Hobo life
> —Labor Movement.

At the end of the month, with *Dawn in Russia* completed, Frank once more turned to his albatross. "And now, quite literally & immediately, the novel is upon you." But Frank was still floundering. Just before leaving for Kentucky on February 6, he fretted about having preconceptions of his novel and the "danger, that by so doing the action of the characters may be somewhat arbitrary—and this form, in consequence, too intellectual & unconvincing." Then, almost as an afterthought, he concluded: "I am on the point of a brief visit to the mines of Kentucky—the great strike. I expect, primarily, to win of this, the renewed Taste of America. . . . On my return, a couple of speaking dates—& thereafter I want [to] shut myself away and begin to write." Clearly Frank believed that he might learn something by going to Kentucky. Along the way he would also be acting much like the novel's main character, which would make him an organic part of the process he was writing about.

The trip to Pineville may have unleashed Frank's blocked creativity, for he did resume work on *The Death and Birth of David Markand* immediately after returning from Kentucky. He completed the novel by July 1933. The final section of the novel as well as Markand's social and spiritual rebirth are all related to events Frank witnessed in Kentucky. Frank, unlike other committee members, may have found what he was looking for while helping deliver groceries to hungry miners, but from the start his determination to awaken a slumbering muse defined his approach to the cause.

Malcolm Cowley, who was nine years younger than Frank, followed a somewhat different writer's path. Determined to write since high school, he hungrily sought life experience. In 1917, before America's entry in World War I, he felt a need to become a part of the most important event of his time. Cowley volunteered to drive a munitions truck for the French army. He stayed in Europe at the war's end but eventually returned to the United States to live in the Village and become a writer. His wartime experiences stayed with him for years to come. Three weeks before the stock market crash in 1929, Cowley had begun to work for the *New Republic* as a copy editor and proofreader. Several months later, he became the magazine's youngest editor and eventually assumed Edmund Wilson's position as book editor when Wilson took a leave of absence in 1931. According to Daniel Aaron, it was the Great Depression and Cowley's trip to Kentucky that truly activated his social conscience.[112] In fact, when he joined the NCDPP in 1932, it was the first organization, political or otherwise, that he had joined since college.

Cowley went to Kentucky to provide both food and publicity for the miners, but, like Frank, personal reasons motivated him as well. As a Harvard undergraduate in 1917, Cowley believed that the experiences he needed as a writer could only be found on the Western Front. Now, as a political radical and an editor of an influential journal, he again felt the need to experience events firsthand. Becoming the kind of person and writer that he hoped to be required that he act in order to learn. He saw the conflict in Kentucky in the same context as his experience fourteen years earlier on the Western Front.

Cowley noticed many images during the trip to Kentucky with remarkable similarities to his war experiences. As he traveled from Knoxville to Pineville, the armed groups of deputies that he watched from the automobile conjured up memories: "Since the War I have never seen so many guns as are now displayed in Bell County."[113] The machine guns aimed at a pro-labor attorney's office in Pineville led Cowley to question why he and his fellow writers were there at all. "I begin to feel that bringing food to the Kentucky miners was like picking daisies in No Man's Land."[114] Cowley's analogy was confirmed when a coal operator in the hotel lobby said in a "hard voice" to those standing nearby: "This is another war."[115] Cowley learned from his experiences in Kentucky just as he had learned from those on the Western Front. This time the learning, more than anything else, helped clarify which side he was on in the class struggle.

Cowley described the trip in a four-page article in the March 12, 1932, issue of the *New Republic*. Like any good soldier who does not want to give comfort to the enemy, Cowley avoided any criticism of how the Communist Party, through the NMU, appeared to be using the writers. In an undated typescript, apparently written shortly after leaving Kentucky, and then again later in *The Dream of the Golden Mountains,* Cowley acknowledged an uncertainty he shared with a few of his colleagues about the strike motives of the party. They had learned early on in Pineville that local intimidation prevented the NMU from holding any kind of a meeting since the second strike had begun. Without informing the writers, the NMU had called the miners into Pineville not only to get much-needed food but also to "hold a speaking." When the people of Pineville learned that scores of angry miners were coming into their community "they believed that they were fighting now to save their property, their homes and their God from the Red menace, from the Soviet horde; any measures of defense were justified, even shooting men in cold blood." These events surprised the writers, for as Cowley wrote at the time, "Our committee, arriving innocently on the scene, was like a party of civilians wandering into no man's land just when the firing was about to begin."[116] As he so often did, Cowley again used a war metaphor to describe the writers' situation instead of the miners'.

Daniel Aaron was likely correct in arguing that Cowley's interviews with the miners and observations of the mine owners led him to appreciate the seriousness of revolutionary ideas. Yet considerably more resulted from Cowley's trip than a heightened sense of commitment. He had gone to Kentucky as a writer—a writer who wanted to learn more about the depression as well as labor and management. Along the way he had learned how ineffectual well-meaning people could be in the face of raw power or cynical manipulation. It seems apparent, then, that when Cowley left the security of his desk at the *New Republic,* even briefly, the resulting experience was sure to affect him in a permanent way. There was, as well, a strong continuity in both his youthful and more mature thinking. Cowley had gone to the coalfields in 1932 for many of the same reasons that he had gone to Europe in 1917—reasons that had more to do with his development as a writer than anything else.

At the time of the Kentucky trip, Edmund Wilson, unlike Cowley, had been traveling through depression-stricken America. From the beginning, again unlike his younger colleague, he had gone to Kentucky as a writer not an activist. Cowley had temporarily taken time off from his editorial duties to make the trip, while Wilson initially joined the expedition in his capacity as a reporter for the *New Republic.*[117] It might be argued that the Kentucky trip was but a continuation of the earlier travels on which Wilson had sent articles of his impressions and observations to the magazine. Fiercely independent and never much of a joiner, Wilson wrote elegantly and often bitterly about injustice. Yet the role of critical observer rather than active participant suited him best. At the pre-departure meeting in Knoxville, he was predictably uneasy about the party's attempt to set the agenda for the delegation. He also insisted that he did not want to get arrested. These were real concerns that defined the parameters of his involvement. Wilson was more than willing to bring food and clothing to the striking miners. But the more important reason why he was there, as was true at other times throughout his life, was to write about what he saw and awaken his readers. Wilson believed that the miners' problems were part of a much larger, universal series of events that substantiated Marx's prediction of the inevitability of social upheaval. His trip to Kentucky had a larger sense of purpose, just as it had for Frank. "The place to study the present crisis and its causes and probable consequences is not in the charts of the compilers of statistics," he wrote in *The American Jitters,* "but in one's self and in the people one sees." [118] Wilson had previously visited and written about striking miners in West Virginia whose determined independence reminded him of his own ancestors in upstate New York. The Kentucky trip was part of a continuing investigation.[119]

Wilson, the diligent researcher and diarist, produced more thorough accounts of the Kentucky trip than any of the other participants. But he scarcely noted his own involvement in food distribution efforts. This was to be expected. While aiding the miners was important to him, informing the American people of their plight was always his real objective. He believed that all writers should do the same for a cause. In a letter to Walter Lippmann, published in the November 11, 1931, issue of the *New Republic,* Wilson not only denounced Lippmann for his general lack of enthusiasm for the Soviet Union but also suggested that writers had a responsibility to inform the public: "And at this time when the American public—one of the worst educated politically in the world—needs political education so much, isn't it a serious matter for a writer of your rank to allow it to remain in ignorance of the fundamental issues involved?"[120]. This need to shed light on the "fundamental issues" explains why Wilson recorded events in such detailed notes in his journal. Ultimately it also explains why he was so angry about communist attempts to exploit the writers for their own purposes. As he wrote to his friend Dos Passos shortly after returning from Kentucky. "The whole thing was very interesting for us—though I don't know that it did much for the miners. . . . I came back convinced that if the literati want to engage in radical activities, they ought to organize or do something independently—so that they can back other people besides the comrades and so that the comrades can't play them for suckers."[121] Being played for a sucker would destroy his credibility as an independent writer whose primary task was to educate, not propagandize. The miners' cause was important; their story needed to be told, but from Wilson's position as a writer the integrity of the teller was more important than the tale. From this perspective, the miners remained one example of "otherness" in Wilson's mosaic of the oppressed in a country overwhelmed by economic catastrophe and political drift.

Like Wilson, Mary Heaton Vorse was an unlikely candidate to join any group of writers going to yet another labor upheaval. She had already witnessed the hopeless strike at Gastonia and written a novel, *Strike,* about it. Charles and Adelaide Walker invited her to join the Dreiser group in the fall of 1931, and though she tentatively agreed, Vorse decided to travel in Europe instead. After returning to her home in Provincetown in late January, 1932, she received another telegram from the Walkers, this time asking her to join the food-distributing expedition to Kentucky.[122] As much as Vorse sympathized with the struggles of workers everywhere, she knew that any outside group would not be welcome in Kentucky. Her own experience at Gastonia had taught her that there was little writers could do to help the miners or their cause.

For the next few days Vorse could not make a decision. Even before the Walkers' telegram arrived, she had recorded in her daily notes parts of a conversation with Dos Passos: "Dos thinks if the communists lose the Nat. M.U. fight—they will have lost in the unions. I would like to be doing that, but I can't do everything."[123] Dos Passos, who lived in nearby Truro, visited Vorse three times during the last three days of January, urging her to go. Still she could not make up her mind. She continually "mulled-stewed."[124] Finally, Vorse methodically wrote a list with separate columns of arguments for and against going. She listed financial concerns, her health, and the loss of a speaking engagement as reasons for staying in Provincetown. In column two she noted the need to take a stand, the fact that her train fare would be paid, and her present lack of a consuming literary project. Above all, Vorse wanted to write a story about coal mining. She wrote down questions about whether or not the trip to Kentucky would help her do that. She had been thinking about writing such a story even before the arrival of the Walkers' telegram, and in December 1931, she recorded her ambitious plans: "I shall write a story of a coal miner that will be the story of bituminous coal."[125] The Walkers were now offering her an opportunity to visit the mining regions of Kentucky. The issue that seemed to concern her most was whether or not the trip would be creatively productive.[126] By January 31, she had finally made up her mind to go. But her search for copy was by no means the only reason for doing so. "I have temporized about going. . . . I feel I am missing something. It is something I should be in on." Then, like a modern-day Thoreau, she concluded: "I think if we are worth anything—all of the civil libertarians & all the liberals should be arrested. I think I should be arrested. I say to myself at just this time—I have no money or time for arrests."[127] Having finally made the decision to go to Kentucky, Vorse still felt lingering doubts: "I have a feeling that this trip is going to be tiresome and fruitless."[128]

For Vorse, the Kentucky trip proved to be a political and creative disappointment. Since nothing was required of her in Pineville, she remained on the periphery of the action. She sat in an automobile chatting with a local woman while the trucks were unloaded. Later that evening, when offered safe conduct out of the county she refused.[129] She did write a short, fictionalized account of the trip that suggests, at the very least, she thought about its meaning more deeply than the other writers. Vorse remained concerned with the moral ambiguities of the writers' activist efforts. Always unclear about the moral responsibilities of writers as social activists, Vorse knew clearly what direction her own writing should take. "Apparently Hemingway said to himself, I will write about life and death," she confided to her daily notes in November 1932. "I have never said anything. I want to write the industrial history of my time about—the I.W.W., the Big Fight for unionization—the betrayal of people like [Frank] Farrington, like [John L.] Lewis."[130] Given her literary goals, it made sense for Vorse to plunge into strike-ridden Kentucky, even without knowing much about the region or its people. Inadvertently, she and her fellow writers had wandered into the midst of a class war. Two months after the trip she still believed that there was something "inappropriate about our brazen attendance among those Kentucky workers." The mine owners, the local officials, and all those who opposed the strike were apparently fighting for something larger than merely keeping a communist union out of the region. They were fighting, she believed, for the tribalistic preservation of their culture and were willing to use any means at all.[131] Vorse had seen in Gastonia how an entire community can be rallied against both "outsider" intellectuals and strikers who, although members of that community, are perceived as being influenced by an interfering group.

In her roman à clef short story, "Rendezvous," Vorse is Sidney Moore, a New York writer who questions his fellow writers' belief that they are helping others by going to Kentucky. Moore feels particularly guilty when one of the writers, Quinn, argues that their group has nothing to fear even though Harry Grimm (Harry Simms) has been shot. "Sidney knew that Quinn was thinking 'we're too distinguished a crowd, too well known, they wouldn't dare do anything to *us!*'" Sidney speculates that Grimm's murder may have authenticated the presence of their group in Kentucky. The group also endangered others, including one of the truck drivers who had been wounded and the mining families who faced increased intimidation and violence. Ultimately when a miner suggests that one of the writers go to the hospital to visit the dying Grimm, Sidney volunteers. And, in the style of 1930s proletarian fiction, he then finally understands why he had come to Kentucky in the first place. "Now Sidney knew what he had come for. He had come to find that his world was divided into two camps. He was on the side of his murdered friend Harry Grimm, on the side of his friend, Jim, the miner."[132] Vorse ends the story in a way that validates Sidney's efforts and those of the Frank Committee as well. But her style is too contrived and unconvincing. Her own notebook confessions and the agonized reflections of Sidney Moore suggest that she still had doubts about the trip. Vorse questioned her ambitions as a writer in relation to the struggle for social justice, and she wondered whether the miners had been helped or exploited by the delegation. The story did not answer these questions. Even more significantly, the story did not explore the extent to which Vorse continued to see the miners and their cause as "the other." They were workers who needed her assistance and she was a writer who needed their stories, but, notwithstanding the mutual dependence, mining people remained in the background of both her activism and imagination. Like extras on a movie set, they were occasionally seen but never heard.

In his masterful analysis of power and powerlessness, John Gaventa notes that neither group of writers who went to Kentucky knew much about the region or coal mining.[133] The same is true of most of the other writers examined in this chapter. Yet from Dos Passos's perspective, neither regional nor professional knowledge was a prerequisite for activism. In a letter to the *New Republic,* Dos Passos noted a kind of universalism in the commitments of writer/activists. "After all, if a Kentuckian who happens to be a miner has a right to defend himself against attack by hired thugs of the coal operators, even if they happen to wear deputy sheriff's badges, why in the name of common sense hasn't a lumberjack in Washington state the right to defend his union hall or a textile worker in Gastonia the right to defend a tent colony?" He then concluded that if the national conscience could somehow be awakened to the inequities revealed by economic conflict, the future would be dramatically different from the past.[134]

Dos Passos and the writers who journeyed to coal mining regions obviously hoped that by spending time in Pennsylvania, Colorado, or Eastern Kentucky, they were pushing the issue of workers' rights into a very public forum. Yet to paraphrase Hanna Arendt's statement about German guilt for the Holocaust, if everyone were guilty then no one was. The same can be said about the universality of workers' causes, especially those of coal miners. If they were all essentially the same (or part of larger issues) then unique conditions did not require unique responses. Although the involvement of Lloyd and Weyl are exceptions, brief appearances and symbolic gestures felt sufficient for the others. In addition, virtually all of the writers intended that there would be a direct correlation between their writing and their participation. Thus, driven by the universality of their ideologies and the particularity of their creativity, these well-intentioned writers or groups of writers defined what needed to be done for the striking miners instead of asking: "What can we do to help?" "Are there ways our talents can serve your cause?" "What do you need?" "Does our presence help or hurt your efforts?" Instead they appeared, did what they thought best, and departed. Their activism reflected a controlling consciousness that, according to Gayatri Spivak, "will consolidate it*self* by imagining the other, or, as Sartre puts it, 'redo in himself the other's project,' through the collection of information."[135] That the activism of these writers was idiosyncratic is not surprising since the ideological, professional, and personal baggage most brought with them to the coalfields encouraged them to view the various strikes in ways that encouraged working *for* but not necessarily *with* coal mining people.

Chapter 2

Two Appalachians: Don West and Denise Giardina

Unlike most of the other writer/activists, Don West and Denise Giardina were born in the coalfields. Both also were closely associated with coal mining during important periods of their lives. For a short time in the 1930s, West tried to organize while he worked as a miner in Harlan County; and Giardina spent her early years in coal mining camps in southern West Virginia. Their common Appalachian background is also reflected in their creative efforts. Much of West's poetry deals with the problems faced by working people in southern Appalachia. Giardina's best-known novels, *Storming Heaven* and *The Unquiet Earth,* focus on the struggles in the coal regions of West Virginia and Kentucky. Finally, and perhaps most important of all, West and Giardina were both activists who lived in Appalachia and felt a responsibility to both its people and problems. Their commitments have been deeper and more enduring than those of most of the other writer/activists. They have also been less inclined to view those with whom they worked as "the other." When West and Giardina ended their activist efforts and it was time to go home, they were already there.

West and Giardina attended theological school after college, although neither followed a conventional career in the church. As an ordained minister in the United Church of Christ, West mixed organizing and preaching activities until the 1940s, when he decided to leave the ministry. Giardina graduated from Virginia Theological Seminary. Although she participated in various social projects affiliated with the Episcopal Church, she never took the final vows that would have led to ordination. For both West and Giardina, the social gospel played an important if unconventional role and, to some extent, guided their activism and creativity.

If West and Giardina shared a social conscience, there was little else about them that was similar. West was born on June 6, 1908, in Gilmer County, Georgia, on a small farm in the mountains fifteen miles from the closest town or store. No other writer/activist experienced poverty so acutely as West.[1] He was one of nine children. His mountain boyhood was interrupted in his teens when his father turned to cotton sharecropping. West came close to following in his footsteps. But the teenager impressed an uncle with his precocity and enormous desire to read. The uncle enrolled him as a work-study student in a Christian industrial boarding school at Rome, Georgia. The Berry School, founded at the turn of the century, reflected the pre–World War interest in preserving mountain crafts and what West later derided as the missionary impulse towards mountaineers.[2] West earned his keep by working in the founder's house, but when he tried to organize a student strike over the showing of *The Birth of a Nation,* he was expelled. He then worked for several months stringing wires for Southern Bell Telephone Company. In the fall of 1925, West hitchhiked to Harrogate, Tennessee, to attend Lincoln Memorial University. Dressed in bib overalls with $1.65 in his pocket when he arrived, West took four years to work his way through LMU. James Still and Jesse Stuart were fellow students. They shared his growing interest in writing but not his sense of social activism, which was already becoming a distinguishing part of his personality. Just as at Berry, West was a campus activist and participated in a student strike aimed at enhancing student rights. For the second time in his life, West was expelled from school, this time temporarily. It was also at LMU that he met Mabel (Connie) Adams, an art major from Middlesboro, Kentucky, who he secretly married halfway through his senior year. Jesse Stuart was his best man.

While a student at LMU, West was influenced by Harry Harrison Kroll, a novelist and professor of English, and no doubt by his association with Stuart and Still. He left college hoping to write poetry while continuing his education. Although money was still a problem, West entered the school of religion at Vanderbilt University in the fall of 1929, obtaining a job coaching basketball at the Martha O'Brien Settlement House in Nashville. At Vanderbilt, West took several courses, including one on social ethics from Professor Alva W. Taylor, a native of Iowa who had first begun teaching there at the age of fifty-eight. Taylor believed that the Christian and social ethic were one and the same. He encouraged his students not only to discuss social problems but also to find ways of solving them.[3] West could readily identify with Taylor's views. Years later he recalled that Taylor's "love of God" truly reflected a life dedicated wholly to human welfare and betterment. "His deep, abiding love for Man is the positive evidence of his love for God." West's favorite course that Taylor taught involved an approach to problem solving including "seminars at Fisk; . . . visits to settlement houses and the slum sections of Nashville" as well as involvement in "labor problems and strikes."[4] Having grown up in a sharecropping family, West needed no introduction to poverty. But it was a strike in East Tennessee that first initiated him into the brutal world of industrial warfare and encouraged him to take the activist road that he would travel for the rest of his life.

During a lifetime of social activism, West never focused solely on a particular group or cause. During three different periods in his life, however, he was directly involved in the lives and problems of coal miners. While still a student at Vanderbilt, West got involved in a strike at Wilder, Tennessee. This early activist experience had an important impact on the future direction of his life. Fentress Coal and Coke Company controlled the little town of Wilder. At the beginning of the depression, the company cut wages twice. A third cut in 1931 was prevented when the miners formed a local of the United Mine Workers and threatened to strike.[5] When the miners' contract expired on June 8, 1932, the company announced yet another cut in wages and began systematically firing union members. The miners at Wilder and several neighboring towns immediately went out on strike. The UMWA reluctantly backed the effort, but the strike appeared to be an act of desperation. When some of the miners returned to work in October 1932, violence escalated between strikers and scabs. Eventually, Governor Henry H. Horton sent in National Guardsmen who seemed more concerned with protecting company property than maintaining civil order. With so many forces arrayed against them and the national economy continuing to decline, the strikers ended the effort in the spring of 1933. Most of them faced unemployment and poverty.

Shortly after the arrival of the National Guard, a number of people who sympathized with the miners went to Wilder to assist in the struggle. Howard Kester, southern secretary of the New York–based Fellowship of Reconciliation, and his wife, Alice, organized the Wilder Emergency Relief Committee in the fall of 1932. Alva Taylor headed the Church Emergency Relief Committee, while Norman Thomas, the socialist, made an appearance in March 1933, as did a young radical, Myles Horton, with whom West had recently worked on another project.[6] Taylor had encouraged West to go to Wilder, and, as West remembers, he took the suggestion as a command. "I borrowed an old truck from a fellow student and went about Nashville collecting food and clothes. I went lots of times."[7]

West was introduced to industrial warfare with the violent death of Barney Graham, the strike's most dynamic leader. Graham was gunned down in the streets of Wilder on the night of April 29, 1933. His body was riddled with ten bullets, four in his back. West attended Graham's funeral along with miners and their families. He also helped in organizing meetings to regroup the miners after Graham's death.[8] No one could ignore the failure of state authorities to take any interest in the murder. Several days before Graham's death, Horton received a tip about a hired assassin. Horton took the suspect's picture and carried it to Nashville in a futile effort to show it to the governor. Although the suspected assassin eventually was brought to trial, the jury acquitted him on the grounds of self-defense.[9]

West never forgot the strike or Graham's death, or the three children he left behind. When asked many years later about his own feelings at the time and why he went to Wilder, West considered the question superfluous. "I was interested in them because they were being oppressed. I had grown up oppressed. I came from the poorest of the poor."[10] This recollection of West's suggests that he was already on his way to becoming what Antonio Gramsci calls an "organic intellectual." Such an individual's origins and familiarity with working-class people help him create a nonpaternalistic counter-hegemony against the dominating elite.[11] More important, it encourages writers and intellectuals to recognize the subjectivity of those they are trying to help rather than turning them into objects of concern. West's consciousness had surely been raised by Taylor's discussion on social ethics and reinforced by his own reading and encounters with fellow students. But what he saw at Wilder only clarified what he had known for most of his life—that there was a tremendous gulf between the haves and have nots, the oppressed and the oppressors. For West there was also the bravado of youth, which he believed explained many of his activities. When asked if he had been afraid to go to Wilder after the murder of Graham, he replied, "I was young; I didn't have enough sense to be afraid."[12]

Part of West's youthful social activism emerged, no doubt, from his interest in the folk school movement. While at Vanderbilt, he had read Olive Dame Campbell's *The Danish Folk School: Its Influence in the Life of Denmark and the North* and had planned to visit Denmark to see it for himself. After obtaining a scholarship, he spent part of 1931 and 1932 in Denmark, including three months at the International People's College, a higher-level folk school. He then traveled throughout the country visiting other, smaller folk schools.[13] "What I liked best about the folk schools," he later remembered, "was that in them people were teaching themselves."[14] The Danish folk schools had first appeared in the 1840s, when a bishop in the Danish Lutheran Church had suggested that there was a need to educate and encourage farmers and rural people who for years had lived under a feudal-like system.[15] West "was encouraged by the fact that many of the farmers had come out of a very poor background, and now they were able to organize and do something for themselves."[16] He believed a similar approach could work in the mountains of Appalachia.

Back home by the spring of 1932, West took over the pastorate of a small Congregational Church near Crossville, Tennessee, while he searched for a location for an American folk school. West met a philanthropic resident of Monteagle, Tennessee, who was willing to turn over her farm to someone interested in building a community-based project. He began making plans to open a folk school at this site. In the meantime, West had met a twenty-seven-year-old Tennessean, Miles Horton, who shared many of the same beliefs and ideals. The two young southerners decided to work together on the project, which would become the Highlander Folk School.[17] West's former teacher, Alva Taylor, branded Horton and West "the two young Galahads" and expected that together they would initiate social change across the South.[18] Highlander did become one of the most dynamic of American folk schools, but it was not to be a joint venture, since West left the school permanently in the spring of 1933. Horton apparently felt that West was too much of an individual and could not adapt to institutional constraints. West found Horton to be too authoritarian, and he objected to Horton's perception of Highlander as an organization rather than as an initiator of social change.[19] Years later, West said that he resented all the outsiders, many of them northerners, Horton had attracted while studying with Reinhold Niebuhr at Union Theological Seminary in 1929-30. Horton tended to accept any offer of help to get the school on its feet. West perceived Horton's followers as missionary types, well-meaning individuals who do things for but not often with those they are assisting.[20] Given these differing points of view, the fact was that these radically oriented, individually motivated young southerners could simply not work together in the same institutional setting. Horton's name became synonymous with Highlander. West's dream about starting his own folk school was deferred for another thirty years.

Instead of trying to build an alternate folk school, West left Highlander to rush back to Georgia. There he joined the cause of a twenty-nine-year-old African American communist, Angelo Herndon, charged with inciting insurrection by leading a demonstration against unemployment. The end of the Wilder Strike and his subsequent involvement with the Herndon case was the beginning of the most radical period in Don West's life. During the 1930s and 1940s, he worked very closely with communists and was often branded a communist himself. Yet even though the FBI was convinced of his party membership during these years and although during the 1930s he organized for the National Miners Union and the Workers' Alliance, an organization of the unemployed, he always said that he never formally joined the Communist Party. Neither he nor Claude Williams, a former Taylor student who for several years was the controversial head of Commonwealth College (a labor school in Mena, Arkansas), were much concerned about a fellow activist's credentials. "He nor I either one would never ask a man what his political affiliations were before we agreed to work with him. If the man seemed to have principles and working for a good cause, why, we were ready to cooperate. Now that was not true of all people who were working at that time in the movement. Some people were particularly concerned that somebody might be a communist, you know."[21] West strengthened his accusers' charges by writing a poem during these years, "Listen, I Am a Communist," in which he announced:

I am a Communist
A Red
A Bolshevik!
Do you, toilers of the South,
Know me,
Do you understand?
Do you believe the lies
Capitalists say
And print about me?[22]

He later claimed that even though he sympathized with the communists' cause, he intended the poem to have a level of irony. He was already labeled a communist no matter what position he took. West may have sympathized with the party, but his support was far from absolute. He deplored the party's lack of knowledge about the South and the "missionary" outlook of many of its members.[23] Never much of an ideologue, he was nonetheless willing to work closely with the party despite his not sharing all its views. He appears to have viewed communists as "socialists in a hurry," much like other intellectuals, writers, and activists of the thirties.[24]

Disillusioned with Highlander and radicalized by Wilder, West scarcely hesitated before hitching a ride to Atlanta. His wife went with him, along with their baby daughter, Ann. Within a few days, West was leading the defense committee working for Herndon's acquittal. His family made do on his salary of five dollars a week. They shared a mattress on the floor of a small apartment with another young organizer. Constance mimeographed the flyers and pamphlets that West secretly distributed at night. Although the Supreme Court dismissed the charges against Herndon in 1937, West's involvement in the case had ended in 1934. At that time he went underground and then fled the state to escape charges of insurrection brought against him and several other co-workers.[25] For the next two years, West worked with striking textile workers in North Carolina. He and Constance then returned to Kentucky, where he found work in a mine in Bell County. For the second time in his life he became involved with the mining community. West had no mining experience, but he had gone to Kentucky as a volunteer organizer for what remained of the National Miners Union. Intending to keep his organizing efforts quiet, he was able to get a job loading coal in the Kayjay Mine.

According to West, the nearly-defunct union paid him nothing. "I was sort of a young fool. I thought it was my responsibility to help the poor and the miners of that area were poor." He also recalled that the other miners helped him cover up his inexperience by giving him the job requiring the least skill. Still, even for someone who had not fully considered the consequences, the first trip into the mine was unnerving. He never forgot getting onto a mine car and riding for what seemed like miles into the mountain.[26] West and his family lived in a two-room cabin on Greasy Creek some five or six miles on the other side of the mountain from the Kayjay Mine, and he and two other miners made the daily walk together. Unfortunately, one of the two, Fred Gooden, turned out to be a managerial stool pigeon. West had posed as a nonunion miner in order to get the job, but local authorities soon learned about his organizing efforts. After a little over six weeks on the job, West was arrested and, like members of the Dreiser Committee, charged with criminal syndicalism. Deputies swarmed into the cabin on Greasy Creek one night in late October 1935 and carried both West and Constance off to the jail in Pineville. Their two-year-old daughter, Ann, was left behind and taken in by neighbors. Local officials released Constance the next morning. She immediately took Ann to her parents in Corbin and then returned to Bell County.[27] West was not so fortunate. "I was kept back in the death cell. It was two double deckers and they had three other people. The other three were condemned to the electric chair," he recalled, "but I was kept in there with them. They wouldn't let me run in the bull pen with ordinary rape and murder charges."[28] When he was released after six weeks, West fled the state with Constance, bringing to an end this second and even more futile effort at aiding coal miners.[29]

The next twenty years were hard ones for West and his family. His social activism and efforts to feed his family, including a second daughter, Hedy, born in 1939, occupied most of his time. Yet he still found spare moments to write. A first book of poetry, *Crab-Grass,* appeared in 1931, and a second, *Between The Plow Handles,* aided by a fifty dollar grant from Highlander, was published in 1932. *Toil and Hunger* came out in 1940, and *Clods of Southern Earth* in 1946, which in terms of number of copies sold was surpassed only by Walt Whitman's *Leaves of Grass.* Most of West's poetry and prose is purposefully didactic, for, as he told an interviewer in the 1970s, "My poetry and Connie's painting is not abstract at all. I don't put down anybody who wants to paint abstract pictures, or to write abstract poetry, even those that want to start their sentences with little letters. If they want to do that, OK, but I'm not trying to revolutionize the alphabet myself. I'm trying to communicate, and I regard poetry as a medium of communication."[30] From a creative perspective West suffered because he had so little time to write. "I could have done a lot more writing if I hadn't had other things to do," he later reflected. "I would think about stopping and writing, then, I'd think about those people on the picket line and I couldn't just stop and write."[31]

When West left Bell County, he became Kentucky state organizer for the Workers' Alliance. This job served to confirm the FBI's suspicions about his communist ties. He later earned a master's degree and taught at Oglethorpe University. He also took courses at the University of Chicago and Columbia University. Somewhere, in between, he farmed for a time, worked as a cook on a Mississippi steamboat, briefly served as a superintendent of schools in Lula, Georgia, and, in 1948, worked for Henry Wallace's campaign. As a Congregational minister, he also pastored churches in Ohio and in his native state of Georgia.[32] Throughout his adult life, West's religious and social views were never far apart. He often preached, for example, that Jesus was most concerned with the downtrodden and would have continued to organize in a more radical social direction had he lived.[33] West believed deeply in what he preached. He decided never to pastor another church when a leading member of his south Georgia congregation joined in the whipping of an elderly black man who had brushed against a white woman on a sidewalk rather than yield the customary right-of-way.

During these years West was constantly hounded as a communist. He lost a teaching position at Oglethorpe in 1948 because of his radical views, and his name was mentioned on several occasions before the House Committee on Un-American Activities. When he was subpoenaed to appear before the Senate Internal Security subcommittee in Memphis in the fall of 1957, he took the Fifth Amendment. West believed government committees were engaging in unlawful political harassment. His refusal to testify was based on principle. "I do not probe into a man's politics or his religion. That is none of my business. Nor do I consider it anybody's business what mine are. . . . Regardless of where it has been written or said, I do not assume responsibility for what others say or write."[34] Hard times continued into the 1950s for the Wests. Their situation worsened when the family lost most of its possessions in a 1958 fire in Georgia, allegedly set by the Ku Klux Klan. They finally enjoyed more financial stability when Constance was hired to teach in the Baltimore public school system and West got a job at the University of Maryland. Rather than bask in the comforts of two salaries, they decided instead to live on one and save the other to fulfill a lifelong dream of creating their own folk school.

In 1965, many years after the founding of Highlander, Don and Connie West began building their dream. They were determined that their school would be different from most of the other folk schools that they knew of in the United States. They would use as a model the Danish system West had observed years earlier. The school would have its own unique personality, a curriculum based on Don and Connie's experiences over the past three decades. From the beginning, the Wests did not want their school to be anything like Hindman Settlement School, where both had briefly worked in the early 1930s, Berea College, whose educational philosophy they knew, or even Highlander. West believed that Hindman and Berea reflected the kind of cultural uplift in which "superior" outsiders assist the "natives." "Most of those were millionaires—people coming in from supposedly higher cultures to lift up the hillbillies." Berea was too elitist. West wanted his school to "deal with real problems of people. Didn't want it to be like Berea. Berea only took in a few poor kids and then tried to make them different from everyone else."[35]

Although he would be loath to admit it, ultimately West's school, the Appalachian South Folklife Center, most closely resembled Highlander. His school would encourage mountain people to be proud of their heritage, but he also planned for it to be at the forefront of social change. Ironically, the Wests began creating their school the same year that Presbyterian minister Jack Weller published *Yesterday's People.* West detested the popular work because of its victim blaming and stereotypical portrayal of mountaineers. Weller's Appalachian analysis made West even more determined that his school would correct such distortions. David Whisnant argues that American folk schools were often so caught up in preserving the "culture" of the region that the dominant structural realities of outside exploitation or "class-based inequities" were ignored, and the schools were therefore more therapeutic than reforming in their orientation.[36] Both Highlander and the Wests' school tried to challenge the basic economic and political structures of Appalachia and to implement social justice through change. In reality, their approaches scarcely differed. But in West's mind, Horton and his northern friends were still too much like outsiders. "I always got acquainted with local people whereas Horton was more interested in what was going on in New York. I guess he went there so much because that's where he saw the money coming from."[37]

The Appalachian South Folklife Center resembled Highlander in yet another way. Just as Horton dominated Highlander until his retirement in 1970, the West family was a key and pervasive influence at the Folklife Center. Ann edited the center's magazine, Hedy was one of the stars of the annual music festival during the first week of August, and Don and Connie were the chief fund-raisers and organizers. The Wests bought a three-hundred-acre farm in the small, unincorporated town of Pipestem, West Virginia, almost halfway between Beckley and Princeton. They chose this site for a number of reasons. They liked the people, the scenic beauty, and the name. But Don also hoped to help people there, especially "kids who were being brought up just like I had been—very poor." Summers County was at the time among West Virginia's poorest and possibly one of the poorest in the country. Though not a mining community, Pipestem lay relatively close to mining regions in western Virginia and eastern Kentucky.[38]

Even though West designed his school for all types of working people, he estimated that close to half of the summer students came from mining families. "At the Folklife Center we were interested in all poor kids, but lots happened to be miner's kids. Mining problems were some of the biggest problems in Appalachia. Miners' kids were the ones who were kicked around the most."[39] In order to enrich the lives of these poor children, the center served as an overnight camp during the summer. Although children from mining backgrounds were usually present at the camp, there were two summers when a particularly large number of them attended. West's accommodation of the extra campers that first summer epitomizes his innate generosity as well as the center's institutional flexibility. Since all campers came free of charge, the Wests always spent a part of each winter trying to raise the approximately $300 necessary to support each of the 45 to 125 young people during the four to eight weeks. The number of children accepted depended on the amount of money raised the previous winter. West remembered that at the start of this particular session, when all of the children that the camp could hold had been registered and settled in, a truck full of miners' children from Harlan County, Kentucky, arrived. Instead of turning them back, the staff engaged in frantic improvising. West made more frequent trips to a bakery on the outskirts of Charleston that sold cheap three-day-old bread. He also traveled more often to a federal distribution center on Route 61, which offered food surpluses to places like the center that helped the poor.[40]

During the summer of 1978, the camp was again filled to capacity. This time West expected the crush of people. The Folklife Center had pledged to provide seventy-five additional scholarships for the children of striking miners from Stearns, Kentucky.[41] On July 7, 1976, miners had initiated a strike against the Stearns Mining Company, a subsidiary of the Knoxville-based Blue Diamond Coal Company. Safety concerns and the issue of union recognition had led to the walkout. The company hired armed guards and scab workers, one of whom was shot to death on his way home from work; a grand jury eventually indicted twenty-seven miners for strike-related matters.[42] Rather than join the picket line at age seventy, West may have tried to help by supporting the miners' children at his school.

The crowded summer session of 1978 was fairly typical. West had hated the exclusion of students from institutional governance at schools he had attended and decided to organize the campers, age ten to seventeen, into a student council. This council helped to assign responsibilities for cooking, dish washing, cleaning, gardening, and feeding and caring for livestock. Although students did not receive grades, the staff encouraged them to attend classes on their mountain heritage, including history, crafts, fine arts, and music. Campers could choose a traditional musical instrument—fiddle, banjo, dulcimer, harp, or guitar—and take private lessons from accomplished musicians who were brought in as teachers and performers. West most enjoyed teaching the history courses but would turn them over to students to teach if they had previously heard his lectures.[43]

Travel was also an intrinsic part of each summer's itinerary. Campers might go to an exhibition coal mine in Beckley, West Virginia; to the Indian Reservation at Cherokee, North Carolina, where they could see *Unto These Hills;* or to the West Virginia dramas *Honey in the Rock* and *Hatfields and McCoys* at nearby Grandview State Park. Smaller groups of campers went on camping trips and on visits to poor homes in the vicinity simply "to get them talking together. We wanted them to understand that they shared common problems and should begin to talk about what could be done to solve them." As the Folklife Center gained renown, sponsors brought in campers from outside Appalachia. During the summer of 1973, for example, three students from the Newcastle coal mining area of Great Britain were guests, and in subsequent summers children from Welsh mining families also attended. In 1978, when sponsors from Delaware inquired if an African American child would be safe in West Virginia, West simply sent them a photograph of the past summer showing the racial mix of the campers, a primary objective of the Folklife Center.[44]

Although summers were the busiest times, the Folklife Center remained open year round to meet the needs of the surrounding community. At poor people's workshops, which lasted one or two weeks, participants discussed common problems and concerns. Church groups offered their own workshops, and Volunteers in Service to America (VISTA) held training sessions there. The center's library, which continually grew as a result of donations from around the country, remained open all year for the people of Summers County. A 1972 article about the school appeared in *National Geographic* and aided in fund raising. Supplementing the treasury became a high priority when, in January 1974, a fire destroyed the two-story frame building that served as dining hall, kitchen, and the Center for Appalachian Culture.[45] West immediately began making plans to rebuild. He and Connie ran the center until 1984 when, both elderly and in poor health, they relinquished co-directorship of the day-to-day operations. West never intended for his school to serve the needs of any particular group. Yet his programs at the Folklife Center from the mid-1960s to the mid-1980s touched the lives of more coal mining families than his earlier activism in Wilder and Bell Counties. By encouraging campers to acknowledge their past and future, he helped prepare them for the day when mining would not be their only choice in life. Even more important, however, he instilled in many of the children a belief that inequality could best be confronted by the collective activities of the oppressed.

About the time that Don and Constance West stepped aside as co-directors of the Folklife Center, another Appalachian, thirty-three-year-old Denise Giardina, was publishing her first novel. Born on October 25, 1951, in Bluefield, West Virginia, Giardina and her brother Frank grew up in the coalfields of the southern part of the state.[46] At the first, Black Wolf, her father was a bookkeeper. Several of her uncles worked as miners for the Page Coal and Coke Company, which was located in McDowell County about twelve miles from Welch, where her mother worked for a while as a nurse. During the 1950s the area was relatively prosperous, but economic conditions deteriorated and the company closed in 1963 when Giardina was twelve. The family eventually moved to George's Creek outside Charleston, where her father got a job with the Cannelton Coal Company. After graduating from high school in 1969, Giardina entered West Virginia Wesleyan, a small liberal arts college in Buckhannon, West Virginia.

Giardina's college years prepared her for a career as writer and social activist. Except for trips to Myrtle Beach, South Carolina, she had never been outside West Virginia until 1972, when she spent part of her junior year in England with the Experiment in International Living. This trip sparked an enduring interest in medieval English history and led to her first novel twelve years later, *Good King Harry,* based on the life of Henry V. She also encountered in England the kind of stereotyping that Appalachians often face, when a fellow traveler, upon hearing her southern accent, asked if she was racially prejudiced.

It was also during Giardina's junior year that she heard about the Buffalo Creek disaster, an event that affected her in a powerful way. Early on the morning of February 26, 1972, a makeshift earthen dam built by Pittston Coal Company disintegrated. This calamity released 132 million gallons of water into a mountain hollow mining community, Buffalo Creek, in Logan County, West Virginia.[47] One hundred twenty-five people died, and four thousand homes were destroyed, all in a matter of minutes. Giardina realized at once that Buffalo Creek could happen in any number of communities, including one of the hollows where she had lived as a child. She developed a special dislike for Pittston because it had created an unsafe dam and because of its "business as usual" attitude following the disaster.

The war in Vietnam also affected Giardina's social consciousness. At first she had supported the war, but as her brother neared draft age she began to rethink her position. The tragedy at Kent State in 1970 further solidified her antiwar views. Giardina's opposition, however, remained on a personal level. She never became a student activist at West Virginia Wesleyan.

Giardina's introduction into the world of protest began shortly after leaving college. She returned to Charleston, West Virginia, and supported herself by substituting in the Kanawha County school system. Soon Giardina was involved in a textbook controversy there. The church attendance she had begun in England continued in Charleston, and the rector of St. John's Episcopal Church, James Lewis, played a major role in the episode. Ironically enough—given her future activities—Giardina actually opposed a sizeable number of coal miners who struck in sympathy for the protestors of the textbooks.

The trouble began during the spring of 1974. The wife of a fundamentalist minister on the school board objected to material in several of the textbooks selected for the fall. She claimed the books undermined community, religious, and family values. The protest simmered during the spring and summer, but when schools opened in September it exploded. Protesters held mass meetings and picketed schools and the board of education. They boycotted classes and bombed buildings. Some thirty-five hundred miners in the surrounding areas went out on a sympathetic wildcat strike. The Reverend Lewis, who often acted as spokesperson for the Kanawha County Coalition for Quality Education, opposed any type of censorship.[48] Through Lewis's influence and her own dislike of censorship, Giardina became involved in the controversy. Even though she understood the deep resentments of many of the protestors, she also believed that "people had to stand up and say 'you are not taking books out of schools and not keeping kids from reading books.'" And although she detested the way in which the media stereotyped the entire region, she disliked even more how right wing political groups attached themselves to the pro-censorship side.[49]

On a personal level, the most important result of her participation in the controversy was the close friendship that she developed with Jim Lewis. Over the years he remained both friend and mentor. He was at least partly responsible for her decision to enter Virginia Theological Seminary in 1976. Giardina today believes that her decision to seek ordination had more to do with education than theology. The year 1976 also brought the first authorization that women could be ordained in the Episcopal Church. Lewis introduced Giardina to the notebooks of the German theologian Diedrich Bonhoeffer, who was executed because of his role in the 1944 officers' plot to assassinate Hitler. The inspiration derived from Bonhoeffer's ethics and courage continues to play an important role in both her political and creative activities. During her seminary days Giardina also discovered *Sojourner's Magazine,* which espoused a kind of personal activism similar to present-day liberation theology. For several months during 1977-78, she lived at the Sojourner Commune in Washington.

Giardina's first job out of seminary was to minister to the needs of a tiny church in McDowell County, where she had grown up, and to co-direct the Keystone Mission, which at the time was primarily a center for senior citizens. At the start, she hoped to broaden the mission's activities by taking a more active role in solving the problems of the area. In doing so, she became interested in the question of landownership—not a high priority for some of her co-directors. When they complained to the bishop, he warned her to cease her activism or resign. Giardina resigned from Keystone but continued to pastor her small church until it became obvious that the diocese could not afford to have a single minister for so small a congregation. Rather than accept reassignment, she decided not to enter into the priesthood.

No longer a part of the social ministry of the church, Giardina remained committed to one of the projects that she had started working on at Keystone. She was one of a hundred "lay researchers" who made up a citizens' task force interested in land reform in Appalachia. Research assistance came from the Highlander Folk School and the Center for Appalachian Studies at Appalachian State University in Boone, North Carolina. The Appalachian Regional Commission donated $130,000 to facilitate an examination of landownership patterns in six states: West Virginia, Virginia, Kentucky, Tennessee, North Carolina, and Alabama. Most of the field work was completed by 1980, and in 1983 the University Press of Kentucky published *Who Owns Appalachia?: Landownership and Its Impact.* Giardina did the research for McDowell County, discovering in the process that the Pocahontas Land Company, controlled by Norfolk and Southern Railroad, owned much of the county but paid little in taxes.[50]

During the early 1980s, Giardina was engaged in a variety of activities, including another stay at the Sojourner Commune in Washington. By 1982 she was back in Lincoln County, West Virginia. She lived there with three Jesuit priests trying to start a citizen-oriented reform group to prevent strip mining and spark some local concern for land reform. Aside from these pursuits, she set aside more time to write—especially after a publisher expressed interest in what would be her first novel, *Good King Harry.*

Giardina had long believed that she lacked the ability to write creatively. She was more interested in reading books she had neglected during her college and seminary years. Until her late twenties she wrote only sporadically. When an editor at Harper and Row seemed interested in her book on Henry V, however, she began to gain confidence. Still, at this time in her life, her writing was more a pastime than a career. To make some money while writing, she joined the staff of West Virginia Congressman Bob Wise in 1982. She had met him while working on the land survey. Giardina quit that job when Harper and Row accepted her novel, and used the advance to begin work on a second one combining childhood experiences in the mining camps with a longtime interest in the 1920-21 mine war in West Virginia. She spent most of 1983-84 writing, but as the money began to run out, she took what was essentially a secretarial job for the West Virginia Democratic Party. Later in 1985, she began working for former Congressman and recently elected Secretary of State Ken Hechler. She stayed with him for a year and a half while continuing to work on the novel.

In the summer of 1986, Giardina moved to Prestonsburg, Kentucky, because she wanted to live in the coalfields. Living there would certainly help authenticate her writing, but there was another, more political reason for her choice. Giardina believed that the many writers who stereotyped Appalachians were adding yet another dimension to regional exploitation. She felt an ethical and personal need to be a part of the area about which she was writing. Shortly after moving to Prestonsburg, she joined Kentuckians for the Commonwealth and served as its secretary-treasurer from 1987-1988. The organization's primary concern at the time was with broad-form deeds. These contracts enabled corporations, many of which were absentee landowners, to control the mineral rights under the land of numerous local residents. Many companies holding broad-form deeds had practiced the most destructive kinds of strip mining while polluting the water and virtually destroying the homesteads of hundreds of small property holders.[51] When *Storming Heaven* appeared in 1987, Giardina was quickly recognized as one of the country's best young writers. New demands on her time and energies forced her to step down as secretary-treasure of Kentuckians for the Commonwealth, but her activist impulses remained strong.

From her childhood in mining camps, her activism, and her writings on the mining experience, Giardina developed a focused perspective on the world. Although she wrote for a living from 1987 to 1992 while working on a more recent novel, *The Unquiet Earth,* Giardina still believed that it was not enough just to write about Appalachia. She believed that collective social action and organizational effort were necessary to achieve social justice and institutional change. "The main reason I do things is because of my spiritual beliefs. Although this place [Appalachia] is the focus, I see myself as a citizen of the world. We all need to do things for other people. God is the ultimate authority and not the government and certainly not corporations. I find myself standing up against anything that tries to take God's place."[52] Like many of the young writers who had participated in the 1902 Anthracite Strike, Giardina believed that the reformed United Mine Workers was essential to the well-being of miners and their families. Any efforts to destroy it had to be resisted. When the A.T. Massey Coal Group moved to undermine the union in the fall of 1984, Giardina observed parts of the resulting strike firsthand.

A.T. Massey, the nation's eighth-largest coal producer, had withdrawn from the Bituminous Coal Operators Association in September 1984. Massey had just signed a contract with the United Mine Workers and insisted that since its individual mines were independently run, each was entitled to negotiate separate contracts with its workers. This meant that the workers employed at a mine that closed could no longer preserve their pensions by transferring to another company mine according to seniority. Under the new rules the company could simply close a mine and reopen it with low-paid workers to whom the company had no long-term pension obligations. Since the union had guaranteed pension rights, Massey's strategy was criticized as an outright attack on the UMWA.[53] In October, 1984, the union called for a strike against the Massey mines in the Tug River valley sections of Kentucky and West Virginia. Violence erupted from both sides. Massey hired a security guard company that used helicopters and armored personnel carriers. The miners tried to prevent nonunion workers from mining and hauling coal. Giardina went to the strike areas several times. She recalls a group of visitors from Bhopal, India, brought by John Gaventa to view the conflict, who were shocked by the poverty of the area and completely astonished by bullet holes in a local organizer's house. The atmosphere was so highly charged that Giardina and the Indian visitors, while in the organizer's home, threw themselves on the floor in terror when a car backfired close by.[54] Although she sympathized with the miners, as was apparent in a guest column she wrote for the *Charleston Gazette,* she did not actively participate in the strike itself. After fifteen months of struggle, a National Labor Relations Board agreement settled the walkout in favor of the UMWA. Massey was ordered to bargain as a single employer.[55] The company's violent tactics would help inspire Giardina's involvement in another confrontation four years later.

Giardina moved to Durham, North Carolina, in the late 1980s, hoping for a chance to make contact with other writers. She supported herself with part-time jobs while working on her novel. While in Durham she read about an escalating struggle between a Connecticut company and the UMWA that seemed much like the Massey episode. Giardina did not fail to note that the company was Pittston, the very one whose dam had caused the Buffalo Creek flood in February 1972. The Pittston Coal Company, the nation's seventeenth-largest producer, had withdrawn from the Bituminous Coal Operators Association in 1987, rejecting the union contract that was to run from 1988 to 1993. The company offered its workers a new contract that included a slightly larger wage increase over a three-year period but a 20 percent decrease from the medical benefits provided in the national contract. The Pittston contract also enhanced the company's ability to schedule shifts, including new night shifts on Sunday, and to avoid hiring workers laid off by other company-controlled mines. The company could also hire nonunion contractors to take over traditional union jobs of repairing equipment, transporting coal, maintaining idled mines, and constructing mining facilities.[56] In a break with tradition, the UMWA worked for fourteen months without a contract, but then called the Pittston miners out on strike on April 5, 1989. Pittston hired replacement workers and a security firm, the Asset Protection Team, to shield the scabs from strikers. The UMWA countered with civil disobedience and passive resistance, hoping to avoid the kind of violence that gave the union a bad press during the Massey strike. Union leaders also called for sympathy strikers to join them, to show their support of working people during yet another antilabor action of the Reagan-Bush era. Given her background and interests it is not surprising that Giardina was among the first to join them.

Unlike many writers examined here who joined a picket line, Giardina was motivated by a powerful past. "I am an exile, as anyone from the mountains must be after being uprooted by coal. Black Wolf, the camp where I grew up," she recalled, "passed through a series of hands before being torn down. My family resettled near Charleston, severing close ties with uncles, aunts, cousins, neighbors. What I found, to my sorrow, is that once those ties have broken, once the community has been left or lost, it can never be restored or duplicated." The Buffalo Creek disaster put the coal companies, for her, in a particularly negative light. "Buffalo Creek revealed the coal industry in all its nakedness," she wrote some fifteen years after the event, "an enemy of the people who live in the central Appalachians, the destroyer of not just mountains and streams but of culture, community, family." The Massey and Pittston strikes represented for her a defense against a corporate attack upon a region and its people. The companies were trying to destroy the union, an institution that Giardina believed provided a critical defense for mining communities against the coal companies. "It is equally clear that the industry intends the continued massive depopulation of the Appalachian coal fields, the better to blast and gouge the landscape into oblivion." Giardina's work in McDowell and Lincoln Counties, West Virginia, along with her involvement with Kentuckians for the Commonwealth had long since convinced her of how a rapacious drive for profit could socially and environmentally devour a region. Collective efforts were needed to counter this greed, and, from her perspective, "the only institution which stands between coal field communities and their dispersal, the institution those communities fought for and which has served as a buffer between the miner and the willful neglect of coal companies, is the union."[57]

Giardina's most daring courses of activism involved not only intellectual and biographically related reasons but spiritual ones as well. Long an admirer of Diedrich Bonhoeffer, Giardina believed that there are times in which direct action is needed. When preparing articles for *The Nation* and *Village Voice* about her experiences at Pittston, she warned them that she was not going to be an objective writer. "I went as a witness. I wanted to say: this is what's happening to this region, these people. I wanted to get the word out for the rest of the country. I didn't believe at the time and still don't that the mainstream media was doing this."[58] But getting the word out was not enough. Giardina was willing to engage in civil disobedience even if it might lead to her arrest. Usually wearing a camouflage shirt like the others, she made the trip five times from Durham to St. Paul, one of the little coal towns in the southwest tip of Virginia. Giardina and her friend Jim Lewis were arrested twice, along with other sympathizers and strikers, for sitting in front of coal trucks.[59] She also received a traffic ticket for driving her car slowly in front of a coal truck, thereby obstructing delivery. Giardina's first arrest took place in early May of 1989. She and a large group of sympathizers had sat down in front of coal trucks as they entered the Moss No. 3 preparation plant near Dante, about five miles north of St. Paul. They had chosen this plant because of the large volume of coal that passed through its gates. In her second act of civil disobedience, Giardina joined with a Catholic nun, six Episcopal priests, and over a hundred miners and supporters from the neighboring area. They had gathered at a worship service the night before, and there Giardina had talked about her growing feelings of anger. Pittston's president had compared the strikers to klansman, Nazis, and communists. Giardina had also heard a recording of a visit by a group of miners to Greenwich, Connecticut. One miner, critical of Sunday work, was laughed at when he said that he used "church to get through work during the week." When he called church "my crutch in life, the whole meaning of it, because I hope to go to a better place when this is over," a Pittston executive flippantly invited him to come to Greenwich.[60] Giardina had seen the same kind of smugness over parochial matters at the Buffalo Creek disaster. She shared many of the values that were being disparaged with the miners and their families. At the end of the evening worship, a miner's wife pulled her aside to say that she fully understood Giardina's anger. "My father was killed in the mines. Two years later my brother was killed in the mines. Ten days after that my husband's brother was killed in the mines. I've had reason to hate. But it destroys you so you have to put it aside."[61]

Giardina always realized that she was a writer posing as an activist. She wrote articles for *The Nation* and *Southern Exposure;* the *Village Voice* commissioned her to live with a retired miner and his wife for a week to learn firsthand of the impact of the strike on the area.[62] Never viewing herself as a neutral observer, she had already been arrested and had joined the miners on the prison bus. By getting arrested as well as living with a mining family, Giardina hoped to show the striking families that they were not alone in their struggle. But for all her efforts, Giardina knew that she could never be a full participant in the strike. She was a writer, not a miner. She was fighting for a good cause, but it was not her own. It was not that the miners rejected her support. In fact, to the amazement of Giardina's clerical friends, the striking miners applauded them as they walked down the highway between two lines of pickets. If the miners were distant at all, it was because they understood intuitively that Giardina's kind of support had its limits. "At times I felt very guilty," she recalled. "I got paid by the *Nation* and *The Village Voice* whereas two priests involved lost their jobs, and, of course, the miners' very lives were at stake. I didn't know what to do about it except keep on trying."[63]

Giardina and West never stopped trying to implement social change in the region. At times Giardina's activism has brought her into conflict with some of those she was most interested in helping. During the Kanawha County textbook controversy and again in her present-day campaign against mountaintop removal (an insidious kind of strip mining in which the tops of mountains are removed to get at the coal beneath them), coal mining people have often sided with the opposition. Understanding and sympathizing with community concerns about moral standards and the loss of jobs, she nevertheless believes that problems like censorship and environmental destruction have no boundaries. In a 1992 essay in the *New York Times* she voiced her customary concerns about poverty, absentee ownership, corporate irresponsibility, and widespread unemployment in Appalachia. But she argued that these were not regional problems. "Like the Canary carried underground whose demise warns miners to make a quick escape, Appalachia's distress is an urgent warning. The whole country is facing . . . 'the appalachization of America.' When the American people seek images of poverty and powerlessness on the nightly news, they now see their own faces looking back."[64]

West also believed that the poor, no matter where they were found, needed his support. He may have engaged in a kind of conceptual "othering" by viewing miners' kids as those "who were kicked around the most." Memories of his own impoverished youth undoubtedly colored his views of the world. Though at times inadvertently stereotyping mining families and their children, he remained determined that they speak and act for themselves rather than being spoken for by the various missionary types he so mistrusted. The Folklife Center was intended to be a gathering place in which self-discovery and collective solutions to social problems—rather than proselytization and moral uplift—determined the daily agenda.

Though neither West nor Giardina viewed themselves as regional activists, both believed that they were most effective in the areas that they knew best. Both carried with them a deep sense of obligation toward the people and region they wrote about. The geographic orientation of Giardina's and West's activism suggests the same sense of place that Kent C. Ryden analyzes in *Mapping the Invisible Landscape.* "The depth that characterizes a place is human as well as physical and sensory, a thick layer of history, memory, association, and attachment that builds up in a location as a result of our experiences in it."[65] For both writers, personal connection to the region had intensely political implications. They participated in what Wendell Berry calls a "beloved community." Members of such a community share "common experience and common effort on a common ground to which one willingly belongs."[66] It is not that the other writers lacked a sense of place. Chicago, western Pennsylvania, Virginia's eastern shore, Cape Cod, upstate New York, the Southwest, Denver, and even New York City were deeply embedded parts of the creative psyches of Dreiser, Cowley, Dos Passos, Vorse, Wilson, Frank, Creel, Eastman, Reed, and Ornitz. But the activism of these writers usually occurred in what a folklorist recently has called an "ad hoc region." West and Giardina acted in an "ontic region"—one in which they were familiar and comfortable. Ad hoc regions are usually the mental constructions of individuals from outside an area and often "preclude considerations of 'group,' group consciousness, or folkloric expression of group consciousness." Ontic regions are more symbiotically tied in with geographical, social, and cultural community expressions and experiences.[67]

Giardina's attachment to a specific region has never suggested parochialism or an "us versus them" mentality. In pursuing her career as a writer, Giardina has imagined herself living in different areas of the world for a time; but she can never see herself leaving Appalachia permanently. "One reason I stay in the region is because living here I share in the problems," she says. "I drive the roads crowded with coal trucks, I drink the water, I share the other problems that all of us share by living in a community. I couldn't live with myself if I just wrote about the region and didn't live in it."[68] Giardina's most recent novel, *Saints and Villains* (1998), is based on the life of Diedrich Bonhoffer. When the German theologian took a brief trip to the United States in 1939, he was offered a job along with security and safety from the turmoil of his own country. He chose to return home. Giardina will continue to return to Appalachia. Pittston will not be her last strike. "If it ever happens again," she assured one interviewer, "I'll do it again."[69]

West also lived outside of Appalachia on many different occasions, but like Giardina, he always returned. The Wests eventually left the Folklife Center for the healthier Florida climate, but after a few years they decided to return to Cabin Creek, West Virginia, where as a young man Don had worked and organized. Shared memories as well as shared commitments played a role in their decision to go back. But West may have been disappointed. Mining was no longer a major industry there. The union barely existed. West looked around and saw too many young people growing up without work, and he felt little hope for the future.[70] In the fall of 1991, at age eighty-five, he shared his concerns with a number of friends:

> Cabin Creek is a sad place. Much different from the 1930s when I was a union organizer here. More poverty, less hope by the people. The union is not doing much, if anything. I live on a road that has 26 more dwellings beyond my place but the state never goes or does anything on that section at all. It is a pitiful, deplorable situation. There is only one family that was here back in the 1930s and they are invalids. No body else seems to know there ever was a struggle here. Mother Jones and Mother Blizzard are strange names.[71]

Although he was too old to pursue an activist role like Giardina, West continued to recognize the area's problems and to lament the lack of community solidarity that he believed had once existed.

As much alike as West and Giardina may have been, they differ in an important way. Giardina regards herself as a writer who is also an activist. At work on another novel, she continues to shape her life around her writing. West used his writing to support his various projects. After the founding of the Folklife Center, West devoted every winter to the lecture circuit. He read his poetry around the country to raise money so that poor children might share in the camp experience the next summer. West's poetry is not found in many anthologies, Appalachian or otherwise. Its didacticism, its harsh message, the absence of stylistic innovations may explain its lack of recognition.[72] Perhaps West paid a literary price for subordinating his art to his beliefs. On a drive near Charleston, West Virginia, in the spring of 1992, West noted that "the mountains are so green that they look soft which makes you forget their hardness."[73] Much like the mountains of Appalachia, West's writing was hard in a way that overshadowed the softer side of his life. He devoted that life to helping others seek social and economic justice. No one knew better than West how elusive those goals could be in a commercially acquisitive world.

Chapter 3

Coal Mining in the Novel, the Short Story, and Genre Fiction

Mikhail Bakhtin argues that the novel, of all the creative genres, offers the best description of life. The novel has dialogic potential as it immerses itself in life's daily routine. In characterization, ideas, and social issues, the novel can effectively portray the unfinished nature of human existence.[1] In many of the works in this chapter, mining people are often "characters" rather than "personalities." This literary distinction of Bakhtin's embraces the concept of "the other."[2] No matter how complex or skillfully drawn characters are, for the most part they are "objectivized" and "finalized." They are static and frozen into an unalterable sense of reality. Personalities are not; they are more flexible, more capable of changing their minds as well as their identities. Personalities are incomplete, fragmentary, and forever in a state of becoming.[3] Their complexity suggests depth, diversity, unpredictability, and, perhaps most important of all, "unfinalizability." As Bakhtin argues:

> For the author the hero is not "he" and not "I" but a fully valid "thou," that is, another and other autonomous "I" ("thou art"). The hero is the subject of a deeply serious, *real* dialogic mode of address, not the subject of a rhetorically *performed* or *conventionally* literary one. And this dialogue—the "great dialogue" of the novel as a whole—takes place not in the past, but right now, that is, in the *real present* of the creative process. This is no stenographer's report of a *finished* dialogue, from which the author has already withdrawn and *over* which he is now located as if in some higher decision-making position: that would have turned an authentic and unfinished dialogue into an objectivized and finalized *image of a dialogue,* of the sort usual for every monologic

> novel. The great dialogue in Dostoevsky is organized as an *unclosed whole* of life itself, life poised *on the threshold.*[4]

Novelists, then, seem better able than playwrights, poets, or film directors to involve themselves intimately in the world around them. Given coal mining's significant, controversial place in American life, it is not surprising that writers have produced scores of novels on the subject, over a hundred of which are examined here, since the late–nineteenth century.[5] None of these authors would be hailed as great writers, but their work has a worth of its own. While not held up to the standards of a Dostoevsky, who Bakhtin believed best reflected the dialogic imagination, their works will be nonetheless scrutinized using Bakhtin's dialogical model and the question it poses: Do the people in these literary creations show any sense of their own subjectivity or are they instead the participants in a creative process that forecasts more than unfolds? Whatever the answer to this question, these novels undoubtedly provide a collective insight into a *mentalité* that explores the complexities of the coal mining experience.

Many of the novels written during the last third of the nineteenth century through the 1930s emphasized how dangerous coal mining can be. Although the authors attempted character development, their portrayal of miners and their families seldom rose above stereotypes. Many of these early novelists were both fascinated and disturbed by issues of class, ethnicity, and race in the coalfields; most wrote about these themes from a decidedly middle-class perspective. The concern of more recent novels for environmental issues is absent from these earlier works, which were written at a time when the coal industry was still meeting much of the nation's energy needs. Most of the novels published between the 1940s and 1970s that touch on coal mining themes are similar in character and tone to those of the earlier period. But there are differences. If management is less frequently praised in the later works, unions also receive their share of critical scrutiny. More women take center stage, especially those working in the mines. The impact of strip mining on the environment is also a major concern. Violence continues to be a part of mining life, particularly in Appalachian settings. But as mystery and other popular genre writers increasingly set their narratives in the coalfields, mayhem became more individualized in literature. A number of the novels written during the 1940s through the 1970s are more innovative, experimental, and creatively significant than any of their predecessors; yet from a Bakhtinian perspective, they, like the older works, remain distinctively monological in their views of coal-mining folk. In the 1980s and 1990s a handful of women writers added a new and exciting dimension to the narrative process by using life and work in American coalfields as an imaginative center. Their works finalize neither issues nor lives. Characters in these works, like the human beings they represent, are always in the process of changing, and the problems and dilemmas they encounter are constantly shifting. This type of creativity encourages the unpredictable and indefinable rather than the anticipated and delineated. Many of these later works therefore reduce the sense of "otherness" found in earlier fiction.

It is difficult to characterize the nineteenth-century novels as anything more than a blend of romanticism and local color with an occasional dash of realism.[6] The first eight are set in either the anthracite or soft coal regions of Pennsylvania. They describe the natural scenery and the mining patches and try to recreate the dialects of the miners. Most of these early novels would fit easily into the local color school of literature. But the willingness of these writers to deal with the day-to-day mining of coal in an effort to understand the concerns of the miners suggests a greater realism. Their early attempts at character development, however, are similar to the facades on a motion picture set. Virtually all of these writers wanted to narrate a romance. Coal mining provides an exotic backdrop for middle-class characters to sort out their lives while in romantic pursuit of one another. Even when the main characters are working-class, their aspirations are socially upward. Their experiences are either stepping stones to something better or explanations for failure.

Nineteenth-century novelists tend to describe mining as grim work. In *The Slate-Picker,* a Horatio Alger–type novel set in the Wyoming coal region of Pennsylvania, an incredible number of accidents and mine disasters occurs. Apart from more dramatic events such as explosions and flooding in the mines, in two of these early novels, *The Company Doctor* and *The White Slaves of Monopolies,* miners' asthma is an equally deadly by-product of the job. For writers such as Mary A. Roe, Rev. R.F. Bishop, Henry Edward Rood, and Dan Beard, working underground is a kind of slavery.[7] In each novel the job itself rather than the legal system creates this form of bondage, which adds to the sense of estranged "otherness" between author and subject. These novelists agreed that mining should not be a lifetime job. Even in the novel *Camerton Slope,* an unrealistically idyllic portrait of the life of a mining community, the most able characters are the ones who want to leave. The writers focus on the importance of self-improvement rather than the improvement of working conditions, especially if strikes are involved. Roe, Thornton, and Bishop seem more concerned about the coercion used against nonstriking miners than the issues that caused the strikes in the first place.[8] Beard, Roe, Rood, Thornton, and the author of *The White Slaves of Monopolies* recognized that management should bear some of the blame for work stoppages. The only unreservedly pro-labor novel among the ten is Thornton's, but even in this work there are good owners. In fact, most of these early novelists feared miners in large groups, especially ones associated with a union or under Irish leadership.

The obviously anti-Irish writers considered the Molly Maguires, with its exclusive Irish membership, the most dangerous miners' organization. McMahon, Roe, and Rood portray the Mollies as criminals. Bishop is a bit more moderate. Describing the Molly Maguires he suggests that this "new order was made up of a class of men who, to say the least, were not model citizens."[9] This anti-Irish tone reflected nativistic reactions to the high rates of immigration to America at the turn of the century. "The ignorance, filth, and viciousness of those Poles, Italians, Sicilians, Tyroleans, Bohemians, and Slovaks are absolutely appalling," Dr. Curtis complains to his wife after resuming his duties as company doctor in Rood's novel.[10]

If the best miner is native born, English, or, more rarely, Irish, he is also sober in his personal life as well as moderate in his politics, much like the fictionalized portrait of labor leader John Siney in *The White Slaves of Monopolies.* In short, the fictional miner, at least the good miner, possesses the same middle-class values of his creator. Nothing better points to this fact than the miners' desire for something better, if not for themselves at least for their children. Sweeney, the mine boss in *Philip: or, the Mollie's Secret,* likes the young man his daughter has fallen in love with but advises her not to marry him. "You know he is quite poor, and will always have to depend on the mines for a living." The marriage takes place only after the suitor leaves the pits to become a mining inspector.[11]

The novella *A Mountain Europa* and the novel *My "Budie" and I,* written in the late 1890s, have much in common with the earlier works. Both are love stories in a coal mining setting, both create stereotypes, and the male hero in each is solidly middle-class. Their differences, however, serve as a kind of literary bridge between the nineteenth and twentieth centuries. Unlike the eight earlier novels, these two are set outside the Pennsylvania coalfields, in the southern Appalachians. Aside from the African Americans and immigrants that are negatively portrayed, there is also a new stereotype that emerges in both of these novels—the mountaineer and his culture. While Fox was more interested in mountaineers than miners, Thornton was fascinated by the process of digging coal and fills the first pages of his novels with technical descriptions of various aspects of mining. Though the mine is a brutal place to work, his characters are highly skilled men who depend on one another through the "budie" system. Buddies not only work together, depend on one another, and look after one another, but also "loaf together, drink together, fight together, fish together, and are altogether together." Thornton also acknowledges a mining culture that differs from the middle-class one of his fictional persona. This culture is neither well defined nor developed in the novel, but at least it is briefly posited. It crumbles in the end when all of the main characters get as far as possible from the mining pits. Ultimately, *My "Budie" and I* is set apart from other nineteenth-century mining novels in its realistic portrayal of the "budie" system and in its effort, however weak, to describe a mining culture.[12]

From 1900 to 1920, when Progressive reformers were addressing the consequences of rapid industrialization, mining novels changed in subtle rather than substantive ways.[13] Most of these early-twentieth-century novelists, like their predecessors, believed that coal mining was a grim and dangerous job. They still feared large groups of miners in mobs or unions. All continued to stereotype immigrants and African Americans, as well as miners and their families. In most of these novels, middle-class characters romantically pursue one another while working or living in coal mining regions. The authors are no more skilled in characterizing mining folk than earlier writers, but Will W. Whalen's *The Lily of the Coal Fields* is the first novel to look at a woman in the coalfields.

These novels are also more geographically diverse than the nineteenth-century works. Half are set outside of Pennsylvania: three are located in the Midwest; the two by Upton Sinclair, in Colorado. Strikes are as important to the narratives as they were in earlier novels, but, in keeping with the period's concern with efficiency, labor stoppages are shown in most cases to be as detrimental to labor as management. These Progressive Era writers feared the impact of social polarization and alienation. Even writers such as Newell, Anderson, and Sinclair, who supported industrial unions, believed that working people need middle-class leadership. While Newall describes an organizer who abandons a position in upper management to form a miners' union, Anderson's Beaut McGregor is even more charismatic. Even though Anderson tries to show that working people would have to unite to challenge the economic forces controlling their lives, he never clarifies the purpose of the marching men, leading critics to disagree over what the novel means.[14] Yet it seems that a more important theme in the novel is very clear. Working people, and especially miners in the early chapters, cannot lead themselves. Their minds are not sufficiently developed. Here Anderson shows the same prejudice as other writers of his day.

Apart from brief descriptions of domestic activities and the shared fear for the safety of men, women also remain in the shadows in these Progressive Era novels. Will W. Whalen's *The Lily of the Coal Fields* is a flighty romance in which a young woman samples life's experiences as a maid and a nurse until the coal miner she has always loved finally asks her to marry him. Apart from brief hints about the restricted lives of young women in mining communities, the female characters are as undefined as they are in most other coal mining novels.[15] Union activist Mary Burke, in Sinclair's *The Coal War,* serves as little more than a contrasting symbol to the empty lives of the upper-class women who dominate the society of the hero, Hal Warner. Yet she is attracted to the middle-class life, especially after she agrees to move into the home of one of Hal's socialite friends as a parlor-maid. "Red Mary" predictably abandons her luxurious surroundings to rejoin the fray during the Ludlow strike. Yet from a literary perspective, even more important than Mary's class loyalty is the novel's intent focus on a female character, unrivaled by any other early-twentieth-century work.[16]

Although Sinclair tried, he could not create believable working-class characters in either of his two mining novels. Sinclair, like Henry Demarest Lloyd, was always more concerned with the whole rather than its parts. His real interest was in showing how a predatory industry operated in a capitalist system. He believed that the system more often than not shaped the lives of people rather than the other way around. This left him little creative incentive to focus on the "inner world of his characters."[17] He wanted the country to see the results of unrestricted capitalism. One way to do this was to rush his coal mining novels into print when public interest centered on the death of women and children at Ludlow.[18]

As it turned out, *King Coal* did not appear in print until 1917, three years after the Ludlow strike. To one potential publisher, the novel had seemed more propaganda than fiction. Sinclair rewrote it to meet that publisher's needs. He then wrote a sequel, *The Coal War.* This was a fictionalized version of the Ludlow massacre with essentially the same main characters as *King Coal.* Rejected for the same reason as *King Coal,* the sequel was finally published in 1976 long after Sinclair's death.[19]

Like most authors of mining novels, Sinclair paints a relatively bleak picture of the miner's world. But his description is unique in one way. Unlike other writers, Sinclair believed there could be no good company or manager. No company could act in a socially responsible way if it operated in a capitalist system. He also believed that most companies could not avoid using force, especially during strikes, to maintain production. Earlier novelists had conflicting views on coal companies' use of force, but most feared a mob of miners above all. Sinclair shared some of these fears, but in his two novels, especially in *The Coal War,* the state militia becomes the howling mob and drunken deputies pose a menace to the community.[20] Despite his disgust with capitalist greed, Sinclair never abandoned his belief that all working groups needed responsible leadership with a middle-class outlook on the world. Masses of immigrants, through their ignorance or fears, seem to thwart all efforts at class solidarity in *The Coal War.*[21] Every confrontation involves mobs of enraged workers who ultimately take directions from rational, middle-class leaders.[22] Yet there are hints in both of his coal mining novels that he understood the limits of paternalistic activism. Toward the end of *King Coal,* Hal Warner has not converted any of his rich friends to the miners' cause. Critic Walter Rideout sees the failure as a symbol of Sinclair's belief that class wars will continue.[23] Warner is also unable to convince Mary Burke that by playing "worker" he has significantly bridged or even understood the class chasm. "Ye think ye've come here and been one of us workin' people. But don't you own sense tell you the difference, as if it was a canyon a million miles across," she explains to this well-meaning scion of privilege. "You and I can never work together like we been doing," she warns him as Ludlow nears its tragic conclusion. "There's no use thinking about that—ye'll find it out in time. But there'll be many ways ye can help the miners, and if I can be sure that you won't lose interest, then I'll not feel so bad about losin' ye."[24] Although his fictional creation Hal Warner presumably continued to support the miners' causes, the writer himself was soon caught up in other unrelated causes and new creative projects. Still, he had raised the question of whether writers and intellectuals have any staying power when it comes to supporting working-class causes, and he had looked to his own life for clues. *The Coal War* served as an unpublished epitaph to an unsustained commitment—the same Progressive commitment that never bridged the gulf between middle-class dreams and the "otherness" of working-class realities.

If Sinclair turned away from coal mining themes in his work of the 1920s, other writers turned towards them.[25] West Virginia replaces Pennsylvania as a favorite locale in most of these novels. Portrayals of immigrants and African Americans are again unreservedly negative. In Mary E. Waller's *Deep in the Hearts of Men* (1925), published one year after the passage of the National Origins Act, the attitude of a key character reflects a prevailing national view. Moving from an ethnically homogenous environment in West Virginia to a more heterogeneous one in Pennsylvania, Celia Boncoeur finds a place "teeming with the human life of twenty-six nationalities: citizens born, naturalized citizens, aliens; and of the latter many of them foreign to our ways, our laws, our ideals; and, above all, not able to use the instrument by which we may transmit ideas and so come to an understanding one with another, our English Speech."[26]

It is hardly surprising that most of the coal novels of the twenties reflect the conservatism of the age. These novels tend to view all industrial workers and especially miners as volatile "others" who are dangerous and yet fascinating. They were published at a time when many manufacturers offered the American Plan (an attack on collective bargaining by big business) as the best way of dealing with working people. A common theme in these novels is a permeating fear of unions and union leadership in the coalfields. By the 1920s the Molly Maguires were all but forgotten, but in George Brydges Rodney's novels the Industrial Workers of the World have taken their place. By the decade's end, Will W. Whalen, in the novel *Strike,* shared none of Rodney's obsession with the IWW and his intense hatred of foreigners. But Whalen still suspected the IWW's power was based on foreign workers, who he believed were more temperamentally unstable and easily led than American-born workers.[27] Although D. Thomas Curtin and Arthur Train could imagine both good and bad unions as well as good and bad union leadership, Mary E. Waller and H.E. Danford would only tolerate the initiative and individualism of an open shop. These writers seemed most intrigued by the violent confrontations between labor and management then taking place in a strange and foreboding region of the country. In *Tyranny of Power,* Curtin uses the Paint Creek/Cabin Creek strikes and the march on Logan to dramatize his narrative, while Arthur Train's hero in *The Needle's Eye* arrives in West Virginia in the midst of the miners' march on Blair Mountain. H.E. Danford, in *The West Virginian,* crudely sensationalizes the much-publicized shootout at Matewan, West Virginia.[28] In these three novels, derogatory images of miners are so interlaced with those of West Virginians in particular and Appalachians in general that it becomes almost impossible to separate the stereotypes.[29] Typical is the reaction of the middle-class protagonist in *The Needle's Eye* when getting off the train in Langhorne, West Virginia: "It was a different sort of crowd from what he was used to—lank men with prehensile arms and faces black with coal-dust, stoop-shouldered negroes, frowsy, flat-chested women in calico sunbonnets, half-naked white babies, and totally naked pickaninnies, all staring silently. There was something ominous and menacing in such a silence in that sparkling world full of brimming sunlight."[30] "Otherness" suggested danger, especially in areas of the country that appeared to be out of the mainstream.

Yet it was not just in West Virginia that coal mining was negatively viewed. This fact raises a paradoxical question. If coal mining was so essential to the well-being of the country, why did so many of these novelists in the 1920s show a prejudice against it? This pervasive negativism stands in sharp contrast to the overall optimism of the era. Agnes Smedley disparaged the world of coal. In her autobiographical novel, *Daughter of Earth,* she recalls that often quarrels between her father and mother concluded with her father threatening to become a miner. Life in the mining camps is portrayed as relentlessly bleak. To escape the monotony "there was the saloon for the men; for the women, nothing."[31] In Waller's *Deep in the Hearts of Men,* mining families are portrayed sympathetically, but by the novel's end, all of the main characters have left the mines. Happiness is found only by escaping the hideous way of life. Characters go out of their way to ridicule coal mining. A young woman in *The Girl from Mine Run,* for example, comments on the reading habits of her coal-mining boyfriend. "Well, your reading Miles, is like a miner's life; all the poetry left out, and the prose run in."[32]

This kind of negativism has something to do with the "three D's" of coal mining: dirt, darkness, and danger. These elements enthralled the novelists and repelled them. Fears about industrialism may also have troubled them. Yet none of this offers an adequate explanation for why a job that was so often praised for its economic rewards and national necessity was so often debased in fiction. During and after the Civil War, white southerners inexplicably praised King Cotton while they denigrated and stereotyped their black workforce. Perhaps an analogy can be drawn to the late–nineteenth and early–twentieth century, when the nation's industrial health seemed tied to coal and those who mined it. The slave analogy to miners appears often in these novels.[33] This may stem from a widespread uneasiness about any national dependence on foreigners, Appalachians, African Americans, and the working classes in general. To the extent that many of these pre-1930s coal mining novelists reflect the preoccupations of the larger society, their concerns suggest that the dialogic process has as much to do with fear as with pity. The unnerving end result of that perception was the fear that these diverse working-class groups would organize.

While a negative image of coal mining is common in these 1920s novels, one novel stands out for its improbable romance. Jack Bethea's *The Deep Seam* features the first coal-mining female in American literature. The main character is determined to be by the side of the man she loves. She learns how to be a powder monkey by listening to the talk of miners in the office where she works. Eventually, disguised as a man, she joins her unsuspecting lover in the mine. In creating a strong, imaginative, female character, Bethea challenged traditional gender relationships; but he went only so far. By novel's end the disguised female miner is injured, losing all desire to work underground and, most of all, wanting the security of male support.

Although the coal novels of the twenties and thirties were similar in many ways, the authors of the Depression Era were better known and generally wrote better novels.[34] Most of the works of the 1930s are considerably more liberal in outlook than the earlier novels. Nearing, Conroy, Frank, Olsen, and Tippett all wrote novels that reflect the decade's increased literary radicalism. Though Gilfillan and Dos Passos were hostile toward communists and the National Miners Union in their novels, at this stage in their careers they were still far to the left of the earlier novelists. Only Rowan's *Black Earth* is openly antiunion. In *Red Neck,* McAlister Coleman and Stephen Raushenbush emphasize the growing conservatism of unions in the character of a labor bureaucrat who gradually loses contact with the rank and file. Strikes also play a uniquely significant role in these 1930s novels. Given the decade's heightened sense of class consciousness and economic frustration, this comes as no surprise.[35] In these novels, strikes are not just a tool to bring characters from different backgrounds together or to describe economic structure. Instead, they often dominate the narrative. Virtually all of these depression-era novelists have a negative view of management. Even from the conservative perspective of a writer like Thomas Rowan, whose villains in *Black Earth* are labor leaders, management usually bears some blame for labor upheavals.

If management is portrayed somewhat more evenhandedly in the novels of the 1930s, the job of mining coal is not. Miners are sympathetically described in Gilfillan's *I Went to Pit College,* but the would-be writer Johnny Carsil is ambivalent about his mining job. He is proud to be a miner because it is "the hardest work there is." Like a virus, it has gotten into his blood. But he also suggests that a sign ought to be hung over the entrance to all mines: "he who enters here must leave all hope behind."[36] In Jack Conroy's autobiographical novel, *The Disinherited,* his coal-mining father tries to dissuade him from working underground: "The mines is a tomb and once the earth gets over you, it's hard to hump up and cast it off. It crushes them all in the end."[37] Tillie Olsen's *Yonnondio: From the Thirties* is a more sophisticated and widely read work than either Gilfillan's or Conroy's. Yet miners' lives are tragically restricted. Early in the novel, in one of the most lyrical but damning sequences, the narrator describes a thirteen-year-old boy who is going underground for the first time after his father's death in a mining accident:

> And no more can you stand erect. You lost that heritage of man, too. You are brought now to fit earth's intestines, stoop like a hunchback underneath, crawl like a child, do your man's work lying on your side, stretched out and tense as a corpse. The rats shall be your birds, and the rocks plopping in the water your music. And death shall be your wife, who woos you in the brief moments when coal leaps from a bursting side, when a cross-piece falls and barely misses your head, when you barely catch the ladder to bring you up out of the hole you are dynamiting.[38]

Even John Dos Passos, who went out of his way to praise the sturdy independence of the miners and their families, has something less than positive to say. In a conversation with Glenn Spotswood, the protagonist in *Adventures of a Young Man,* a miner's wife limits the world of Appalachian coal diggers to a kind of cultural reductionism. Spotswood is surprised that although the woman is younger than he, she already has two children. The miner's wife, Pearl, amusedly responds, "Up in these mountains we don't have nothin' to do but work and git chillun."[39] Spotswood and Pearl have met for a brief instance, yet Dos Passos portrays the mountain woman as though her destiny is frozen in time. As she dismisses the complexities of all cultures and human relationships, she also fails to confront the messiness, the flux of life's "unfinalizability," that Bakhtin believes is intrinsic to human existence. All four of these writers use the mine as a pejorative metaphor—a form of social and economic construction that distorts and silences the miners' voices.

Gilfillan, Frank, and Dos Passos were far less interested in describing coal mining life than in analyzing how their middle-class protagonists reacted to events in mining communities. After graduating from Smith College in 1931, Lauren Gilfillan went to New York in search of a job in the publishing business. An editor challenged her to live for a while in the Pennsylvania coalfields and then write about her experiences.[40] Gilfillan made no effort to alter her middle-class values. She wrote what a recent critic calls one of the most "self-reflective" proletarian works of the entire 1930s.[41] The novel traces a young, college-educated woman's transformation during a coal strike from a wide-eyed observer to a committed journalist. The author empathizes with many of the mining families, especially the women, but her analysis of their lives is often superficial. To her credit, however, she recognizes her status as an outsider, a middle-class voyeur who peers into the lives of people she cannot understand. A Communist Party member in the novel reminds her, "You don't feel sorry for these people. Their misery is just so much grist for your mill. You're going to write a book."[42] Gilfillan would not argue against this point. She understood that she was in Pennsylvania to write. Her goal was not so much to help as it was to learn—but to learn primarily about her own reactions to events rather than anyone else's.

Like Gilfillan, Waldo Frank saw the coalfields as a place to develop a writing topic. He and his committee failed to accomplish much for the striking Harlan County miners, but Frank personally derived some real benefit from the experience—it helped him to finish the novel that he had been writing on and off since 1927. *The Death and Birth of David Markand* traces an intellectual's tortuous quest for ultimate meaning.[43] Only in book four of the novel, "The Mountain," does coal mining play a role. Markand arrives in Kentucky to help striking miners. "The Mountain" section is not only a recapitulation of many of Frank's personal experiences in Kentucky but also a reflection of his active role on behalf of the miners. Markand, like Frank, believed that the miners needed leaders who could help them articulate their ideas, but this was not the primary reason that he went to Kentucky. The journey was another part of Markand's continuous search for self-understanding. Just as Frank left the area for good in 1931, Markand develops no enduring relationship either.

By the time John Dos Passos fictionalized his Kentucky experiences in *Adventures of a Young Man* (1939), he too viewed the miners' plight as politically entangled with the American Communist Party. Dos Passos's persona in the novel, Glen Spotswood, is a member of the party. During his stay in Harlan County, he has trouble keeping party leaders focused on the miners. Yet by novel's end, he hints at a parallel between the arrogance of the communists and that of writers, such as himself, who went to Harlan with the Dreiser and Frank Committees. When he returns to New York, the disillusioned Spotswood seems to abandon his activist bent: "It's the workers who are going to do it anyway, not a lot of soapbox sobsisters."[44] Just as the party lost sight of the people it was trying to help, these three writers paid little attention to the depth of the coal mining life. The writers gave coal-mining people little creative opportunity to speak for themselves. Their characters were convenient props or fictionalized "others" for middle-class intellectuals trying to confront troubling personal and political issues.

Larger issues of agency play a key role in one of the most interesting novels about mining and miners written in the 1930s. Although critic Barbara Foley claims that Tom Tippett's *Horse Shoe Bottoms* fetishizes the proletarian origins of its main character to create an exemplary working-class hero, it is an enduring piece of fiction with a unique treatment of coal-mining people.[45] Written by a Brookwood Labor College instructor and organizer, this novel realistically describes mining life and unionizing efforts in the Illinois coalfields in the 1870s, when John Siney was setting up the Workingmen's Benevolent Association and later the National Miners' Association.[46] The novel traces the life of a young immigrant, John Stafford, as he advances from miner to organizer in true 1930s fashion. What sets this novel apart is its willingness to examine how the members of a mining family, especially the wife, react to one another and to life's uncertainties. Ellen understands that the men in her family will always be miners because they want to be. When a friend urges her to persuade her husband to look for another kind of work, she responds: "My John likes the coal; he is somehow a part of it. There's coal in him. He'll never leave. My sons will be miners." Ellen does not naively dismiss the dangers of mining coal. A sense of agency emerges as her family endures poverty and danger. They care for one another and they allow nothing to destroy their resiliency or to let anything "quench the laughter in their hearts."[47]

Horse Shoe Bottoms is also a rarity among the coal novels published between the 1870s and the 1940s. The main characters are not trying desperately to escape from the mines or to own one. Tippett never idealizes the mining life. He portrays its dangers in many different ways. Yet the family never sees itself as part of a degraded workforce. When Stafford is blacklisted, the family moves close to a small mine owned by a farmer willing to hire him. They live in a house in an isolated hollow surrounded by rural beauty. Ellen is content here, but John is restless. When the blacklist is lifted, they move back to Horse Shoe Bottoms "where sparrows, streaked gray like the mice, fought over the tipples, where smoke coiled low and hovered near the ground." Later, as her husband is dying from black lung, Ellen realizes that the family is home, not just her sons but her daughters as well. After a lifetime of doubt, she can now face a truth she has always known: "We are miners."[48]

During the 1940s and 1950s, a number of factors helped sustain literary interest in coal mining themes: the World War II coal strikes, the turmoil in the coalfields following the war, and the irascible and powerful personality of the head of the United Mine Workers, John L. Lewis.[49] Many of the writers of the forties and fifties chose the coalfields as a convenient fictional setting. The novels of Cain, Salisbury, Graham, Burke, and the Boltons are good examples. Graham's *Swing Shift* is a picaresque description of the organizing efforts of a character from a coal mining background. Burke's *Sons of the Stranger* is an involved romantic epic in which mining is incidental to the story. Cain's *The Butterfly,* Salisbury's *The Clay Hand,* and Stanley and Jeanette Bolton's *Black Blood in Kentucky* are novels set in mining areas of the Appalachian mountains. All three portray the region as an American heart of darkness. Cain, apparently, was influenced by a 1922 visit to the Big Sandy area of West Virginia. He worked there for a while in the mines and was fascinated by tales of the mine wars. Still, he never wrote the novel he intended.[50] Instead, twenty-four years later he published *The Butterfly,* which features violence, incest, illegitimacy, moonshining, and ignorance. It is an improbable story of mistaken identity in which a father lusts for a daughter who, it turns out, is not related to him. As implausible as the plot is, Cain obviously hoped that his readers would accept the tale because of its location.[51] Davis likewise chose an isolated Appalachian coal mining town as the setting for her mystery novel, *The Clay Hand.* Superstitions and moonshining are as entangled in the plot as in *The Butterfly,* but it is the miners' xenophobic dislike of strangers and their tendency to attack outsiders that helps create a tense murder investigation. Davis's and Cain's descriptions are subtle in comparison to those of the husband and wife team who collaborated in writing *Black Blood in Kentucky.* The Boltons' book is essentially a western novel in an Appalachian setting: a sadistic, antiunion killer takes over an isolated coal camp in eastern Kentucky, where the only justice comes from the barrel of a gun. With the cold war at its height and recent coal strikes suggesting the growing power of the UMWA, it is not surprising that several of these novelists focused on historical themes, especially labor disputes involving communists or strong leaders like Lewis. Caldwell, in *Tender Victory,* William Bradford Huie, in *Mud on the Stars,* and Harris, in *The Trouble at Hungerfords,* wrote novels in which communists or communist-like groups played nefarious roles in coal town power struggles. McKenney, in *Jake Home,* and Lawrence, in his four novels set in New Mexico, are far more supportive of the organizing efforts of communists. McKenney is also more sympathetic toward the Molly Maguires than most earlier writers, but so too are such non-radicals as Atherton (*Mark's Own*), Idell (*Stephen Hayne*), and Graham (*Swing Shift*).[52]

There is little agreement among these writers about the need for strikes, the role of the UMWA, and the nature of its leadership. In *Mud on the Stars,* Huie attacks both the union and its leader; Burgan (*The Long Discovery*), Atherton, Lawrence, and George are more sympathetic, while Caldwell specifically praises Lewis for his anticommunist stand. Writing from a more conservative perspective in *The Right to Live,* a romance set in a mining community in eastern West Virginia in the 1920s, Smith is less concerned with the lives of miners than with the wastefulness of strikes and the need for reconciliation between labor and capital. Burgan hoped that athletic competition might unite the various factions in a mining community. In his novel, the town's baseball team is the creation and hobby of the mine owner. The team brings the community together and offers an escape from the mines for its more talented players. Yet, it is unclear whether work itself or a specific kind of work is held accountable for dehumanizing the workers, and Burgan fails to develop this theme or explore fully the importance of baseball to coal mining towns.[53]

A far more gifted and better-known writer than any of the above is James Still, whose *River of Earth* and *On Troublesome Creek* both go beyond mining issues in their emphasis on such themes as birth, death, and love. A farmer, a native Appalachian, and a teacher at Hindman Settlement School in the Kentucky mountains, Still has always been interested in the coal mining experience and seems to dislike it intensely.[54] What troubles him most is how the mining culture separates human beings from the soil and nature, how it fosters economic dependence, and how it undermines a traditional way of life. None of his works more forcefully expresses these themes than *River of Earth.* In the novel, the mother represents a traditional relationship with the soil, that of farming and mountain life; the father pleads the economic and social advantages of working underground. The story is often told from a child's perspective. The family's younger members, like a jury hearing both sides of a case, are caught between opposing viewpoints. Although proud and enduring, Still's characters live in a deterministic world. They struggle to maintain their dignity in the face of a changing culture and an economic structure that offers them only blind chance. Still abhors the mining culture not so much because it brutalizes and degrades but because it threatens to destroy a traditional way of life he cherishes. It is this master craftsman's defense of the traditional that adds a degree of "otherness" to his characterization of many who live in a coal mining setting. There is something lacking in their lives and experiences. They are confronted with detours at every turn. All horizons may be limited, but none more so than those of the characters in Still's mining camps.

In many respects Myra Page, whose novel *With Sun in Our Blood* appeared ten years after *River of Earth,* loathes coal mining as much as Still, but her reasons are more conventional. Page had a vital interest in the plight of working people. She was an organizer for the Amalgamated Clothing Workers Union, a labor journalist in the early 1930s, and she published *Gathering Storm* in 1932, a novel based on her observations of the 1929 strike at Gastonia, North Carolina.[55] While coal mining fascinated her, Page believed it had a brutal impact on mining families. Page's coal camps are dreary settings, and the work is portrayed as dangerous, but characters are sustained by the concern they show for one another as well as their continuing hope for change.[56] Yet for an activist like Page, membership in a caring, vibrant community cannot compensate for the dangers of mining coal. Only social change would produce any meaningful improvement for miners and their families. The life of the main character in Page's novel comes full circle as she, much as her father before her, tries to improve the miners' plight. Dolly is scarcely reconciled to the senseless grief around her. But at a community gathering a newly installed pump that Dolly helped acquire serves as a ritualistic baptismal hope for the future. With the installation of this relatively simple device, there is a kind of rebirth in the community as the clean water improves life for the people there. By novel's end, Page seems considerably more optimistic than Still, for human effort has made a terrible job better.[57] Much like Still, however, she essentially rejects digging coal as an acceptable way of life.

In writing about the 1960s, critic Frederick R. Karl reminds us that "its examples of the new do not necessarily supersede those from the previous decade."[58] This statement is relevant to the novels of the 1960s and 1970s in which coal mining plays a substantial role. Five novels written during the 1960s use the background and image of coal mining and miners to narrate a story that has little to do with the job.[59] Three other coal-related novels appeared in the 1960s.[60] What makes these three novels different is their authors' intention to create stylized, larger-than-life characters. Few miners have been more vividly portrayed as superhuman than the characters Matt Matthews, in *Danger in the Dark,* Jan Volkanik, in *Black Fury,* and Benjamin R. Holt, a mine-worker leader in *Power.* Known primarily for his historical fiction, Howard Fast published *Power* in 1962. One of his lesser-known works, *Power* centers on a fictionalization of the United Mine Workers and President John L. Lewis (Benjamin R. Holt). The narrative follows the union leader's career from his failed organization of West Virginia in the early 1920s through the creation of the Congress of Industrial Organizations and the sit-down strikes at General Motors in the mid-1930s. For the most part, Fast portrays Holt sympathetically; though he has little good to say about the miners' world. Michael A. Musmanno's *Black Fury* is an enhanced screen script that first appeared as a highly successful film in 1935. Musmanno was much like the writers who helped the UMWA during the 1902 strike or accompanied Dreiser and Frank to Harlan County. He was interested not only in writing about the miners but in helping them as well. As a member of the Pennsylvania Legislature in 1929, he introduced a bill bearing his name that called for the repeal of a law allowing management to use coal and iron police in the coal regions.[61] His larger-than-life character, Jan Volkanik, symbolizes the union's leadership on the local level during the years 1925 through 1928, as it battled both management and communists.

The majority of the novelists of the 1970s whose work centered on coal mining themes were interested, as was Fast, in real characters and events. They showed a continuing fascination with turbulent eras of the past.[62] Whereas James Lee Burke, in *To the Bright and Shining Sun* (1970), and John Sayles, in *Union Dues* (1977), wrote about the 1960s, John Rolfe Gardiner's *Great Dream from Heaven* (1974) and Michael Novak's *The Guns of Lattimer* (1978) were set in the 1890s, when class warfare periodically erupted. Davis Grubb, in *The Barefoot Man* (1971), James Sherburne, in *Stand Like Men* (1973), and Charlie Ward, in *Silk Stockin Row* (1975), wrote about miners and their families struggling to survive the economic and labor upheavals of the 1930s. Events in Michael Quigley's *April Is the Cruelest Month* (1971) spill over from the 1930s into the 1940s. The novel reads like a fictionalized version of Jack Weller's *Yesterday's People,* which stereotyped more than analyzed Appalachian culture. In *Vein of Riches* (1978), John Knowles examines the mining scene from management's perspective over the years 1909 through 1924, during which the coal industry went from boom to bust. John O'Hara wrote about the anthracite region of his youth, but the occasional miner appearing in *Gibbsville, PA: The Classic Stories* (1992) is usually a drinker, gambler, spender, and womanizer—far less interesting than his better developed middle- and upper-class characters. Gene Marvin, in *Vestige of Valor* (1973), continues the tradition of writing mystery novels set in coal mining country. This whodunit occurs in eastern Kentucky during the 1960s, with flashbacks to the 1930s. Finally, Charleton Ogburn's *Winespring Mountain* (1973) is an old-fashioned novel about a relatively recent phenomenon: the fight in Appalachia over strip mining. In this novel, set in an indeterminate post–World War II time frame, the miners—or at least the operators of the heavy machinery—are no longer portrayed heroically. The authorial voice emerges in a long speech by the main character at a public hearing: "We have to make our living from the earth, yes. It can't be wrong to mine coal. But what must be wrong, and evil, is to act like vandals, to have no consideration for God's creation." In its claim that "it can't be wrong to mine coal," *Winespring Mountain* suggests a more positive approach to digging coal than many of the novels that preceded it.[63]

Robert Coover's *The Origin of the Brunists* is a comparatively innovative novel of the 1960s. Nonetheless, it creates a sense of "otherness" in describing strange events in a small mining town in western Pennslyvania. Coover uses shifting points of view and the fusing of religious imagery with caustic satire to examine the impact of a chiliastic cult on modern society.[64] The Brunists take their name from an Italian miner, Giovanni Bruno, who miraculously escapes a mine explosion that kills his entire crew.[65] Bruno is a cross between Nicholas Hasek's the good soldier Schweik and Jerzy Kosinski's gardener, Chance, in *Being There.* In a vision he has after the explosion, he learns the day and hour the world will end. As Karl points out, Coover masterfully describes the passion of the cult, "the readiness of normal people to give themselves over to something that will pour meaning into their lives."[66]

Coover chose a mining community for his novel for a variety of reasons. The mine appears to provide a particular setting, and readers recognize the danger involved with the disaster-prone mining industry. Yet Bruno could just as easily have survived an air crash as a mine explosion. Just as John Grisham knew that his readers would instinctively understand why a young attorney from the coalfields works so ambitiously, Coover believed that his readers would appreciate why miners and their families try to add meaning to their lives. *The Origin of the Brunists* implies as much. As Bruno begins his ascent into notoriety and prophesy after emerging from the mine, Coover suggests that the hero "was a little short on style maybe, but this town was long accustomed to making do with less than the best."[67] Coal mining communities, so infused with quiet desperation, can more convincingly become the source of improbable events.

Violence has always played a prominent role in coal mining fiction, but violence is exceptionally graphic in some of the mining fiction of the sixties and seventies. The hills of Appalachia are portrayed as the last vestiges of the American frontier. This emphasis on violence can be tied to such events as the brutal killing of Jock Yablonski, whose Miners for Democracy challenged the UMWA leadership, in 1969. Violent scenes in coal mining novels usually emerge from management-labor confrontations. Novak, Knowles, and Sherburne treat such episodes as the Lattimer massacre, Blair Mountain, and the Battle of Evarts as parts of a larger saga. Much of the violence in *Great Dream from Heaven* surrounds the brutal treatment of convict miners. Several of the other novels describe gruesome murders or savage fights, notably graphic in comparison to earlier works. Charlie Ward's chapter "The Red Onion Café," for example, is filled with alcoholic-induced mayhem. Terrible beatings and an explosive confrontation between the local bully and the hero play a key role in Ogburn's *Winespring Mountain.* All of these novels pale in comparison to the graphic violence in Marvin's *Vestige of Valor,* Burke's *To the Bright and Shining Sun,* and Grubb's two novels.

While Appalachian miners are heavily stereotyped in the 1970s novels *Stand Like Men,* by James Sherburne, and *Union Dues,* by John Sayles, Sherburne is more concerned with the destructive role that outsiders have often played in Appalachian labor struggles. He fictionalizes the entire period of the mine wars in Harlan County during the 1930s. He describes Dreiser as an insensitive blunderer who did more harm than good in Harlan County. He likewise portrays the condescending and often doctrinaire attitude of the Communist Party toward the Appalachian miners it was trying to organize. Nothing better symbolizes the party's narrowness and lack of understanding of the region's culture than its attack on organized religion. Yet an organizer who understood this misstep erred himself when he explained the miners' lack of class consciousness. "Hell, they're all feudists at heart! They'd rather shoot their next-door neighbor than the employer who's screwing them blind!"[68]

Although he never defines such condescension in terms of "otherness," John Sayles describes similar displays of stereotyping in *Union Dues.* Hobie McNatt lives in a commune in Boston where he has to listen to a 1960s radical rant about the support McNatt's father gave to UMWA reformer Jock Yablonski. "'I think he's an evolutionist. A coopter. I think you people are being taken in by a dime-store liberal.' Hobbie slapped the floor with the mop and pushed away from Schenk. You people." Much like his father, Hobie was learning that his background stamped him as different. People saw him as politically naïve and, as he discovered in an intimate moment with Tracy Anne, a member of the commune, even primitively erotic. A sixteen-year-old runaway, Tracy Anne enjoyed the sexual freedom of the commune as much as anyone. It was only a matter of time until she discovered Hobie, and when she did, it was his tales of the dangers of coal mining, especially black lung and mine disasters, that most excited her. She believed that making love to a miner's son would be a new experience.

> She turned on her belly, then raised her bottom up in the air with her knees. "Come behind and fuck me."
>
> Hobie got up on his knees behind her and held himself and tried to find the right opening, the wet one.
>
> "Fuck me like they do back home," said Tracy Anne, "fuck me like the hill people do."
>
> He hunched and squirmed and pushed till Tracy Anne reached back to start the head into her. It fit, it fit so perfect, oh so

> hot and perfect around him, why didn't people do this all day long?
>
> "Fuck me like they do in the hills," she said, "fuck me like a *mule.*"[69]

These negative and stereotypical views of coal mining that encouraged readers to view mining folk as "the other" persist into the 1980s-1990s. Both change and continuity are evident in the more than thirty short stories and novels written on the coal mining experience during this period.[70] William Diehl, in the legal drama *Primal Fear,* hoped that his readers initially would sympathize with his demoniac creation, Aaron Stampler. An investigator defending Stampler for the murder of an archbishop in Chicago visits Crikside, Kentucky, to gather background information for the trial. He is stunned by his conversation with a local teacher:

> "I teach eight grades here, Mr. Goodman. One to three over there; four, five and six there; seven and eight here. You know what that's like? I feel I've accomplished something if I just get them into high school. If they don't make it by the time they're fourteen, fifteen, the boys end up in the mines. The girls get married."
>
> "At *fourteen*?"
>
> She nodded.
>
> "Did you talk Aaron into leaving?" he asked.
>
> "I told you," she said. "I'd like to think I had something to do with it."[71]

Several mystery writers of recent decades have also used coal mining themes. Unlike Elmore Leonard's lawman in *Pronto* and *Riding the Rap,* who merely grew up in eastern Kentucky, Frank C. Strunk's Berkley Jordan of *Jordan's Wager* (1991) and *Jordan's Showdown* (1993) actually lives there. Gerald Tomlinson, author of *On a Field of Black* (1980), allows the treacherous reputation of the Molly Maguires to complicate a murder investigation that leads back to the Civil War. John Douglas, in *Blind Spring Rambler* (1988), uses the hermetic isolation of an early-1920s West Virginia mining camp as the setting for his investigation. Jess Carr, in *Inheritance in the Wind* (1987), and K.C. Constantine, in his Mario Balzic novels, such as *The Man Who Liked Slow Tomatoes* (1982) and *Always a Body to Trade* (1983), write about events closer to the present. More an adventure novel than a mystery, Carr's story focuses on a kidnapped infant and a deranged Vietnam veteran in an Appalachian locale. Constantine's Mario Balzic is the Sheriff of Rocksburg, a bituminous coal mining town in Pennsylvania where most of the coal has run out. Although miners or ex-miners appear in all of these novels, most of the protagonists do not want to dig coal for a living. Strunk's Berkley Jordan, for example, worked as a miner for three weeks and hated every minute. Balzic becomes physically ill when he even contemplates working underground. There is a grimness permeating these novels. They are filled with a profound brooding ready to explode. There is nothing unique or even unusual about locating mystery novels in a mining setting. To be sure, there is no area of modern American culture that has escaped recent mystery writers. Coal mining communities have merely joined Native American reservations, the bayou country of the Cajuns, or the lands of the national park system as a setting for foul play. In choosing their locales, all of these writers hope to ensnare readers by offering them tidbits about a culture or an environment different from their own. Yet all who place their characters in a coal mining world seem to agree that no one digs coal unless he has to.

The same is true of less genre-oriented novels written during the same period. The writers of these works seemed most concerned with recreating historical eras in which coal mining played a significant role. Writing at a time when the industry is declining, they attempt to recapture its former importance. Sophia Yarnall's *The Clark Inheritance* (1981), Jay Kubicki's *Breaker Boy* (1986), Catherine Gourley's *The Courtship of Joanna* (1988), Ellis Wynne Roberts's *Flames and Embers of Coal* (1990), and Ed Campbell's *Between Heaven and Hell* (1989) all return to the Pennsylvania coalfields of the nineteenth and twentieth centuries. Sue Halsey's *Hannah's Dream* (1990) describes life in the southern West Virginia mining fields in the early–twentieth century, while John Young's *Hardcastle* (1980) depicts the metamorphosis of a drifter from mine guard to mine activist in the same state during the 1930s. Tom Hillstrom's *Coal* (1984), also set in West Virginia, tries to include everything that has happened in the coal industry since the 1950s in a rehashing of the Cinderella motif. The title story in Harry M. Caudill's *The Mountain, the Miner, and the Lord* (1980) and the selection "Little Thuggie" take place in strife-ridden eastern Kentucky during the 1930s, while Robert Louis Nathan's ambitious but not wholly successful novel, *Coal Mine No.7* (1980), unfolds in the southern Illinois coalfields in the late 1940s, when events in the mining industry still made national headlines.

The native West Virginian writers Jayne Ann Phillips, Richard Curry, and Breece D'J Pancake also employ coal mining themes in several of their shorter pieces of fiction.[72] Place plays an important role in the work of each. With the exception of Pancake, whose suicide cut short a promising career, all have written long as well as short fiction. Relatively young when their mining-related stories first appeared, these three writers shared an interest in coal mining and a similar attitude toward it. They grew up in West Virginia during the 1960s and 1970s when the coal culture was beginning to decline. Their creative responses reflect less the nostalgic decrement of poet P.J. Laska (discussed in chapter six) than one of sorrow tinged with bitterness. None of them shows any interest in explaining or dwelling on the coal mining life. Their characters dwell instead on unfulfilled dreams, the nature of human relationships, endurance, and alienation.[73]

Although four other writers of modern coal-related fiction—Cathryn Hankla, Lee Smith, Mary Lee Settle, and Denise Giardina—also share Appalachian backgrounds, they differ from Phillips, Currey, and Pancake. Each has written a novel or novels in which coal mining plays a significant role. Each has developed coal-mining characters more fully and less stereotypically than any of the above writers. And finally, gender may also be an important influence in the creative dimensions of their work.

From a literary perspective Hankla's work ought to stand alone. In a first novel, *A Blue Moon in Poorwater,* this poet, writer of short fiction, and teacher has tried to do what the others have done better. The story is narrated by ten-year-old Dorie Ann Parks, whose father is a miner. Her observations offer occasional insight into the life of a mining family in the later 1960s, although at times her story seems more like a Nancy Drew mystery or neighborhood adventure by Beverley Cleary. Neither Dorie nor her brother, David, likes living in a mining town and there is little in the narrative structure to distinguish it from earlier coal mining novels.

Like so many writers before her, Hankla incorporates a major mining disaster into the novel—the incidents of November 1968 in Farmington, West Virginia—but it is a much smaller accident that destroys the order in Dorie's world and adds a unique dimension to the story. Her father is seriously injured in a rock fall. Dorie and her mother rush to the hospital not knowing the extent of the injury. The most poignant sections of the novel describe Dorie's reaction to her father's loss of an arm. His maiming seems to turn her against him. She purposely ignores him at a neighborhood party celebrating his release from the hospital. It is only when he slips into her room that night to tell her that he understands her anger that she finally speaks.

> He turned to leave as I peeked out from the covers. Light outlined his body. Where the curve of his arm should have continued alongside his hip, the shape came to a stop, squared off. From behind it looked like he must be holding something in his arm, with his forearm bent in front of his stomach as he walked.
>
> "Daddy," I asked, "will there always be miners?"
>
> "What kind of a question is that?"

> "I was just wondering if there would, still—all the time."
>
> Daddy laughed. I was talking to him again. "As long as the Wye flows and green grass grows," he said.
>
> "I'm serious. You're laughing at me."
>
> "Laugh at you? Never. Sleep tight. Good night."[74]

As sophisticated as she may have been in other ways, Dorie could not figure out life's injustices. Her future is unknown and her father's injury has already affected her life. Yet this exchange between father and daughter transcends the work world and adds an intimate, if indeterminate, dimension to these characters. In its compelling simplicity this conversation focuses on the relationship between a daughter and her father who happens to be a coal miner—not, as in many earlier novels, a coal miner who happens to have a daughter.

In Smith's novels, neither miners nor mining has an important place, but mining scenes and situations enhance the development of her characters in ways that tie the present to the past. *Oral History,* one of her more acclaimed novels, is essentially a love story along the lines of Fox's *A Mountain Europa.* Richard Burlage, the young and handsome son of an old Virginia family, comes to the mountains to teach and to forget a broken love affair. He falls in love with Dory Cantrell and she becomes pregnant, though he does not know. Caught up in a swamp of conflicting social mores, he finally leaves for home, vowing to return. Eleven years later, Burlage is back. This time he is a priggish photographer who hopes to capture the mountain setting of his youthful love affair. Burlage does not appreciate the fact that everything has changed. He is appalled by the Blackey coal camp where Dory lives with her miner husband and their twin daughters. "I had never seen anything like it. . . . Trash, rusting machine parts, and bodies of cars lay everywhere, along that road, in all the yards where no grass grew," he observes with disgust. An unemployed miner approaches him, resenting the condescending curiosity of the outsider. It becomes clear that Burlage, like characters in the novels of Sherburne and Sayles, is incapable of understanding what it is that he hopes to capture in his photographs or recognizing that locals might feel he is prying into their lives. The miner draws a pistol and symbolically shoots out the rearview mirror on his expensive car. Burlage drives off quickly, then stops for a moment to get a closer picture of Dory's house. He is convinced that he has already captured the "essence of the mountain town in depressing times" with the carefully framed photographs he took earlier that morning. Burlage is not at all pleased with these final shots. "By this time, the light was nearly gone. This series of photographs has an indistinct, grainy surface, as if coal dust were blowing palpably through the air." Reality is not what he is after. The photographic mirror-image distorts the idyllic memories of his youthful romance, and like the many writers who thought they knew mining culture, Burlage cannot understand what he saw during the visit. The grainy surface of the photographs reveals less about coal camp life than it suggests that memories shadow the present. He simply cannot appreciate a way of life that has no reality for him beyond his idiosyncratic youthful recollections.[75]

Five years after completing *Oral History,* Smith published an epistolary novel, *Fair and Tender Ladies,* that is possibly her finest work to date.[76] Beginning shortly before World War I and ending in the mid-1970s, the novel traces the life of Ivy Rowe through a series of letters that she wrote to friends (real and imaginary), relatives, and anyone else who entered her life. In her youthful years she resembles an amalgam of James Still's characters, both male and female. She loves the natural beauty of the mountains and the warm society of coal town life. For a period during World War I, carrying the child of a man she does not intend to marry, Ivy lives in Diamond Fork coal camp with her sister and brother-in-law. Her initial enthusiasm for the camp is exceeded only by her naivete. "Oh, it *is* like paradise! So orderly and everything done for you, it is hard to beat. It is hard to believe the company will treat their own so good." Several months later, her initiation into the realities of the coal economy changes her attitude. She loathes the company officials who lay off miners after the war. What bothers her even more is the inability of the miners to adjust. "They have given up their land, those hardscrabble places we all came from, and they have no place to go back to. They have lived here so long they have forgot how to garden anyway, or put up food, or trade for goods, or anything about how they used to live." When she marries a miner, they decide to move back to her home on Sugar Creek, where life is anything but easy. Ivy makes an observation that James Still formulated almost half a century earlier: "When you go down in the mine so long, something happens in your head so that you cannot imagine another life. It's the only thing you know to do, the only way you know to live. You get scared of the mine and scared of everything else." Like so many other characters in novels dealing with coal mining culture, Ivy has to leave.[77] On the surface this novel is thematically traditional in its portrayal of contrasting ways of life. Yet there is something about Ivy's leaving that transcends the usual condemnation of digging coal, that adds a dialogical dimension to the novel. Margaret Atwood argues that all authors are trapped by "time and circumstance" and can never escape the present.[78] Smith is particularly adroit in writing about the Rowes in ways that transcend the parochial descriptions of mining families so common in earlier works. In this postmodern industrial society, many Americans cannot grasp that there are ways of life other than their own. Dealing with changing mores, hostile takeovers, and a capricious market economy universalizes Ivy's struggles. Her family's own particular hardships are a microcosm of modern society. If their uneasiness with life's uncertainties makes them "characters" rather than "personalities," then so are we all.

The supremely skilled Mary Lee Settle and Denise Giardina have written novels that to some extent illustrate the characteristics Bakhtin believes separate "personalities" from "characters." Their characters are less authorial "others" moving within the confines of a creatively determined stasis than fictional personalities whose subjectivity invites indeterminate dialogical dimensions. The net result is to illuminate the "unfinalizability" of their existence. The novels of Settle's Beulah quintet cover an enormous sweep of time stretching from the English Revolution in the seventeenth century to the contemporary setting in Charleston, West Virginia, of the most recent, *The Killing Ground* (1982). In the novels she explores the often neglected periods before cataclysmic events, such as the Cromwellian dictatorship, the American Revolution, or the mine wars in West Virginia.[79] This complex saga defies precise definition. Brian Rosenberg identifies three dominant themes as "the tension between freedom and obedience, the interchangeability of oppressor and oppressed, and the contrast between reality and dream."[80] Any of the five novels can stand alone, and it is the last two, *The Scapegoat* and *The Killing Ground,* that most directly pertain to Appalachia and mining. In these two works, Settle shows how class antagonism, like the run-off from a strip mine, can poison an environment and carry over from one generation to the next.[81]

The Scapegoat may be the most complex of the novels in the quintet. The narrative unfolds in 1912 during a twenty-four-hour period at the beginning of a coal strike in the vicinity of Paint Creek, West Virginia. Eighteen different characters provide conflicting versions of the events. The only certainty by novel's end is that miners and operators, once neighbors, are now enemies.[82]

Beverley Lacey is forced by his father to work in the family-owned Seven Stars Mine. He must learn every aspect of its operation and, in the process, comes to know many of the men who work there. When the UMWA begins its West Virginia organizing campaign, he is willing to negotiate to avoid a costly, disruptive strike. But he finds little support from other owners. Most of the mines in the area are controlled by corporate outsiders, who bring in hired guns to break the strike. Jake Catlett, whose wife cooks for the Laceys, is one of the strike leaders and also a good friend and distant relative of Beverley. As the strike intensifies, Mother Jones arrives to boost morale. She soon becomes involved in a bitter quarrel with Catlett over the culpability of the Laceys in the strike.[83] With the inevitability of a Greek tragedy, the two sides begin to move towards confrontation. Class hostility overwhelms local issues, as civility in this West Virginia valley evaporates. The Baldwin Felts, guards hired by coal companies and hated by miners, are angered by warning shots fired at them from the mountains and set out to take revenge. In the first bloodshed of the strike, they murder a young Italian immigrant, a recent arrival to the tent camp. For Essie Catlett, Jake's wife, this brutal death becomes a kind of moral watershed in the valley's history: "They had killed a man, and nothing was ever going to be the same. She could hear the change like a creek swell, flooding nearer and nearer, and all the former things were passed away. It wouldn't never be the same, she kept saying over and over like a prayer, not knowing she was saying it out loud." This murder symbolizes the class hatred that eventually erupts in the West Virginia mine wars. It also hints that deep-seated resentments will flow from the past into the present. Caught in the midst of change is the headstrong, high-spirited, and most intellectual of the three Lacey daughters, Lily. She has returned from Vassar a suffragette and is sympathetic to the needs of working people and intent on helping the less fortunate—including the young, handsome Italian immigrant Eduardo Pagano. By the time of the strike she has also secretly helped the miners by gathering information from the party line of her family's phone. During the strike, however, Lily is torn between her work for the miners and her loyalty to her family. To make matters worse, no one takes her seriously. Her parents believe her radical ideas are the fantasies of an immature school girl. Mother Jones, skeptical of her privileged background, accuses her of acting out of "curiosity and boredom." Both sentiments have a ring of truth. But Lily is capable of action even if she is at times erratic and naive. Courageous, even foolhardy, she goes where no Lacey woman has ever gone before: into the mine, to a meeting of striking miners' wives, and into the tent city itself. Yet she is often so oblivious to the class chasm that she cannot understand the hostility of those she has come to help. When Mother Jones shoos her from a meeting of miners' wives, Lily's departing cry of "VOTES FOR WOMEN" is as inappropriate as her presence.[84] Lily shows the same naivete as she tries to lift Pagano from the mines by reading him Montaigne. Though she eventually helps save his life, the young activist still cannot appreciate the class constraints that divide them or fathom the dangers she has subjected him to by knowing him. As they travel together toward New York and safety, she is blissfully unaware of what Richard Sennett and Jonathan Cobb call "the hidden injuries of class."[85] In the train's dinning car, Pagano eats grapefruit for the first time and grimaces at the bitter taste. When Lily whispers that he is supposed to use the sugar to make it sweeter, Pagano replies that he knows how to eat it. "It was better with the sugar but he told himself he never was going to eat grapefruit again except when he was in a dining car and everybody expected him to. His hand trembling, the spoon was the center of his being and he knew everybody on the dining car was watching him."[86]

Despite Lily's good intentions, she never comes to understand the inequalities intrinsic to the coalfields. Given that the personal is so intricately tied to the political in her thinking, this would be impossible for her to do. Much like her family, she cannot see how the past is influencing the present and haunting the future. When Lily eventually leaves West Virginia—the only Lacey emotionally capable of leaving home—she insures her own freedom and Pagano's safety. But as the train reaches the outskirts of Cincinnati and he disembarks, Lily has no real interest in his plans. She thinks about her own future instead. "She didn't know where he was going when he got off at Covington, but she knew at last where she was going. She leaned back and dreamed and didn't care what Montaigne said. There was clarity in dreams, too. She dreamed, lulled by the train, of getting off at heaven or New York City, whichever she got to first." The relationship between this daughter of a mine owner and the immigrant miner Pagano, intertwined with infatuation, class differences, misunderstandings, and youthful exuberance, remains compellingly "unfinalizable." Comfortable with this, Settle has created "personalities" rather than "characters" and, in doing so, given them a greater degree of indeterminate freedom than any other writer of coal-related fiction.[87]

Hannah McKarkle, the narrative voice in the last of the quintet's novels, *The Killing Ground,* like Lily Lacey, asserts her independence by leaving her well-to-do family in Canoa (Charleston), West Virginia, to pursue her career as a writer in New York. In 1978, now a well-known writer, she returns to her native city to speak at an art gallery fund-raiser. The suicide of an old family friend unleashes memories of her brother's senseless death eighteen years earlier. While reconstructing Johnny's death, she begins to face the self-indulgent way in which the two of them had lived. "Johnny and I had done the same thing, followed the urge to break taboos, using with our charm the passion, the vitality, of the earthly born, giving nothing except a sex we didn't care much about, silencing anyone who loved us with our mild, wandering insistence, our cold arrogant kindness. Johnny," she bitterly continues, "had escaped and left me to bear the knowledge that we had strip-mined every stranger who had let us in." Unlike her brother, who escaped only in death, Hannah had used her own life decisions to escape their smugly parochial family and the social responsibilities associated with their mining investments.[88] Her brother had not, and he had punished himself and those around him by living a debauched and purposeless life. After one of his usual drunken sprees he is arrested and placed in the drunk tank at the local jail. There, when another inmate slugs him for no other reason than he is well dressed, Johnny hits his head against an iron bench and dies.

Hannah goes to the jail to see the man who killed her brother. He turns out to be Jake Catlett, an unemployed thirty-eight-year-old miner and the son of the Jake Catlett who had led the striking miners in *The Scapegoat.* The younger Jake is also a distant relative on Hannah's mother's side of the family. Hannah's anger and his reticence prevent any kind of exchange, but eventually she is able to ask him how long he had thought about hitting Johnny before he did so. His answer of "Just about all my life" catches her so by surprise that she begins to laugh until he, insulted, more fully explains what he meant. Jake and his folks, having had to sell most of their farm, now live on a few hilly acres. He lost his job in the mines to a mechanized "joy loader," and the union has refused to pay the hospital bills of his seriously ill wife because he has been unemployed for over a year. He could not find work in Dayton, Akron, or Detroit. All the while his family's hardships have been mocked by symbols of prosperity, including a golf course built on their farm. Hannah's response is as lame as those offered by Lily a generation earlier. "We didn't know." Yet when she, like Lily, offers to help by telling his family where he is, Jake snaps at her: "you gwan back to that there gold cradle you're livin' in and leave us alone." Her anger rekindled, she explodes: "You people won't walk across the hollow. Let people ride roughshod over you and you just back a little further up your hills and whine because you haven't guts enough." Later, their anger spent, Jake accepts her offer. Hannah begins a personal journey that will not be complete until twenty years later. She runs into Jake, along with his family, at an aunt's funeral. Jake tells Hannah how her Aunt Althea not only obtained his release and persuaded her father to drop all charges but also helped set him up in a small strip mining business that had prospered. Althea acted because she believed, as Catlett heard her say more than once, "This has gone far enough." She knew intuitively that there are individual and collective responsibilities for the suffering and class antagonisms in the coalfields.[89] As Brian Rosenberg reminds us, these responsibilities stretch across the three centuries of the quintet.[90] Althea sees so clearly the exploitation of her family's livelihood. Hannah eventually sees it too. Like her aunt Lily, Hannah at times feels close to her family and at times feels like an outsider. But her brother's death and Althea's generosity toward the Catletts forces her to acknowledge that she too is as bound by the past as they. As she looks down from the plane carrying her back to New York, the scarred ground below evokes memories of many lives caught up in coal mining. Sadly, their "arrogance and lack of care toward its riches had grown into arrogance and lack of care for each other."[91]

It is this lack of caring for one another that seems to influence Settle's most recent novel, *Choices* (1995). The main character's life spans the years from World War I to the nineties. Melinda Kregg is the daughter of one of Richmond, Virginia's social elite. Similar to Lily Lacey in *The Scapegoat* and Hannah McKarkel in *The Killing Ground,* she is expected to marry well and remain close to home, embracing the family's standing in a society more caught up in the past than the present. Shocked by her father's suicide during the Great Depression, she naively volunteers for Red Cross work in the eastern Kentucky coalfields. There she begins an odyssey of service and commitment that includes participation in the Spanish Civil War, World War II, and the civil rights movement.

The novel is dedicated to "southern liberals past and present." It is one of Settle's most accessible in its narrative structure. She is more concerned with the story than with how she tells it. Kregg is socially, politically, and racially naive, as are many of Settle's female characters. She eventually sees the contradiction in many of her activities and comes to understand that she is often an observer at someone else's war—be it in Kentucky, Spain, or Mississippi. Armed with this understanding, she focuses on practical ways of supporting each cause rather than making Dreiser's mistake of serving a personal agenda.

Her first encounter with miners occurs several years before her Red Cross work. She travels to the Kentucky Derby with a young man. When she cries at the sight of the flickering lamps of miners on the way to work, her companion's response is: "They're digging my Packard and your pretty clothes, my dear sweet silly child. Your daddy and mine are in the coal business up to their necks."[92] She decides to go to eastern Kentucky after finding stock certificates of the Straight Creek Coal Company in her deceased father's desk. Continuing the roman à clef tradition in the Kentucky sections of the novel, Settle writes about a lecherous and insensitive Dreiser and briefly refers to Sheriff John Henry Blair, editor Herndon Evans, and Aunt Molly Jackson (whose multiple roles included miner's wife, midwife, and folksinger). She also fictionalizes the incident in which locals placed a toothpick against Dreiser's door to allege that his female companion had spent the night. But Settle's real interest is in the murder of Harry Simms, who she transforms into an idealistic activist from Yale named Johnny Bradford. His murder is the culminating event in the Kentucky section of the novel. Notably absent are coal miner characters like the two Jake Catletts in *The Scapegoat* and *The Killing Ground.* Instead Settle universalizes the theme of choice among her middle- and upper-class characters.

In the Kentucky section of the narrative, Melinda is dismissed from the Red Cross when she refuses to distinguish between unemployed and striking mining families. She works with the National Miners Union to feed the striking families, is arrested and briefly jailed, and watches from her prison window as irate deputies burn the car in which she carried supplies. These are significant experiences for Kregg but hardly as serious as losing a job or getting blacklisted. There are other qualitative moral issues, in which Settle is more interested, that relate to one's social responsibility to confront intolerable situations. The owner of a local boarding house helps Kregg by sharing a homespun philosophy she can use for the rest of her life. "My husband used to say you can argy all day long, but when you wake up at three o'clock in the morning a thing is wrong or it's right, and either you take to drank or do somethin about it."[93]

Settle's final two books of the Beulah quintet as well as *Choices* are far too complex and multidimensional to be called coal mining novels. She simply uses the relationships of the coal mining world to explore larger issues that transcend time, place, and status. Yet in doing so she also humanizes and personalizes all those associated with the American mining experience. Settle shows that arrogance and greed are not unique to the West Virginia and Kentucky coalfields. Whether Kregg encounters injustice in Harlan County, Spain, or the Mississippi Delta, it can only be changed through intense human effort. Still, if the characters in Settle's novels reach varying degrees of understanding about the nature of the human condition, neither the problems, solutions, nor characters themselves are finalized in ways that are predictable and limiting. If at the conclusion of *The Killing Ground,* Hannah and Jake understand one another better than did Lily and Pagano in *The Scapegoat,* they still have not solved all of their personal problems, nor bridged the class issues separating them. Hannah could see that conflicting interests and ambitions were intrinsic to human struggle: "Finally I knew that I had joined the wanderers . . . all of those who have set out alone, perhaps self-deluded by necessity. But it was the wanderers who had given us a country, and left the scars behind. Deep within us there had been instilled an itch, a discontent, an unfulfilled promise, perpetually demanding that it be kept. . . . And all of us, would always fail and always win, and eternal vigilance and our sense of loss, of being unblessed, were the price of freedom."[94] All of Settle's major fictionalized creations in these novels are in one way or another "wanderers," which insures that they will be Bakhtinian "personalities" rather than "characters." It is this sense of freedom and its indeterminate direction that so distinguishes Settle's fiction.

Denise Giardina, in *Storming Heaven* (1987) and *The Unquiet Earth* (1992), writes less self-consciously within the modern tradition than either Smith or Settle, but she is also interested in how her characters respond morally and ethically to one another.[95] In the first of her two novels relating to coal mining, *Storming Heaven,* she explores how both individuals and groups reacted to class antagonisms, economic exploitation, and power struggles in the southern West Virginia coalfields. *The Unquiet Earth* is less event-driven and more probing in its examination of social tensions in a postindustrial setting. Like Settle's *The Killing Ground, The Unquiet Earth* delves into the impact of the past on all human relationships, especially those between men and women.

Both of Giardina's novels are stories of tempestuous love affairs in which men and women struggle to reconcile social responsibility with their deepest feelings of affection and commitment. The star-crossed lovers of *Storming Heaven* are labor organizer Rondal Lloyd and nurse Carrie Bishop. Their story provides the novel's primary narrative structure. The story ends with the West Virginia miners' march on Blair Mountain. With Carrie marching by his side, Rondal suffers a horribly crippling injury.

Giardina fictionalizes other aspects of Appalachian mining culture. She writes about the coalescence of religious and political commitment as well as the use of organized sports—especially mining camp baseball—as a means of social control. The issue of withdrawal versus activism in the face of social injustice surfaces repeatedly throughout her novel. The political dominates the personal. Beneath a thin narrative veneer lies the author's determination to reveal the brutal misuse of power that has long plagued southern West Virginia. Key events in *Storming Heaven* demonstrate a violent history—Rondal's grandfather is murdered for refusing to sell his land, a black UMWA organizer is burned alive, Baldwin Felts guards kill Isom Justice and Albion Freeman (Sid Hatfield and Ed Chambers) on the steps of the McDowell County Courthouse. Major characters as well as minor ones are often larger than life in their commitments, sacrifices, and heroism.[96]

The Unquiet Earth is a more complex and compelling novel than *Storming Heaven,* though it is in many ways a continuation of the former, with Carrie and Rondal's son, Dillon Freeman, as a main character. Like many other writers before her, Giardina writes about real events. What makes this novel exceptional is the interplay of diverse, resonant characters in a coal community undergoing profound social and economic change. Giardina strongly believes that those who care the least about mining communities in Appalachia have caused the greatest harm. *The Unquiet Earth* is tied together by parallel love stories. In each of Giardina's novels there is a tension between the practical and the political, often transmitted through gender differences. Dillon's lover, Rachel, explains to him: "There's some that would save the world and think nothing to hurt those around them, and you're that way." Dillon Freeman is a miner like his father and an organizer as well. But he is a more interesting mix of sensitivity, emotional obtuseness, courage, obstinacy, introversion, and concern for others coupled with a blindness to the needs of those closest to him. Giardina's creation of this complex character is one of the most skillful in American coal mining fiction. Rachel is also strong-willed, but she is more insightful than Dillon. What sets her apart from the man she loves and, at times, deplores is her realization that she has a very different relationship with the region. She uses her nursing skills to help those around her in ways substantially different from the political approach of her lover. Their irreconcilable differences are clarified during a strike when Rachel will not join him on the picket line. "I am involved. I nurse the families of those men every day. . . . But I can't wear out a truck driver with a switch. You are asking me to go against my nature and I just can't do it. I'm not a miner's wife either. I don't even spend much time with them." Much like Settle, Giardina is comfortable with the "unfinalizable" discourse of her characters. Even when drawn together through love, their conflicting ways of relating self to society inevitably keep them apart.[97] Rachel and her daughter eventually leave Dillon. She marries Arthur Lee Sizemore, a local boy, once poor, who is now a manager in the business office of the American Coal Company. Giardina does a better job here of drawing his strengths and weaknesses than she did with a similar character, Miles Bishop, in *Storming Heaven.* Less defensive of life in the coalfields than in her earlier novel, she neither romanticizes poverty nor overlooks human flaws. The dysfunctional Bringham Lloyd family, the greed of Arthur Lee, the self-centeredness of Doyle Ray and his wife are juxtaposed with the kindly, enterprising abilities of Hassel Day, the courage of Sim Gore, and the gritty determination of Day's niece, Ethel Day, who as a single mother supports her child by digging coal. To a VISTA volunteer like Tom Kilwecki, the trailers and houses of mining camp Number Thirteen are symbols of rural poverty and social degradation. But to Jackie, the daughter of Rachel and Dillon, they represent a kind of security and belonging that she has found nowhere else in the world. "I never cared for the long walk along the railroad track but I miss everything else about Number Thirteen. In Number Thirteen you could go right in someone's house without knocking," she recalls, "just sit on the couch and watch what was going on. No one would think a thing of it. Out in the world you will be by yourself, but not at Number Thirteen."[98]

Giardina believes that the mining culture has come to terms with its troubles. It angers her that outsiders make decisions about the mining world based on misinformation, stereotyping, and greed. The collusion between the national government and private interests destroys Tom Kilwecki's organizing efforts against strip mining. Kilwecki's Washington supervisor, sent to the area to rein him in, has this conversation with Hassel Day, a supporter of the young volunteer:

> "Yes, Mr. Day. Part of Tom's job is education. And he's supposed to be addressing the problems of poverty. I can hardly see what strip mining has to do with poverty. Tom can't just turn people loose to harass government officials and business leaders. Those are the very people in the community you should be cooperating with."

"Naw," I say. "That ain't the way it works down here."
"Mr. Day, I believe I know my job."
"Yessir, but you ain't never lived in a coal camp have you?"
"Mr. Day, I have a master's degree in sociology from Brown."
"I don't know no Brown," I say, "But I know Arthur Lee."[99]

In the last cataclysmic event of the novel—the Buffalo Creek disaster—Giardina proposes that the real villains in Appalachia are the outside corporate interests. At the time of the flood both Dillon and Arthur Lee are retired, but Dillon has not lost his social conscience. After a rainy winter, he becomes concerned about the American Coal Company's makeshift earthen damn at the head of the hollow. Early on a cold, drizzly February morning in 1990, he calls Arthur Lee to tell him that the situation is dangerous. The company has not properly monitored the dam. Arthur Lee tells him not to be concerned, he is retired now. Dillon drives up the hollow to check on the dam anyway. Much as he had feared, he sees that the stick Arthur Lee used to measure the water level is gone and the sides of the dam are crumbling. At this moment, his old nemesis appears. Whatever his failings, Arthur Lee also feels a personal connection to the area and its people. The two old warriors go their separate ways but, this time, on the same mission—to warn the hollow's people that the dam might break. Both of them have heard the company's public statement on the safety of the dam. They have also heard the company's charge that the union was harassing management by refusing to accept the company's word. Here is Giardina's powerful message that not just Appalachians but all Americans are at the mercy of those whose overriding concern is profit.

Although *The Unquiet Earth* concludes with two old male antagonists cooperating to save the valley they love, women play a significant role not only in the novels of Giardina but in those of Hankla, Smith, and Settle as well. Elaine Showalter suggests that an examination of women's culture is more conceptually productive than theories based on biology, linguistics, or psychoanalysis.[100] In her study of proletarian fiction in the 1930s, Barbara Foley discovered that women writers focused on questions of identity and selfhood in their novels and showed through character development that the class struggle did not occur "'out there,' in the mill or on the picket line, but as dialectically embedded in, and mediated through, everyday experience." Women more so than men viewed the political as personal. They were willing to expand Marxism into areas where it had never been before.[101] Bridging this argument to the present, sociologist Dorothy E. Smith argues that women are more closely attuned to the everyday world because of the historical nature of their culture.

> I proposed women's standpoint as one situated outside textually mediated discourses in the actualities of everyday lives. This is a standpoint designed in part by our exclusion from the making of cultural and intellectual discourse and the strategies of resorting to our experience as the ground of a new knowledge, a new culture. But it is also designed by an organization of work that has typically been ours, for women's work, as wives, secretaries, and in other ancillary roles, has been that which anchors the impersonal and objectified forms of action and relations to particular individuals, particular local places, particular relationships. Whatever other part women play in the social division of labor, they have been assigned and confined predominantly to work roles mediating the relation of the impersonal and objectified forms of action to the concrete local and particular worlds in which all of us necessarily exist.[102]

Even though strikes, mine disasters, and unionizing efforts play important roles in their novels, these four writers are more interested in probing the inner lives of their characters. Some of their creations are therefore uniquely complex, multidimensional, and, at times, enigmatic. In short, their characters have voices of their own that express a subjectivity often lacking in other coal mining novels. Some critics argue that the traditional concern of women writers with concrete issues of family and personal relationships is limiting. Tonette Bond Inge as well as Showalter, Foley, and Smith disagree. Inge argues that southern women writers have a greater affinity for time and place than many of their creative sisters elsewhere. They have not so much avoided the world as brought it kicking and screaming into local settings and situations. This approach is neither accidental nor forced. Most southern women writing in the modern era, Inge says, "know very well who they are, thank you, and consider their imagined houses more as daily manifestations of reality than as refuges from reality."[103] In an interview with the *New York Times* in 1984, Settle explained her attempt to personalize great events in her five-volume Beulah quintet. "Both time and space are distances, and they work for historians and novelists in the same way—not as a gulf, but as psychic force. Hindsight—which revises, tears down, discovers trends and explains by concept—has little place in fiction. To try to see, to hear, to share a passion, to become contemporary, is its task. Who said that 'history tells us what happened; fiction tells us how it felt.'?"[104] Settle knows that the political is invariably personal. As do Hankla, Giardina, and Smith, Settle explores how her characters personalize events affecting their lives. These writers in one way or another affirm Balzac's contention that "talent flourishes where the causes which produce the facts are portrayed, in the secrets of the human heart, whose motions are neglected by the historians. The characters of a novel are forced to be more rational than historical characters. The former must be roused to life, the latter have already lived."[105] The stories of these "roused to life" fictional characters, according to novelist Margaret Atwood, are about "human nature, which usually means they are about pride, envy, avarice, lust, sloth, gluttony, and anger. They are about truth and lies, and disguises and revelations; they are about crime and punishment; they are about love and forgiveness and long suffering and charity; they are about sin and retribution and sometimes even redemption."[106]

The willingness of Hankla, Smith, Settle, and Giardina to confront the complex issues affecting the lives of mining families involves their going beyond professional and class determinism and instead confronting the human panorama with its messy inconsistencies and Bakhtinian "unfinalizability." It may also have something to do with their common Appalachian heritage. As poet and critic Jim Wayne Miller notes in the timely essay "Nostalgia for the Future," in the last two decades many Appalachians have made an effort to "intervene" in their own lives and culture from within. Underlying this effort is a new awareness of and appreciation for the region's literature. "Our literature is a tool for inspecting our lives individually and collectively," Miller writes. "Our literature is a way into knowledge or who we have been, how we got to be the way we are. It is a means of empowering ourselves for our common future."[107] All of these writers have lived in Appalachia. All incorporate the historical impact of coal into the mainstream of their fiction. This is their way of trying to understand the influence of the past on the present.

What is refreshing about Giardina, Settle, Smith, and Hankla is how they portray coal-mining people from a dialogical perspective. Whether they are exploring gender differences, class conflicts, the relationship between parents and children, or the tension between rural versus industrial ideals, these writers create complex "personalities" whose concerns, inconsistencies, and emotions invite the reader's engagement. In keeping the conversation going, they neither defend nor attack coal mining culture. They do not romanticize or relegate coal miners to the limbo of creative "otherness." Instead, they skillfully illustrate the "unfinalizability" of all human beings—no matter how they work and live.

Chapter 4

Stage and Screen

Film and poetry share what the critic Robert Richardson calls a "logic of imagination." Charles Eidsvik suggests that theater is the only modern art whose existence has been threatened by the appearance of the cinema.[1] What may be commercially true in the world of theater and mass culture, however, is neither analytically nor conceptually important to this discussion. Plays and films relating to coal mining are analyzed primarily from a thematic perspective, and these two very different media ultimately complement one another. This is true even though the analytical tools used here do not always reflect the creative dimensions of camera or stage. What is important is that the major dynamic in mass culture is entertainment, and both coal mining plays and films typically seek to entertain. Viewers are invited to lose themselves in the drama unfolding on screen or stage and to experience the realities of coal mining lives. Cathartic release ensues as they leave the theater thankful that they do not have to mine coal or live with anyone who does.[2] As a result, theater and film exaggerate the stereotypes and pervasive sense of "otherness" found in fiction.

Nuances are clearly lost when a play is read rather than viewed. But broad themes relating to coal mining are as readily available from reading a drama as seeing it performed. Apart from Robert Schenkkan's *The Kentucky Cycle,* the plays in this chapter have been analyzed through their scripts rather than their stage presentations. The analytical emphasis is upon the playwright rather than the director, on the written word rather than that which is spoken or enacted.

Unlike dramas, many screenplays are not published and frequently have little life outside the films themselves. It can also be more difficult to identify the writers of screenplays since, as the editors of the American Film Institute suggest, the designation of "author" for screenplays may refer to the head of the filming company.[3] Screenplays are often the collective effort of a team of writers, including those associated with the production and direction sides of filmmaking, rather than the work of a single individual. Susan Sontag writes that there is far more to creating a film than cinematizing a script. Every scene, image, camera angle, and detail reflects the intentions of the director. In this respect theater and cinema are quite different since, in Sontag's words, "theater allows only the loosest approximation to this sort of formal concern and to this degree of aesthetic responsibility on the part of the director, which is why French critics justly speak of the director of a film as its 'author.'"[4]

In spite of this obvious difference, plays and films can both exploit the enclosed environments of mines and mining camps. The thematic index of a recent guide to films about labor listed eight working categories: farm, garment, steel, waterfront, auto, mine, office, and trucking.[5] None of these occupations lends itself as readily to dramatic performance as does the mining of coal. As in wartime films or prison dramas, diverse groups and personalities can be brought together amid excitement and tragedy. Riding a mine car deep into the earth or encountering the total darkness of the underground are experiences that most people can witness only in the safety of a theater. To capture the cinematization of coal mining, this chapter analyzes feature rather than documentary films. On the other hand, plays of all kinds are examined, regardless of length or intent. Since plays are read as well as watched, playwrights can experiment a bit more than script writers or directors and, in a Brechtian sense, encourage audiences to sever themselves emotionally from the drama in order to think about what they are viewing. By necessity a similar approach is used in this chapter, and thinking about the playwright's intentions in writing about mining culture, rather than experiencing the play on stage, is the chapter's primary thrust.

Thirty-one plays were selected for this analysis, with the intent of showing how the playwrights have creatively envisioned the coal mining experience. While all the plays were written in the twentieth century, several of the dramas take place in the late–nineteenth century, when coal mining was maturing as both an occupation and a way of life. The plays include a number of sub-genres—melodrama, closet drama, agitprop, musical, as well as historical and experimental efforts. For the most part, however, the writers use traditional methods of plot, staging, and characterization. Some, like a number of the poets in chapter six, use a coal mining setting for its ambience of darkness, dirtiness, and dampness, while others are fascinated with the dramatic impact of mine-related disasters, such as explosions and underground fires. Most writers stereotype the mining life, though a few try to genuinely understand it.

John Howard Lawson's *Processional* (1925) and Bonchi Friedman's *The Miners* (1926) are both set in West Virginia, whereas a series of six plays by Leo B. Pride, published in *The Shadow of the Mine and Other Plays of the Coal*

Fields (1928), as well as two other plays by the same author, *The Haunted Coal Mine* (1929) and *The Miners' Christmas Eve* (1929), all take place in the coalfields of southern Illinois early in the twentieth century. Frederick Schlick's *Bloodstream,* which opened at the Times Square Theater on March 30, 1932, is set in a prison mine in Alabama and dramatizes the brutalities of the convict labor system.[6] The one-act melodrama *Trouble in Tunnel Nine* (1937), by S. Sylvan Simon, portrays the frantic efforts of trapped miners to survive an explosion. In 1934, Samuel Ornitz published in the *New Republic* an eleven-page closet drama, *In New Kentucky.* This play is about the kind of strike he would like to have found rather than the one he actually experienced. Albert Maltz's *Black Pit* (1935) is not only one of the best plays dealing with coal mining but, because of its sympathetic treatment of a scab miner, also one of the most controversial. Nine years before publishing her novel, *With Sun in Our Blood,* in which Tennessee coal miners battle state authorities over the use of convict miners, Myra Page dealt with the same issue in a short radio play, *The March on Chumley Hollow* (1941). Marlene Brenner dramatized the agony of a group of women awaiting news after a mining disaster in *The Wait* (1958). Jason Miller, in *Nobody Hears a Broken Drum* (1970), portrays labor struggles in the Pennsylvania anthracite fields shortly after the Civil War. E.J. Eustace also focused his dramatic efforts on the anthracite coalfields, attempting to telescope the struggles between management and the Molly Maguires into a three-act melodrama, *The King of the Mountain* (1975). Popular songwriter, poet, and dramatist Billy Edd Wheeler has written two plays dealing with mining. The first, *Slatefall,* which he wrote while a student at Berea College, describes life in a coal mining community during the time of a tragedy. *Mossie and the Strippers* (1980), Wheeler's second, features the efforts of a retired miner's wife to stop the strip mining of the land around her home.[7] By far the most experimental of the dramatists who have written about coal mining is Kentucky playwright and poet Lee Pennington. He has published several short plays in which mining is an important topic, including *Appalachia, My Sorrow* (1976), *Coal Mine* (1976), *The Spirit of Poor Fork* (1976), and *The Scotian Women* (1984). In 1980, Mat Williams's *Between Daylight and Booneville* dramatized the major changes taking place in coal mining by concentrating on the families of strip miners in Indiana. Paula Cizmar uses a traditional theme, mining disaster, to analyze the life of a nontraditional Appalachian miner, Mary Alice Hager, in *The Death of a Miner* (1982). West Virginia playwright Jean Battlo wrote a musical, *The Creeks,* that dramatizes Mother Jones's activism in the Paint Creek/Cabin Creek strikes of 1912-13.[8] This work was first performed in front of the building where the legendary labor leader was incarcerated in Pratt, West Virginia. Another of Battlo's plays, *A Highly Successful West Virginia Business,* is a three-act comedy that shows how a mining family tries to adjust to the closing of the last mine in the area. The last four plays of Robert Schenkkan's 1992 Pulitzer Prize–winning *The Kentucky Cycle* offered an overview of Kentucky mining from the 1880s through the 1970s, arousing a good deal of regional controversy in the process. Finally, Tennessee playwright Jo Carson's *A Preacher with a Horse to Ride* (1993) dramatizes the Dreiser Committee's trip to eastern Kentucky. The play examines Dreiser's motivation and analyzes the committee's impact on the lives of the striking miners. Although all plays touch on a wide variety of coal mining topics, including strikes, disasters, mining-related disease, and efforts at unionization, most of the playwrights seem more intent on demonstrating that coal mining is an exploitative, brutalizing, and dangerous profession than on developing complex characters with lives, minds, and voices of their own. As in much fiction, coal-mining characters are portrayed as industrial pawns who are acted upon and, like the characters in a Zola novel, appear helpless in an uncaring universe. It is this debased helplessness that imparts a sense of the miners' "otherness" to reader and viewer alike, which transcends the artificial perimeters of the stage.

The theme of exploitation is multifaceted. It may involve management, management in collusion with other sources of authority such as government or the church, or the parasitical greed of bar owners, gamblers, and prostitutes. All of these groups in one way or another exploit mining communities. Labor-management struggles—often involving issues of poor safety, starvation wages, inadequate company social services, as well as strong-arm efforts to thwart unionization—drive the action on stage in *Processional, The Miners, Black Pit, The March on Chumley Hollow, Nobody Hears a Broken Drum, Bloodstream, The Death of a Miner, The Creeks,* and *Fire in the Hole* of the *Kentucky Cycle* series. The odds are stacked against coal miners when government collaborates with management in *Processional, The Miners, The March on Chumley Hollow, The Creeks,* and *Fire in the Hole* and equally so when church and management conspire in *Nobody Hears a Broken Drum* and *The King of the Mountain.* On a more personal level, in *On the Way Home,* a roadhouse owner in collusion with local authorities pilfers the wages of miners while keeping them away from their families. A Fagan-like bar owner in *The Miners' Christmas Eve* encourages the children of destitute mining families to steal coal off railroad cars during a strike, though he knows that guardsmen will shoot them on sight. Many of these playwrights are angered by the double bind of mining life—the uncertainties of a hard and dangerous job coupled with institutional and personal exploitation. Digging coal for a living seems bad enough, but doing it while being preyed upon turns the way of life into a nightmare, a literary perspective separating us from them.

The psychological pressures borne by coal miners can be as treacherous as the exploitative ones. Yet there is some disagreement on whether mining brutalizes the miner or whether only certain kinds of workers are suited for the job. The issue is not so much that of Eugene O'Neill's Richard "Yank" Smith (*The Hairy Ape*) questioning his personal worth and social role, but a deterministic, stereotypical "otherness" that implies characters cannot be fully human in such a debilitating work environment. Scramer Hicks of *The Haunted Mine* is described as "the giantlike motor driver with a face like an ape's," and the African American miner Juke Taylor (*Bloodstream*) has "the gait of a gorilla, and a slanting forehead." Dave, in *Trouble in Tunnel Nine,* is similarly described as an insensitive, "hulking young miner of eighteen or twenty," and a fellow worker castigates him as someone with "all back and no brains." In Leo Pride's *Fortune's Hired Man,* Milt Fortune is consumed by a raging bitterness that, as he tries to explain to his wife, stems from his years working underground. "It's that damn mine that's done it," he explodes, "that hell dungeon down there in that damp an' the cold." In another of his plays, Pride is equally explicit in showing how digging coal seems to drain the life out of miners. Here he describes a busload of miners pouring into a local roadhouse: "Each face—white, black or dark—has the stolid, unimaginative expression of the prisoner—the isolated workman. . . . While each has about him his own rough, dynamic individuality, he carries with him bodily the atmosphere of his trade; and remains a type as inseparable from his fellows as a blade of grass in a meadow." In a 1970s play, *The King of the Mountains,* a local priest sympathetic to the plight of the miners believes that their work virtually destroys them: "And if his eyes are not torn out of his head by the powder blast, or if he's not buried alive by the rock fall, he lives, a beast in a stinking den . . . humpbacked like an ape from grubbing in the black rat holes . . . an ape in overalls." Even Jason Miller's more subtle characterization in *Nobody Hears a Broken Drum* still suggests that there is something innately debilitating about having to work underground for a living. Pat, one of the two Beckett-like commentators on the play's denouement, explains to his cohort Mike: "I'm just sayin' that death could mistake you for me and never know the difference. We've had little lives and so we'll have little deaths."[9]

Death haunts coal mining dramas like violence does the modern film. In almost half of the plays, a family member or friend is either killed or injured, or an earlier fatality or injury serves as a symbolic backdrop for the next scene. As a method for bringing diverse groups of people together or dramatizing life-and-death struggles, mining disasters are to coal mining drama what main street gunfights are to western films. Such disasters play major roles in *Shadow of the Mine, Barbarians, Trouble in Tunnel Nine, The Wait, Nobody Hears a Broken Drum, Between Daylight and Booneville, Bloodstream, The Scotian Women, Coal Mine, The Death of a Miner, Slatefall,* and in two plays of *The*

Kentucky Cycle, Fire in the Hole and *Table Salt and Greed.* The terror of being trapped thousands of feet below ground and the anguish of awaiting news of the fate of loved ones are frequently confronted in coal mining dramas. Audiences viewing a darkened stage, awaiting the next tragic twist of plot, cannot help but recognize that affliction is an intrinsic part of this way of life.

No playwright shows more concern for the impact of accidental death on communities than playwright Lee Pennington in *The Scotian Women.* Like *Between Daylight and Booneville, The Scotian Women* is a play about women written by a man. It is set in a bathhouse in which five women and the father of one have gathered to await news about a mine explosion. The use of masks, a chorus, biblical names, and the simple chime of the triangle as well as thunder (to announce mood and scene changes) all suggest a kind of timelessness in the suffering of the waiting women. The seamless tragedy of human existence is reflected in a pregnant woman who compares the trapped miners with the child in her womb—one living, the others dying, all in darkness. As the waiting continues, the oldest of the women, Hester, appeals to a deity of arbitrary will: "Please, God, don't let it be him. Let it be anyone but him!" She has already lost her husband and all of her sons except the one now trapped in the mine. Unlike the others, she has experienced a life of despair: "You always expect something to happen. I have spent my life waiting, expecting." Like the hell of Sartre's *No Exit,* the mine offers no hope for those who enter it. The play ends with Hester, whose life will become the life of the others, alone on stage addressing the audience as the lights fade: "Deep within my bones I feel the chill. [She looks toward the mine.] In the bloodstone month. They are all Picean—all in bondage. They cannot speak for themselves. They can only speak through us. And we can no longer speak." Similar to fellow Appalachian James Still, Pennington hates what coal mining does to human beings, but his anger leads to an unintentional kind of "othering." In his plays, miners, like Oedipus, are ill-fated, but it is their profession rather than an ancient curse that sets them apart.[10]

"Little lives" and meaningless deaths may be the nature of the human predicament, but no one consciously seeks this. Escape is the only alternative. What kind of a person, for example, would choose to live in the environment described by Albert Maltz in *The Black Pit*? "This is a coal camp: It sits on a mountainside, it's shut off in a lonely ravine, it straggles the bank of a river rusty with the wash of sulfur. It looks like a scab on living flesh and the miners call it a 'patch.'" Little has changed in Robert Schenkkan's 1990s version of an Appalachian coal camp in *Fire in the Hole*: "The set is now darker and dirtier looking, almost as if a healthy outer layer of skin has been ripped off and some essential 'essence' had been bled out of it. There is no hint of the forest that once stood here. The ground is barren and covered with slate and mud. Looming over it all is a huge metal structure, the coal tipple."[11] The image in both cases is that of a wound, not so much like those suffered by a Hemingway character in a manly defiance of fate, but one that is more pervasive, debased, and inevitable. Coal mining is not the kind of job in which one takes pride, nor a career children are encouraged to pursue. Instead it is a job from which escape is eagerly sought, for to accept it is to lack imagination or even humanness. To mine coal when there are other alternatives available is to cross the boundary into "otherness." Carla, a central character of *Between Daylight and Booneville* not unlike Sinclair Lewis's Carol Kennicut, feels stranded in the little trailer court where she lives, a surrogate location for the traditional mining camp of so many other plays, with no car and no outlet for her energies except the care of her eight-year-old daughter. Her bitterness spills over as she tells her two friends and fellow camp residents why she refuses to have a second child. "You want to know why me and Larry ain't had another baby? I don't want one. I don't want to raise another baby if this is all they'll ever get out of life. All they'll ever know."[12]

The escape theme is even more explicit, however, in the mining disaster play *Trouble in Tunnel Nine* by playwright S. Sylvan Simon. Pete Novak desperately wants out of the mine and has been studying on the sly to become a radio operator on an oceangoing ship. Novak is opposed by his father, Jan, the foreman of the work crew, and his hulking brother, Dave, who believes that Pete is demeaning the family's tradition by trying to find another way of making a living. When Jan, the experienced miner, makes an error in judgement that causes the three to be trapped by a cave-in, it is Pete who stays calm while Dave cowers in a corner. When Pete realizes that all of the lighting in the mine is on a single circuit, he uses the Morse code he has secretly studied to send a message to those above. This act facilities a rescue. Now impressed by his son's skills, Jan agrees that there are better things to do in life than dig coal. Even Dave is happy to see his brother off to school where he can use his mind rather than muscles.

Escape is not a theme in Robert Schenkkan's Pulitzer Prize–winning *The Kentucky Cycle,* but the characters in the two mining-related plays, *Fire in the Hole* and *Which Side Are You On?,* are as wooden and one-dimensional as portions of the play's language are lyrical and engaging. *The Kentucky Cycle* is a nine-play attempt to dramatize two hundred years of Kentucky's history. Schenkkan maintains that the play is less about Appalachia than it is an attempt to capture the entire vista of the American saga.[13] The histories of three families, two of which are white, the Rowens and Talberts, and the other African American, the Biggses, provide a unifying motif for this panoramic narrative.

Schenkkan purposely wrote *Fire in the Hole* as a thirties-like drama by telescoping events from the Paint Creek/Cabin Creek and Harlan County strikes into a single episode centering on the fictional Blue Star Mines. Within this ritualized structure there are villainous managers, pliable but courageous mining families, and a heroic union organizer who gives his life for the cause. A montage of mining experiences—the corrupt company doctor, the preacher who speaks the company line, an explosion in the mine, and life in a tent city during a strike—introduces the audience to the world of the miner. To make doubly sure that the audience understands how dreadful life in a coal camp is, the main character, Mary Anne Rowe Jackson, describes her never-ending battle with coal dust: "Durin' the day I swept and mopped the coal dust out of the house, but every night, while I slept, it crept back in with the shadows, like my daddy's bad dreams, and ever mornin' I started all over again. And always there was that smell: like you'd took a corn-shuck mattress, soaked it in piss, covered it with garbage and coal, and set it on fire."

As with many thirties dramas, the play centers around a strike for unionization that the miners eventually win, but not without considerable outside help. The union organizer, Abe Steinman, rooms at the Jackson house. Unlike most of his fellow Kentuckians, he has been out of the region, has fought in Europe, and knows what it takes to bring about change. When Mary Anne Rowen angrily tells him that he is bringing trouble to her family, he replies, "Seems to me whatever trouble you got was here a long time 'fore I showed up." Ultimately Mary Anne sees the wisdom of Abe's words, and she becomes a strike leader after learning that her husband has sold the miners out, an act that leads to Abe's murder. As always, mining people, especially males in this instance, need outside help. This time it comes in the form of Mother Jones, who was known to hector men into action by appealing to their sense of courage: "Boys, when I got in town today you were afraid to look at me, like a buncha damn cowards. Well, I been in jail more'n once and I expect to go again, and if you are too cowardly to fight, I'll fight by myself!" But Mother Jones is not needed at the Blue Star Mines, for the men eventually join Mary Anne and the other women, who have been beating pots and pans, in an expression of union solidarity. As the curtain falls Mary Ann calls out to her son, Joshua, "Ain't Union grand! *Ain't Union grand!*"[14]

In the next *Kentucky Cycle* play, twenty years later, the union has become a grand bureaucracy. That is the problem. Joshua, now forty-four, heads the UMWA local in district 16, where the Blue Star Mines operate. Institutional and personal idealism have long since disappeared. *Which Side Are You On?* explores the cynical world of a union bureaucrat who has lost touch with the rank and file. Joshua works more closely with management than he does with his own constituency. He drinks too much, supports a mistress, and neglects his wife. He appoints his son, Scotty, who has just returned from serving in

Korea, as a UMWA field representative for District 16; but Joshua intends his son to maintain the status quo rather than address safety concerns in the mines.

Joshua is a composite creation of former United Mine Worker presidents—Tony Boyle in particular. When a build-up of coal dust, ignored by the union and management to save money, causes an explosion at the Blue Star Mine, Joshua tries to cover up the disaster even though his own son is one of the victims. His lines are a paraphrase of Boyle's unfeeling statement in the aftermath of the 1968 Farmington Mining disaster in West Virginia.[15] "I can say that the Blue Star is a safe, responsible operation with a good record. What this says to me is that thing we all know but nobody likes to admit. And that is, that mining is a dangerous business and we just have to live with this."[16] In these two dramas, Schenkkan is clearly proclaiming that the union of the 1950s was as damaging to the miners as management had been in the 1930s. Schenkkan's story, told within a dramatic framework, tends to compress complex issues into statically simple ones. In the mining plays, union leaders are either heroic or evil. The UMWA, at least in District 16, is a bureaucratic miasma whose only goal is self-perpetuation. Mining people are equally one-dimensional—even when they are inclined to take action rather than be acted upon, as is Mary Anne Rowen Jackson and Joshua's son, Scotty, who encourages outsiders and returning veterans into protesting. The mining world is dreary, as in most plays, and mining lives are either lost or circumscribed. These two plays differ little from those that precede them. This approach is as stylized and shallow as John Howard Lawson's was over half a century ago, when he tried to capture the American processional.[17] Such dramatic congruence suggests that little has changed in the coalfields over the years. It may also reflect how little playwrights at the beginning and end of the century have changed in their understanding of this fascinating, and yet elusive, way of life.

Over half a century before the production of Schenkkan's plays, Albert Maltz's *Black Pit* offers a uniquely sympathetic portrayal of a scab worker.[18] Like Upton Sinclair's *The Jungle,* Maltz's *Black Pit* begins with a wedding, but there is no time for celebration as the groom is whisked off to prison for his strike activities. Innocent of the charges against him, Joe Kovarsky emerges three years later and tries to resume his life. Having been blacklisted, he cannot find steady employment. He and his pregnant wife, Iola, live with their friends, the Lakavichs, who scrape by on the ten dollars a month the company pays Tony, the head of the family, for his crippling mine injury. Iola fears that she will die in childbirth like her mother unless attended by a physician. Their precarious lives are further threatened when the local mine superintendent, Prescott, who is also Iola's cousin, tries to enlist Kovarsky as a company stooge. Prescott eventually prevails by reminding Kovarsky that the company doctor only serves employed miners and that he can evict the Lakavichs if he so chooses. The play ends appropriately for a socially conscious drama of the 1930s. A shamed Kovarsky leaves his wife and child behind to wander the world alone, while the virtuous Tony stands by his commitment to the union and his principles.

In some respects Maltz's Kovarsky, like Milton's Satan, is too sympathetically portrayed throughout the narrative to be so totally pilloried by its end. Neither his confused explanation of why he became a stool pigeon in the first place nor his sudden shift of anger toward the company in the closing scene is convincing. What is persuasive, however, is his anguish for his crippled friend's family and his own pregnant wife, as well as his self-loathing for surrendering his principles. Unlike the stock characters in Schenkkan's plays, in *Black Pit* Maltz has created an all-too-human miner who buckles under terrible odds. As dishonorable as his decision is, we suffer with him in his shame. We understand his rationalization that he will stool for only a little while and lie to Prescott in the process. We hope that in similar circumstances we would have stood firmer, but wonder if it would have been humanly possible to do so. The curtain falls on neither hero nor antihero but on a stool pigeon who, in spite of his fall from grace, remains one of the most tragic and believable characters in mining literature.

Although written from a contemporary perspective, Jo Carson's "Preacher with a Horse to Ride" is also set in the 1930s. The play analyzes political and professional "othering" by considering how the Dreiser Committee barged into Harlan County without asking the miners what needed to be done. Convinced that the miners were harmed rather than helped by the committee's visit, she examines the motivation and tactics of Dreiser himself. Carson's Dreiser is more concerned about his declining career than class issues. Struggling with writer's block, he goes to Kentucky to rekindle his creativity. "I've been working wrong for so long I'd almost forgotten how I work," the aging writer recalls. "Newspapers, magazines are not my medium. They are too short and too little. My stories are bigger than they are. And Kentucky is such a story that this nation will weep."[19]

As Carson demonstrates, it is Dreiser's rather than the miner's story that ultimately captures the nation's attention. As the play unfolds, Dreiser's sexual exploitation of the secretaries he hires and discards serves as a thematic counterpoint to the control of the companies over the miners. Ironically, Dreiser's traveling companion, Marie, who inadvertently sparks the Comstockian uproar by spending the night with him, seems to aid the strikers more effectively than the committee by distributing peppermints to the mining families. The peppermints, though a fleeting gesture, help boost morale and do not endanger the families as do the committee's inquiries. Yet the scandal she and Dreiser create ultimately has a wider effect than her generous and kindhearted nature. Carson leaves it up to Aunt Molly Jackson, who knows more of life and death than anyone else in the county, to evaluate the overall impact of Dreiser's committee. She tells a story learned from her mother about other well-meaning outsiders of earlier times. During the years of early settlement, no congregation could afford a regular preacher, and circuit-riding ministers were regional mainstays. Although communities welcomed a preacher, his presence could be a hardship on those families who took him in:

> Well, food to feed a extra man was hard and you'd kill a chicken you couldn't afford to kill just yet or something like it to have enough to go around. You didn't say nothing. It was a point of honor with my mother that the man didn't know what a chicken meant to her. Now, he was there with good intentions, the saving of souls, but the truth was he made it harder on the day by day. Well, say he got him a horse to ride. He could do his circuit that much faster, get to your place that much more often, keep a better check on your eternal soul. There was folks that bled their cows almost to dying and drank the blood to keep from starving themselves. I know what you are thinking: they had cows and we don't. Well, we got preachers with horses to ride, a whole bunch of 'em and all of them setting down to eat hardy with the best intentions.[20]

While Carson was primarily interested in outsiders who visited mining areas, Paula Cizmar's *The Death of a Miner* is more in the tradition of Settle and Giardina in its exploration of the inner depths of its main character, a thirty-two-year-old female miner. This drama opens with Mary Alice Hager already dead in a mining accident. The scenes continually switch between present and past. Mary Alice leaves behind a husband, Jack, and a daughter by another marriage, Sallie. Her survivors battle for her death benefits, which, by law, are denied to the families of female workers.

In production notes, Cizmar wants Mary Alice to remain on stage throughout the play. Cizmar hopes to simulate the process of remembering, with images and ideas merging one into another. Traditional Appalachian music played on folk instruments underscores her monologues. There are no blackouts during scene changes. Cizmar wants to suggest life's continuous flow. The production's mood is to be upbeat and "filled with the joy of living" even while portraying the dead. Neither Mary Alice nor any of the other characters are meant to be tragic. Her monologues in particular "should be spontaneous outpourings of her love of the land, her hopes for a better future—outpourings filled with humor, bitterness, excitement." Mary Alice's presence on stage is intended to unify the play's action, but her monologues are intensely personal—neither poetic nor sentimental—delivered with the "gutsy, lively observations of a woman who is sensually aware of the world around her."[21]

Having ended a marriage, Mary Alice takes her daughter and moves from Detroit to Pea Ridge, West Virginia, not because she knows what she wants to do but because she knows where she wants to be. "I can never understand why anybody would want to live anywhere else, why anyone would want to live, say, on the ocean. That ain't living in the earth." Mary Alice's career decision follows a stint as a waitress and her marriage to Jack, a local carpenter. Against Jack's wishes, she decides to be trained as a miner. But it is while they are discussing the prospect of marriage that she explains her visceral connection to the surrounding hills, which will eventually influence her to work underground:

> *Jack.* You come to a new town, not knowin anyone. Just take a chance. Take care of yourself and your kid. Get a job. Make friends.
>
> *Mary Alice.* Meet you.
>
> *Jack.* Meet me. yeah. Up to somethin all the time. I just wonder what you'll be doin on Saturday.
>
> *Mary Alice.* Saturday? Well . . . well I was hopin to spend some time with you.
>
> *Jack.* I was hopin we could get married.
>
> *Mary Alice.* Jack!
>
> *Jack.* Think maybe we can have a real nice life. I feel real comfortable with you. I feel real comfortable in this place.
>
> *Mary Alice.* It's the hills.
>
> *Jack.* Think so.
>
> *Mary Alice.* Old Mama Mountain throwin her arms around us, huggin us, protectin us from the wind.
>
> *Jack.* Even animals are afraid of the wind.
>
> *Mary Alice.* Yes.
>
> *Jack.* Yeah. I *do* feel protected here. You know once, went all the way up to—what the hell's the name of that place in Ohio—Lordstown? Went up to Lordstown to work in the auto plant. Was making 12 bucks an hour. Didn't feel right though. Hillbilly is as low as you can go up there. Don't feel good you know.
>
> *Mary Alice.* I know. I was at this weddin in Detroit once, workin in the kitchen and—Oh, I told you that. Yeah I told you that.[22]

Mary Alice's choice to become a miner is neither romanticized nor glamorized. Each day she is conscious of the mountain over her head, and she understands and accepts the dangers of the job. None of the men in the play, including Jack, supports her decision to work underground. Her marriage is complicated by this disagreement. Tensions at work are even worse, and a coworker, Chester, the archetypal "good ole boy" whose grandfather and father were also miners, exemplifies the attitudes of most of the men. They refuse to accept women in the mines. They blame Mary Alice and her friend and fellow miner Winona for any problems that occur. Mary Alice rationalizes that the miners are no worse than many of the male diners she served at the Blue Sky cafe, where she had to "bat my eyelashes just to get a tip."[23] Economic realities probably led to Mary Alice's decision to work at the Blue Sky just as they influenced her decision to dig coal. But there is no self-sacrifice involved here. She hopes that Sallie will have a better life, but mining also gives her a personal sense of self and place; as she explains in one of her early monologues: "Well, you know, that the earth, the land, is takin care of me—that I've got a job to do and I'm damned good at it, and I take my livin out of these hills."[24]

The play appears to be heading to a predictable end when the union leadership supports the payment of Mary Alice's death benefits to her husband and daughter. Surprisingly the rank and file vote against the payments, showing their contempt for women miners. Working-class solidarity unravels over gender issues. At the same time, the steadfastness of family is affirmed as Jack and Sallie stay together. Jack thinks about leaving town. He is crushed by his wife's death and uncertain of his affection for his adopted daughter. But Jack and Sallie are brought together by the callousness of both the company and the union's rank and file. They learn that they are still Mary Alice Hager's family with roots in Pea Ridge, West Virginia. As the lights fade, Mary Alice offers her blessing: "This is where you belong. In these hills. Somethin about the dirt—thick and red and soft like that. Or black. Nice, rich, black . . . not dirt that has the life washed out of it. The earth seems so ancient here. And down in the mines—I feel it sometimes. I just know it's been here forever. Look at that! Just look at that! Changing again. This has got to be the most beautiful sunrise I have ever seen."[25]

Mary Alice Hager is more of a "personality" with her own voice than the "characters" in most of the other plays in this chapter. Like the visiting circuit riders in Carson's *Preacher with a Horse to Ride,* many of the men and women who have written plays with coal mining themes have acted with the best of intentions. Whether writing out of compassion or curiosity, drawing upon creativity or personal familiarity, they dramatize those aspects of the coal mining experience that most attract, repulse, or simply interest them. At their best, they avoid stereotypes and portray miners as normal people pursuing a unique, if difficult, way of making a living. The mining families in such plays experience the ordinary joys and sorrows of life. At their worst, playwrights stereotype mining families as helpless pawns caught up in a relentless, destructive process for which escape is the only relief. In either case, as Hamlet says, the play's the thing. The dramatic process always tells us more about the creator than the creation. Americans have written plays about coal mining with thematic similarities, but this does not mean that they truly understand or represent the mining world. Instead, they react personally and professionally in imaginative ways to what they perceive as the reality of that world. In truth, they are often writing about a subject, a dramatic "other," that continues to stimulate and elude their creative faculties. Mining environments and situations are realistically portrayed, but the inhabitants of these plays, like the characters in a Japanese No drama, are often stylized; since miners are characterized according to their occupation, we lose sight of the fact that they are not industrial mutants but fellow human beings with all of the complexities and inconsistencies that such a status implies.

Screenwriters and directors of American feature films have creatively responded to the coal mining experience in ways both similar and different from those of playwrights. Many of the differences are primarily technical and relate to the camera's mobility as well as the innovative ways it can be used. As dramatist Arthur Miller reminds us, the visual dominates cinematography in ways unknown to the stage. Virtually anyone would be "hard put to remember the dialogue in some of the great pictures that you've seen. That's why pictures are so international. You don't have to hear the style of the dialogue in an Italian movie or a French movie. We're watching the film, so that the vehicle is not the ear or the word, it's the eye."[26] Film crews can go to coal mines for realistic footage. They can provide panoramic scans of mines and mining camps. They can simulate mine disasters and the human reactions to these disasters in ways unavailable to dramatists. Rapid scene shifts are also more easily facilitated on film. As a result, script writers and directors enjoy much dramatic discretion. Cinematic historian Robert Rosenstone agrees with Miller that film images are capable of conveying ideas and information that cannot easily be managed by the spoken or written word. From this perspective the medium becomes the message. It is a message capable of creating for mass audiences "the look and feel of all sorts of historical particulars and situations—say farm workers dwarfed by immense Western prairies and mountains, miners struggling in the darkness of their pits, mill workers moving to the rhythms of their machines."[27] While many of the nineteen mining films in this chapter try to authenticate "the look and feel" of digging coal by showing men and women at work underground, more often they use mining disasters or strikes to replicate life in the mines. While *Matewan, The Molly Maguires, Act of Vengeance,* and *October Sky* are historically grounded, most of the other films clearly seek a wide audience by cultivating the sensational or sentimental. As a result, these films of popular appeal seem more melodramatic and certainly far less political than many of the plays. If Steven Mintz and Randy Roberts are correct in *Hollywood's America: United States History through Its Films* that "the movies have taught Americans how to kiss, make love, conceive of gender roles, and understand their place in the world," some of these films have also shaped America's perception of the coal mining world.[28] Still, there is an overall continuity between screen and stage, for in both, coalfields are often envisioned as so hermetically different that audiences might well imagine their inhabitants arrived from another planet.

The nineteen feature-length films addressed here range from the beginning of American cinema to the present.[29] The earliest is *Threads of Fate* (1917), a silent melodrama in which mine owners and miners remain on the periphery during most of the film.[30] A silent film that has even less to do with mining, *Human Hearts* (1922), dramatizes the efforts of a few villains to seize control of valuable coal deposits. A third film, *Little Church around the Corner* (1923), provides fascinating impressions of both miners and mine owners along with a brilliant recreation of a mining disaster and rescue efforts. Equally as interesting is an early sound picture without dialogue, *The Toilers* (1928), which offers a close look at the lives of three mining buddies. In the 1935 film version of Michael A. Musmanno's *Black Fury,* directed by Michael Curtiz, Paul Muni plays the role of Joe Radek. Director Lewis Seiler assembles an all-star cast of John Wayne, Marlene Dietrich, and Randolph Scott in *Pittsburgh* (1942). In this bleak film, two miners and their lovely sidekick (Dietrich) often remind one another of their dreary, dead-end life. Six years later, *The Miracle of the Bells* (1948), based on Russell Janney's novel of the same title, narrates the story of a dying actress who returns home to offer hope in the otherwise desolate lives of the people of Coaltown. Although released in 1970, Martin Ritt's *The Molly Maguires* has a definite 1960s quality about it with its looting scene, cynicism towards power, and ambiguous differentiation between good and evil causes. *The Christmas Coal Mine Miracle* (1977) reveals many of the failings of telemovies in its efforts to portray a coal mining family. So too does the soap operatic *Roses Are for the Rich* (1987), the first parts of which are set in a coal mining town. Two other run-of-the-mill films made for television are *Kentucky Woman* (1983), which focuses on the life of a female coal miner, and *Burning Rage* (1984), a story filled with love and avarice in an Appalachian town sitting over a slowly burning abandoned coal mine. All four of these movies oversimplify complex issues and create a middle-class veneer for most of their characters. They also try to avoid tragedy by distorting the real disasters, sickness, and oppression of the mining world. An exception to the other made-for-television films is *Act of Vengeance* (1985), in which Charles Bronson does a credible job of portraying United Mine Worker reformer Jock Yablonski. Although the film centers on Yablonski's reforming efforts and his subsequent murder, director John MacKenzie was clearly fascinated with the motivation and blundering efforts of the murderers themselves, much like Truman Capote's novel *In Cold Blood* and the Coen brothers in the more recent film *Fargo.*

Coal Miner's Daughter (1980) was the first of a number of credible films with a coal mining setting released in the 1980s. The film follows the life and career of country music singer Loretta Lynn (brilliantly played by Sissy Spacek). The next year another biographical film, *A Winner Never Quits,* narrates the career of one-armed baseball player Pete Gray. He learned to play the game in the Pennsylvania coalfields, where he eventually returned to retire. John Sayles's *Matewan* (1987) was the most discussed coal mining film in recent decades until the appearance of *Germinal* in 1994. A year later, a film that has not been widely distributed because director and producer could not agree on the finished product, *Made in USA,* brilliantly portrays in its opening scenes a desolate Pennsylvania coal town on the economic downswing since the closing of its deep mines. Although the latter half of the film does not hold together, the opening sequences showing the departure of two sons of former coal miners are filled with poignant images of a dying culture. A less successful movie appearing that same year, *The Prince of Pennsylvania* (1988), revolves around the uneasy relationship between a coal miner father (played by Fred Ward) who tries to make a man of his eldest and free-spirited son (Keanu Reeves) by forcing him to work in the mines. Released in 1990, *Montana* is aptly set in the West, where so much of the country's coal is now being strip mined. The plot revolves around a husband and wife who agree on little, including whether or not to sell their ranch, which is rich in coal deposits. The miners in this film spend their workdays operating machinery above rather than below ground. Finally, Joe Johnston's popular *October Sky* (1999) takes place in a West Virginia coal mining town in which a father-son relationship parallels the efforts of the local "rocket boys" to achieve an impossible dream.

This chapter also looks at screenplays or synopses of eight other films found in the copyright files of the Motion Picture, Broadcasting and Recorded Sound Division of the Library of Congress. *Through Fire to Fortune; or The Sunken Village* (1914), a Horatio Alger story about a young man who replenishes his family's fortunes by working his way upward through the coal mining ranks, is a particularly impressive early film because of its visual images of work inside of mines and mining disasters.[31] Plot synopses found in the *American Film Institute Catalog, The Moving Picture World,* and J.W. Williamson's

Southern Mountaineers in Silent Films reveal a number of other films that contain coal mining themes. Few of these films deal exclusively with the mining world. For example, a favorite plot in early films involves efforts to either preserve or gain control of valuable coal deposits.[32] Few of the early silent films, such as *Through Fire to Fortune,* resist the attraction of a disaster below ground. These films place explosions, cave-ins, and trapped miners at the center of the action. In these films, miners who use their skills and courage to rescue fellow workers are heroically portrayed.[33] Miners who work in groups, however, are usually to be feared. In many of the early films in which strikes occur, miners are a rough lot, volatile and easily led by unscrupulous men. Collectively they appear to be caught up in a destructive kind of mob psychology. Yet they are capable of repentance and reason under the firm leadership of the middle or upper classes.[34] A notable exception is *The Dawn of Freedom* (1916). In this film, the miners are justifiably angry because they are not paid a living wage. Their struggles are favorably compared with those of their revolutionary forebears. Finally, in several of these pre-1930s films, coal mines become proving grounds for manhood or a litmus test for good character, the assumption being that life's other hardships are minor when compared to digging coal underground.[35]

The same emphasis on the brutal and dangerous aspects of mining life found in plays is also found in film. The exploitative nature of the industry usually centers on management in more recent films, though mine owners and managers are often heroic in the silent film era. They are capable of changing and showing concern for the workers even in such mid-century films as *Little Church around the Corner, Jeepers Creepers,* and *Pittsburgh.* More recently, however, they are typically greedy. They undermine safety and consistently underpay their workers. The men they hire to carry out their orders and protect their property are even worse. In an earlier film, *Black Fury,* the Coal and Iron Police are particularly vicious and capricious. They are a little better but considerably more cynical in *The Molly Maguires.* Local police in *Burning Rage,* who are in the pockets of management, are murderous but bungling in their villainy. Whether the malevolence of the two Baldwin Felts guards in *Matewan* is inwardly or outwardly directed is never entirely clear, but they carry out their orders with a chillingly banal brutality.

It does seem odd that such a conservative segment of American popular culture as the film industry would portray the management side in such a negative way. Yet most of these films are relatively modern ones. George Baer's paternalistic myopia has become part of the coal industry's folklore in the same way that greedy cattle barons are acknowledged villains in many westerns. With the continuing decline of the coal industry in recent times, films can safely attack the coal barons. Yet none of the films attacks the industry nationwide. Instead, individual owners and managers on the local level are usually held accountable for the worst abuses in the mines. Explosions, rock falls, and fires result from rare acts of greed or an attempt to ignore the safety regulations that normally protect the miners. Many of these films, in the Hollywood tradition, still end happily.

Just as miners in the 1923 production of *Little Church around the Corner* are seen as a rowdy and violent lot, the rugby game in *The Molly Maguires* and the fighting in the voting precincts in *Act of Vengeance* are reminders that the mining scene is a brutal one. Yet, in film as on stage it is the psychological rather than the physical that predominates. In *The Miracle of the Bells,* the priest of a miners' parish, Father Paul (Frank Sinatra), and an outsider named Bill Bunnigan (Fred MacMurray) stroll to a cemetery overlooking the town to work out the arrangements for a funeral. As they gaze over the dismal industrial scene below, Father Paul tells Bunnigan that the "people in Coaltown are almost too tired to come to God." When Bunnigan replies that the town does not look too bad from where they are standing, the priest quietly says: "Coal dust doesn't blow up here." The longer Bunnigan looks at the town below, the more he begins to feel that Father Paul is right. If he lived like most of the townspeople, Bunnigan says, he "wouldn't mind coming up here for a great long sleep." "Perhaps most of them do," the priest replies.

Unlike in the 1940s when *The Miracle of the Bells* appeared, by the 1970s coal was a dying industry, but the negativism associated with miners was still very much alive. In *The Molly Maguires,* Martin Ritt explores the motivation of Pinkerton infiltrator James McParlan (Richard Harris), alias James McKenna. Set in the anthracite coalfields of the 1870s, the film looks closely at a man who knew about management's exploitation of its Irish workforce and empathized with the miners' suffering; Ritt asks, how could such a man act as an industrial spy by selling out his close associates? McParlan pays lip service to his opposition to terrorism. He reveals his true thoughts when he secretly meets deep inside a mine with the Welch police captain who serves as his pipeline to the authorities. Obviously bothered by what he is doing, McParlan tells the police captain how much he hates working underground. "I have to get out—I'd kill somebody if I couldn't," he exclaims and then asks: "How would you like to spend your life down here?" When the captain says that he tried it for awhile but found a way out by making himself useful in other ways, McParlan hears what amounts to a reaffirmation of his own actions. The end justifies the means, especially when digging coal for the rest of his life is a future he cannot accept. Later in the film, the unsuspecting daughter of a crippled miner with whom he is boarding warns McParlan that there is no future for him but hell if he continues to associate with the Mollys. He replies: "I'm a miner now. I've been traveling in that direction anyway just out of habit."

Using their technical abilities to recreate mining disasters in far more believable ways than on stage, filmmakers often suggest that digging coal is a kind of living hell. Ironically, no modern attempt laden with special effects has reproduced the tensions, terror, and collective anguish of the early silent films. In *The Toilers,* for example, a spreading mine fire and the frantic effort of retreating miners to save themselves creates powerful dramatic tension. Primitive as it may appear on film, the surging wall of flames is terrifying, and the frantic efforts of the trapped miners to save themselves are utterly believable. The subtitles sharpen the drama: "All through the night they kept building barricades against the onrushing flames." An equally impressive recreation of a mining disaster appeared in a film made five years earlier. Scenes rapidly alternate in *Little Church around the Corner* between trapped miners below ground and a crowd of anxious onlookers and loved ones above. Even more impressive is the initial reaction of the town to the alarm whistle, as people rush to the mouth of the mine in a way reminiscent of the crowds Sergei Eisenstein skillfully used in *Battleship Potemkin.* The silence of the film dignifies the anguished families and heightens the terror felt for the survivors below.

The dense clouds of dust surrounding coal workers, though difficult to simulate in a play, frequently supply imagery and atmosphere for the movie screen. The dust, at least in more recent films, suggests a heightened awareness of the dangers of black lung. John Sayles created a magnificent opening scene in *Matewan,* with a solitary coughing miner enveloped by darkness and dripping water. Pete Gray's mother in *A Winner Never Quits* walks from the mine at the end of her shift, coughing along the way. Loretta Lynn's father in *Coal Miner's Daughter* tells his oldest child that he cannot estimate his weight because of all of the coal dust that he has inhaled while working underground. Maggie, in *Kentucky Woman,* decides to become a coal miner to support herself after her father is forced into early retirement because of the ravages of coal dust on his lungs. In *The Miracle of the Bells,* actress Olga Treskovna is doomed by the tuberculosis she contracted as a child living in a Pennsylvania mining town. While these dramatic interpretations contain varying degrees of truth, even in scenes that are pejorative to a people and culture, they by no means depict the dominating reality of mining life. Yet the overall impression in film and theater is that they do, and audiences cannot help but view coal mining people as tragic "others" who should, like all rational beings, search for better ways of earning a living.

Long before McParlan explained spying for the police as a justifiable way of getting out of the mines, director Lewis Seiler creates a comparable situation in his star-filled film *Pittsburgh.* In an early scene, Pittsburgh Marcum (John Wayne) is flirting with Josie Winders (Marlene Dietrich), but she wants nothing to do with him because he is a miner. "They say coal means warmth and life," she tells him. "All it means to people like us is death if you stay around it long enough." He quickly defends himself by promising, "I ain't always going to be slinging a pick." Marcum later tells Winders that they are cut from the same cloth. She caustically dampens his ardor again by alluding to his job. "Yeah. Dirt, smoke, hunger, strikes, and life as black as the bottom of those mines." Winders eventually lures Marcum and his buddy out of the mines by daring them to make something of themselves. Even though Marcum ultimately loses the contest for her affection, he knows she has changed his life: "Why I'd still be digging coal if you hadn't sunk the spurs in me."

Pam Marshetta, the mother in *The Prince of Pennsylvania* (played by Bonnie Bedelia), takes up where Josie Winders left off in language that would not have passed the censors in the 1940s. She more or less justifies her infidelity to her coal-mining husband by explaining, "Sometimes I feel I married Jimmy Hendrix and he turned into Oliver North." While not explicitly blaming her marital problems on coal, she constantly tries to persuade her lover and her son to leave coal mining behind them. "What are you doing here?" she snaps at her eldest son during a family celebration at a local restaurant. "You want to end up just like me? If I were you I would tell him [her husband] to take his goddamned coal mine and shove it up his ass, and I'd ride the hell out of this miserable little shit hole."

The language in the 1983 TV movie *Kentucky Woman* may be antiseptic in comparison, but the message is the same. Luke Telfort (Ned Beatty) is angry and frustrated. Suffering from black lung is bad enough, but thinking about his daughter taking his place in the mine is more than he can bear. Telfort can no longer join his daughter and grandson in church. "I can't get right with no God that allows coal mining," he explains. "Sunday baseball is my religion."

While film is no less disparaging of mining culture than drama, many directors have made an effort to portray the actual mining of coal more realistically. A playwright might use a darkened stage to suggest a mine. Film directors can take their crews directly there. Time and again these films show men entering and leaving a mine or riding in crowded cars with lights from their hats flickering in the darkness. Briefer scenes show cutting machines attacking a coal face or miners shoveling coal into half empty cars. Yet there is little effort to demonstrate the various skills needed to mine coal, and not all mining films make such adroit use of the camera's mobility. While the faces of Marcum and Cash Evans in *Pittsburgh* are appropriately covered with grime, the two characters seem mainly concerned with speaking into the camera. Whether they are loading coal or pushing a mining car, the work seems like a distraction in their lives. Adding to the contrived atmosphere, Winders enters and leaves the underground mine as though she were at a shopping mall.

If cinema does a relatively good job of capturing the feel of the workplace, it is less successful even than theater in portraying the inhabitants of coal mining communities. According to reviewer Joanne Barkan, not even the characters in the critically acclaimed film *Matewan* show any depth or complexity in their personalities.[36] Two notable exceptions to this shortcoming in films are the coal-mining fathers in *Coal Miner's Daughter* and *Winners Never Quit,* who are pillars of strength and understanding. Although capable of moments of real anger, they are also affectionate and comforting. Nonetheless, the lack of character development in *Matewan* is typical of most coal mining films, though several attempt historical authenticity through the use of ethnicity.

Ethnic diversity plays a role in films like *Threads of Fate, The Man Who Dared, Winners Never Quit, The Molly Maguires, Black Fury, The Miracle of the Bells,* and *Matewan.* On the screen, this diversity blends into the cinematic montage but seldom into individualized personalities. On the stage, stock ethnic mining characters are as stylized as they are common. The major exception to cinematic stereotyping is *Matewan.* Even though character development is muted, Sayles tries to show how deep-seated mistrust and cultural differences in the form of music and sports quickly evaporate. Ethnically diverse groups in the tent colony unite in class solidarity and outrage against their oppressors. Except for James Earl Jones's powerful presence in *Matewan,* African American miners are missing from most mining films and are never found in major roles.

The opposite is true of women, who play significant roles as mining wives, particularly in the 1970s and 1980s, in such films as *The Prince of Pennsylvania, The Christmas Coal Mine Miracle, A Winner Never Quits, Roses Are for the Rich,* and *Coal Miner's Daughter.* Pete Gray's father and mother both work in the mines in *A Winner Never Quits,* and the entire script of *Kentucky Woman* focuses on the life of a female coal miner. Relatively few of these cinematic female mining characters are as well developed as those on stage. Whereas the women in such plays as *Between Daylight and Booneville, The Scotian Women,* and *The Death of a Miner* exhibit strengths as well as weaknesses, those in film are too often larger-than-life or, as is the mother in *The Christmas Coal Mine Miracle,* too good to be true. This syrupy made-for-television story attempts to capture the lives of an Appalachian mining family. Everyone in it, including the mother, Rachel Sullivan, appears to have just stepped off the set of the Waltons. As the story unfolds Rachel is never tired or dirty but always patient, supportive, understanding, and completely unreal. She smoothly glides through a gadget-filled suburban house preparing meals, delivering homilies, and caring for children, neighbors, and elderly parents. Her lifestyle and activities suggest the kind of narcissistic "othering" described by postcolonial critic Abdul R. JanMohamed. Since imaginary mining families have no intrinsically valuable or interesting characteristics of their own, they become a mirror that reflects the values of their creator. With no voices of their own, they merely mimic the values of the mainstream society. As in soap operas or in made-for-television films like *The Christmas Coal Mine Miracle,* despite personal or family problems the middle-class ethos is pervasive and defining.[37]

A comparison can be made between the female miners in Czimar's *The Death of a Miner* and those in a film written, produced, and directed by Walter Doniger, *Kentucky Woman.* Unlike Czimar's Mary Alice, who chooses to go underground for a variety of personal and economic reasons, Maggie (played by Cheryl Ladd) is forced to do so as a result of her father's black lung. Both women are single mothers, but there the comparison ends. If Mary Alice feels a connection with the earth and the mountains and a sense of pride in doing a job well, Maggie never appears comfortable in her work. Mary Alice reflects on her life and decisions while Maggie delivers hard-hitting one-liners that are intended to display her grit and determination. When the mine manager, who is reluctant to hire her, asks what she will do if someone gets hurt, she sweetly responds, "See blood every month, Mr. Varney." Later, after her foreman warns her against "fooling with the men," she again puts a male in his place by replying, "Who'd want to?" Whereas Czimar's play begins and ends with the death of its main character, Doniger's has the obligatory but unconvincing happy ending. Maggie accuses a miner of smoking in a mine believed to be filled with pockets of methane. She sticks to her guns despite opposition from both the union and management. When a small explosion reveals the validity of her charge, the film ends with Maggie's fellow miners calling her "buddy" and carrying her around on their shoulders. True grit and honesty have again prevailed, and working in a coal mine is scarcely different from working anywhere else.

The decline of the coal mining industry was already in a state of free fall by the time John Sayles's *Matewan* appeared in 1988. Set in the spring of 1920 in the midst of a strike over tonnage rates, the film ends in a shoot-out between Baldwin Felts guards and the town's sheriff, Sid Hatfield, supported by many of the miners. Sayles claims that it was mining as much as the gunfight that led him to make the film. "Coal mining is, I think, where the rubber meets the road. It is an elemental act. In World War I, America fought with the coal that these guys pulled out of the ground. I mean, how many movies do you see about cowboys? And that era lasted for a very short period of time."[38] Sayles may have intended to make a film about coal miners, but he ultimately focused on other things. Besides the trapper-boy preacher, Danny Radnor, the central characters are pacifist organizer Joe Kenehan, sheriff

Hatfield, and the two Baldwin Felts heavies, Hickey and Griggs. The scenes from the tent colony of strikers and their families are convincing. Sayles writes in his book, *Thinking in Pictures: The Making of the Film Matewan,* that he wanted the audience to feel what it was like to be a miner: "We do some of our understanding straight from the gut, and if we can be made to feel the damp and cold of the mine shaft, feel the weight of the pick, breathe the dust-thick air, we're going to have more of a handle on a coal miner and his feelings than we could get just from reading and thinking."[39] The film's opening scene clearly accomplishes this goal, but as reviewer Joanne Barkan points out, the film is not about the "daily plight of miners. This is not *Germinal* or *The Road to Wigan Pier.* We witness no graphic depictions of backbreaking labor in the underground tunnels, no detailed portrayal of steady burial under debt to the company store."[40]

As do other directors who portray coal mining themes in their films, Sayles probes the age-old question of who really wants to mine coal. *Matewan,* which celebrates the strength and resiliency of an entire region, offers a very common answer—no one. Virtually none of these films seems complete without a character at some point delivering lines about the insidious life of mining. In *Matewan,* a clan of mountain folk saves the strikers' tent city from the Baldwin Felts guards. "These hill people," says the mother of a striker, "wouldn't be caught near a hole," though she offers no explanation for their aversion to mining. Perhaps they are too free, independent, or noble? Whatever the reason, the viewer knows well that mountaineers are not alone in despising the mining life. In another scene, while Danny Radnor and his friend Hillard are waiting to slip into the railroad yards to steal coal for the striking families, they reminisce about an incident in the Hatfield-McCoy feud that took place below where they are sitting. Danny points to the spot where Cap Hatfield shot three men. He asks his friend if he thinks a bullet hurts very much. Hillard replies that it "beats dying in a damn coal mine."[41] This kind of dialogue reinforces the film's images of poverty and death. Sayles clearly eulogizes the courage and grit of his miner characters but not their decision to work underground. By the film's end audiences can agree with Appalachian mountaineers and young coal miners that no one should electively do this kind of work.

A similar outlook is found in *October Sky,* which focuses on the efforts of Homer Hickam Jr. and his friends to catch up with the Russians by building their own rockets in the late 1950s. Although much of the film is devoted to the building and testing of these rockets, equally important is the relationship between Hickam and his father, who is a mining superintendent. Director Joe Johnston and scriptwriter Lewis Colick alter Hickam's fictionalized memoir by turning this complex father-son relationship into one that emphasizes the son's efforts to escape a life in the mines. The senior Hickam's life is the mine, and he cannot understand why his second son, Homer, desires to do anything else. In the film, the father envisions Homer working his way up from miner to superintendent, while in the memoir the son is encouraged to attend college to become a mining engineer. On the screen, after the father is injured in a mining accident, the son voluntarily goes into the mine to support the family, whereas in the memoir the only time he goes underground is for a brief tour with his father. Throughout the memoir, Homer's father is gruffly supportive of most of his scientific experimentation, yet the film delays the elder Hickam's conversion to this generous spirit until the story's end, as though working in a coal mine had initially hardened Hickam to his son's dreams.

In both film and memoir Homer's mother does not want her son to work the mines in any capacity. But nowhere in the book is found the bitterness about mining or the embarrassment about being Appalachian that seeps into the film. On one occasion in the film Homer shouts at his friends: "We should be trying to get into the science fair instead of acting like a bunch of hillbillies." On another occasion he soberly warns that "the mine will kill you." After quitting his mining job, Homer tells his father that he is never going into the mine again, at one point shouting, "I'll be gone forever and won't look back!" These cinematic liberties, intended to create dramatic tension, need to be balanced with the writer's own memories. Though undoubtedly colored by nostalgia and the passage of time, the memoir gives a more complex understanding of the characters. Hickam recalls the advice of a union official who had supported his scientific efforts even as he opposed the managerial position of his father: "Dubonnet had been right that day years ago by the old railroad track when he said I had been born in the mountains and that's where I belonged, no matter what I did or where I went. I didn't understand him then, but now I do." Like Mary Alice Hager, Hickam realizes that "Coalwood, its people, and the mountains were a part of me and I was a part of them and always would be." And, although wanting to do something other than work in the mines, Hickam does not disparage those who do. "I also remembered that night when Dad had come back from Cleveland and we had argued in my room. I had gone to my window after he'd left and looked out, envying the men I saw going to and from the mine, because they knew exactly who they were and what they were doing."[42] In the cinematic version, the confrontation is more like that between father and son in *Prince of Pennsylvania* than it is faithful to the memoir since it emphasizes not only Homer's triumph over the difficulties of calculus and differential equations but also his escape from the living hell of coal mining.

In the theater and on the screen, even more than in fiction, the images of mining that we encounter are usually negative ones. What we have seen and heard is more graphic than anything we have read. Miners and their families may be admired, but the physical and psychological costs of this kind of work seem unbearable. We are thankful that we do not have to go underground to make a living but perplexed why anyone else would do so had he other options. The fact that coal mining is a dying industry tends to relegate it, like cattle drives, to the past and render the entire process even more unreal, thereby increasing the distance that exists between us and them.

Chapter 5

Coal Mining Fiction for the Young

A good deal of children's and adolescent literature touches in some way on the coal miner and the mining life. There is no intrinsic distinction between this type of literature and that created for adults, although subtle differences do exist. C.S. Lewis, for example, said that he never consciously set out to compose exclusively for children. While first toying with an idea, he discovered that "a children's story is the best art-form for something you have to say: just as a composer might write a Dead March not because there was a public funeral in view but because certain musical ideas that had occurred to him went best into that form."[1]

Still, there are those who argue that real differences in the genre are apparent. Critic and historian Paul Hazard wrote in the early 1940s from Nazi-occupied France, "Children and grownups belong to different worlds. Time, deals so ruthlessly with the body, is only too often just as pitiless with the soul. Adults are rarely free; they are prisoners of themselves. Even when they play it is self-consciously and for a reason. They play in order to relax, to forget, to keep from thinking of the brief time that is still left to them. They seldom play for the sheer joy of playing." Children are "full of the exuberance of life, from morning to night they run, shout, quarrel, make up and fall asleep only to begin again next day at sunrise."[2] Rebecca J. Lukens points out that children "are different from adults in experience, but not in species . . . in degree but not in kind."[3] An author may accommodate these experiential limitations by using simpler vocabulary, clearer language, and shorter stories. Characters, plots, and themes may be less developed than in adult fiction. Linear time and action may be the glue that holds the work together.[4] Children like to identify with the characters of a story, many of whom are the same age as the intended reading audience. Children are also attracted by the heroic: they encounter it on a daily basis. As Diana Wynne Jones suggests, "in every playground there are actual giants to be overcome and the moral issues are usually clearer than they are, say, in politics."[5] Regardless of the perspective from which critics approach children's literature, most of it is still written by adults and often selected and purchased by adults. In fact, Peter Hunt suggests that "we want to select what the children may or may not know, and at which stage in their development they know it."[6] It is from this adult perspective that this chapter will explore whether writers of children's and adolescent literature approach the coal mining experience in ways similar to or different from those of writers and directors with adult audiences. In the children's genre, are miners imaginary "others" or do they have voices of their own? Does the nature of their work define them or are they portrayed as human beings engaged in a kind of work that is merely different? It will be argued that books for the youngest children are remarkably free of the kind of "othering" found in the two preceding chapters, but the authors of books for older children and young adults take on many of the assumptive stereotypes of novelists and the directors of both stage and screen.

Kenneth L. Donelson and Alleen Pace Nilsen, in *Literature for Today's Young Adults,* offer a workable definition of the difference between children's and adolescent literature. Children's literature includes works written for ages from preschool through the sixth grade. Adolescent or young adult literature is written for an audience from the seventh grade roughly through the high school years.[7] The first books to be examined are written for the youngest readers through the age of eight.[8] They are essentially picture books with simple, descriptive narrative structures.

Lillie D. Chaffin's *We Be Warm Till Springtime Comes* (1980) is unusual in how it presents coal mining to young readers. She describes how a small boy saves his mother and baby sister during a severe winter storm in the Appalachians. When they run out of fuel, little Jimmy Joe, carrying a lantern and dragging a rusty pick and toy wagon behind him, goes into a little dog-hole mine to dig its coal. This is Jimmy Joe's first glimpse of a mine's interior. Gloom is his initial impression: "The floor is water, and the ceiling is rock. It's darker in there than two midnights put together." Fear mingles with respect in the young miner. "If the top falls, it'll squash me out like a stepped-on bug. 'Don't you dare fall on me,' I say. Then I add, 'please.'" Although the story focuses on Jimmy Joe's resourcefulness and courage, it also introduces the young reader to mining. This heroic child, who is not a miner but acts like one, teaches the reader about the dangerous, essential job.

Concern for a parent's safety as well as pride in her occupation mingle in George Ella Lyon's *Mama Is A Miner* (1994). Told from a daughter's perspective, this book introduces younger children not only to mining but also to the fact that both men and women work underground. The young narrator envisions what her mother is doing below ground by comparing her mother's job with her own life and world above. "When I'm settled on Bus 34 Mama's crowded into a low car, cap light off, dozing, swaying headed for Black Mountain's heart." She does not dwell on her mother during the day, although "sometimes in gym or reading or math a door will creak, a chair will grate and I pretend it's Mama I hear."

Life in this mining family is warm and secure from a child's perspective. Although the father's job is not mentioned, he helps get meals on the table and helps with homework. Always at the domestic center, the mother works underground despite her daughter's wishes, because the pay is better. "I wish Mama still worked at the store away from the explosions, roof fall, dark," the young girl reflects. "But ringing up grub didn't pay our bills. Hard work for hard times," Mama says. She tells her daughter that during the first part of the shift she is digging for lunch. "Second half's better," Mama says, serving up beans, cutting cornbread. "Then I'm digging for home." In step with the traditional gender roles in the story, Mama views her job as a way to help the family rather than a career to pursue. This distinction makes no impression on her daughter. She fears for her mother's safety but is proud of her mother as well. At bedtime, she burrows under the covers, using a flashlight beam to draw a picture of her mother decked out in mining gear.

Cynthia Rylant, in *When I Was Young in the Mountains* (1982) and *Appalachia: The Voices of Sleeping Birds* (1991), and Michelle Dionetti, in *Coal Mine Peaches* (1991), use mining images as part of an overall narrative structure, whereas Margaret Wise Brown's *Two Little Miners* (1949) tries to teach young readers about coal mining from the perspective of miners. Reminiscing about her childhood years spent with coal mining grandparents in the mountains of West Virginia, Rylant's narrator creates positive images. The home atmosphere is warm, food is plentiful, and a tired, dust-covered grandfather still takes the time to kiss his grandchildren when he returns from work. Dionetti offers an equally loving, more whimsical tale about grandparents that begins and ends with a yarn about coal mine peaches. The storyteller is the writer's grandfather, who grew up in a mining town and worked as a slate picker. To help his young listeners forget about the winter's cold and their red hands, he tells them that in the summer the temperature in the mine got so hot that peaches grew out of the coal. They laugh, of course, but in the summertime, when they eat "small purple plums the size of coal nuggets," the grandfather says, "What did I tell you? Coal mine peaches!" Mining serves as little more than a backdrop in this generational story. By intermixing images of hardship, laughter, and fantasy the story poses many questions about the coal mining life.[9]

Less concerned with images, Brown's *Two Little Miners* is intended not only to entertain but also to instruct about the basic rudiments of the coal mining life. As the title implies, Brown's adult miners are described as though they are children. They are constantly in motion, hurrying to work, "jumping" into the lift carrying them into the mine or "jumping" out of the mining car taking them to a coal face. If the loneliness of their occupation is stressed—"All the rest of the tunnel was dark, and there were only the black shadows of the two miners and their pickaxes blending up and down in the dark coal mine"—the work itself appears to be hard but fun. The end result is almost magical. Their car emerges at the end of the day filled "with bright, shiny coal, like a little black mountain of coal-black diamonds." Brown introduces an element of danger when the "two little miners" use dynamite to loosen more coal and the blast brings down a wall of coal between them. Instead of despairing, they immediately set to work tunneling towards one another and are soon together again. By day's end, these miners are "black as soot, dirty as pitch, black as night, black as a crow, black as black, coal black." They still love their work and their middle-class lives. Their houses are warm and lighted. They wear shirts and ties. They eat a bountiful supper surrounded by pets and plants. In the story's illustrations they are usually smiling, and when they sing, it is always about the joys of the mining life.

Written forty-two years later, Rylant's impressionistic story of the region where she grew up, *Appalachia: The Voices of Sleeping Birds,* is less positive in its mining imagery than any of the earlier books. Suggesting a realism apparent in much of the fiction written for somewhat older children, mining houses are no longer snug and warm but, standing on poles, tiny dwellings "on the sides of which you could draw a face with your finger because coal dust had settled on their walls like snow." Mining itself is "pretty hard," and it takes courage to go two miles "into solid dark earth" to reach the coal. Unlike the two little miners who are so in love with their work that they sing about it, there is a hint here that some Appalachians mine coal because of family tradition, others because they have no other choice. "Maybe some thought they didn't have any other choice but to be a miner, living in between or on the sides of these mountains, and seeing no way to go off and become doctors or teachers and having no wish to become soldiers." By the 1990s a middle-class life for mining families is a dream rather than a reality. It is difficult to imagine Brown's two little miners of the 1940s as comfortable in Rylant's upwardly mobile world of the 1990s. Rylant's story is thoroughly tied into a middle-class, adult perspective—one that is purposefully muted as it is in the most intriguing of the early illustrated storybooks for children, Judith Hendershot's *In Coal Country* (1987).[10]

Like Rylant, Hendershot grew up in a coal mining family. Her father and grandfather worked in the mines of Neffs, Ohio. Using her parents' as well as her own memories, she creates a narrative describing a year in the life of a young girl growing up in a coal camp. She mixes the pleasures of childhood in a matter-of-fact way with some of the more difficult and unpleasant aspects of coal camp life. Hendershot includes only those events and images that would have meaning for a six to eight year old. In the opening paragraph, pride as well as economic awareness are reflected in the child's view of her father's job. "Papa dug coal from deep in the earth to earn a living. He dressed for work when everyone else went to bed. He wore faded denims and steel-toed shoes and he walked a mile to his job at the mine every night. . . . It was important work. He was proud to do it." As in the other storybooks for younger age levels, she emphasizes the dirtiness of the job. She also highlights the humanity of the person beneath the coal dust. "Sometimes I walked up the run to meet Papa. He was always covered with grime and dirt, but I could see the whites of his eyes smiling at me. He let me carry his silver lunch bucket." The houses, like her father, are covered with dust. The coal-burning fires inside cause the paint of the exterior to peel. Inside is comfort and warmth. Her mother always has "a jar of spring flowers on the kitchen table." The book's descriptive didacticism is based on concrete images. The water in the nearby creek, for example, is blackened from the runoff of the nearby tipple, which drains into it and "turned it black as night." When a pile of slate catches fire it smolders for weeks. These same "gob piles" are playgrounds for the kids. Even the trains loaded with coal, which rumble by day and night, make a greater impression on the children than does work at the mine itself.

The last part of the story explores the natural beauties of the countryside: waterfalls, autumn woods, snow on Baker's Ridge. Work and pleasure are symbiotically united in this delightful book. The first image is that of a miner returning from work; the concluding one, a family celebrating Christmas. "The house smelled of Christmas tree and roast goose and all the good things that Mama had made. No whistle called Papa to the mine. Everything felt so special. And it was." *In Coal Country* neither romanticizes nor sentimentalizes coal camp life. Hendershot simply and successfully portrays it through the limited yet acute vision of a young child. Unlike Rylant, who has something to say about why Appalachians mine coal, Hendershot does not venture beyond a child's viewpoint. What she does say is that bad smells, dingy houses, and laborious jobs exist in all mining camps. But family and the beautiful world of nature makes life full and special, at least from the perspective of a young child.

In most of the children's books for the younger age levels, mining is simply described as one of many kinds of work to be found throughout the world. Its only distinctive qualities are dirt, darkness, and location beneath the earth. Miners work underground because they choose to—Rylant is the only of these authors to suggest otherwise. Her perspective may have more to do with limited mobility in the 1990s and a general lack of agency for all Americans than coal mining's economic coerciveness. Miners in most of these stories are happy with their jobs, and families are secure in the comfort of their homes and communities.

Authors writing for older audiences, the third through the sixth grades, often intertwine instruction with various kinds of adventure and history. Ethel Augusta Eliot's *Little Black Coal* (1923) is one of the few books that mixes didacticism and fantasy, while Ellen Wilson's *Three Boys and a Mine* (1954) is descriptively didactic.[11] Catherine A. Welch's *Danger at the Breaker* (1992) is a story about the first workday of a young boy in the anthracite fields during the latter portions of the nineteenth century. Lois Lenski, in *Coal Camp Girl* (1959), Alvena Seckar, in *Trapped in the Old Mine* (1953), Annabel Johnson, in *The Bearcat* (1960), Francis William Rolt-Wheller, in *Boy with the U.S. Miners* (1922), and M.A. Jagendorf's short story "The Haunted Mine" all instruct the reader about mining techniques, lore, and lifestyles in the context of exciting adventures. A relatively short novel by Seckar, *Misko* (1956), describes the adventures of a Slovak family trying to find a new place to live after the father is killed in the mines. Strip mining is common in this story, but the author treats it as simply another way of obtaining coal. Marguerite de Angeli's *Up the Hill* (1942) faithfully describes life in an immigrant Polish family. Mining is incidental to the plot as the oldest son leaves his job as a mule driver to become an artist. Upward mobility is also a theme in Burton Egbert Stevenson's Horatio Alger–type novel, *Tommy Remington's Battle* (1901). Here the son of a miner surmounts the liabilities often associated with a working-class background and makes his way into Princeton. Like Stevenson's novel, Homer Greene's *The Blind Brother: A Story of the Pennsylvania Coal Mines* (1887) is also intended for older readers. Set during the Molly Maguire era, this work offers a positive portrayal of miners and a negative description of their job. Dareen Rappaport's *Trouble at the Mines* (1987) is based on actual events in a miners' strike in Arnot, Pennsylvania, during the late 1890s. Betsy Byars's *Good-Bye Chicken Little* (1979) and Cynthia Rylant's *A Blue-Eyed Daisy* (1985) belong to some degree in the category that Sheila Egoff adroitly dissects and labels the "problem novel." These novels emerged from a 1960s frankness and willingness to discuss virtually any theme relating to childhood problems. At best they brought about a sense of "urgency and forcefulness" to the genre, while at worst they have led to banal formula writing that has little to offer their young audience.[12] Byars's narrative is about a pre-teen boy who has to deal with his father dying in a mining accident and his favorite uncle dying as a result of a senseless bet. Mining itself is scarcely mentioned. Rylant's *A Blue-Eyed Daisy* describes a father-daughter relationship that deteriorates when the father loses his job in the mines after a debilitating injury. The father's drinking divides them even further, until a shared interest in a hunting dog draws them together. Mining serves little purpose other than providing a context for the problems. Scott O'Dell, author of the Newberry Award–winning *Island of the Blue Dolphins,* likewise writes about a parent-child relationship in his short work *Journey to Jericho* (1969). Nine-year-old David Moore sees his father leave a home in West Virginia and a coal mining job that he loves in order to move to California and work in a sawmill. David's mother had been consumed by fear of her husband's work underground. Eventually the rest of the family moves to California. David accepts this because he will be reunited with his father. Unlike so many of his fictional counterparts, he is sorry that he will never be a miner himself. A character created by Michelle Green, Willie Pearl Mahone, is a year older than David. She and her African American family cannot afford to move. They stay in their depression-ridden West Virginia mining town, where her father works for the Consolidated Coal Company. In two simple yet clever stories, *Willie Pearl* (1990) and *Willie Pearl: Under the Mountain* (1992), Green skillfully portrays from a child's perspective the economic deprivation of an isolated mining community as well as the compassionate values of a struggling family. Green focuses more explicitly on mining practices in the second story, describing safety precautions, the danger of tunneling too close to the surface, and the various work shifts and what is done on each. She also enumerates the duties that the children have in a family of seven including two boarders who work in the coalfields.

Stories written for older children clearly differ from those intended for younger readers in a number of significant ways. Literature for older children is more descriptively judgmental about mining homes and villages. These stories offer more realistic portraiture of relationships in mining families. They are far more explicit in their descriptions of the dangers and hardships of digging coal for a living. Miners and mining are often positively characterized, but there is more ambiguity than in the earlier books about mining as a way of life. Most important of all, like adult fiction, theater, and film, these books lead children to believe that coal mining is an exploitative profession and that most of those who do it would prefer a different job. Whether intended or not, the agency and even joy in the lives of the two little miners no longer seems as important as the sympathy readers are encouraged to feel for those engaged in this kind of work. There are still many positive images to be found, but pity, hardship, danger, and, above all, departure are so intricately intertwined in many of these stories that young readers cannot help but view mining people as a working-class "other."

In many of these books for older children, part of the inevitably exploitative nature of the profession is that mining people do not live well. Snug houses, rooms filled with pets and plants, and hot suppers are replaced by less idyllic mining homes and villages. If Rylant earlier suggested a less-inviting view of mining houses and communities in *Appalachia: The Voices of Sleeping Birds,* Burton Egbert Stevenson's turn-of-the-century youth novel *Tommy Remington's Battle* begins with as dreary a portrait of a coal town as any adult novel of the same era: "It was not a pretty scene, this part along the river which man had made, with its crazy coaltipples, its rows of dirty little cabins, its lines of cokeovens, and the grime of coal-dust over everything." In *Three Boys and a Mine,* when the company owned the houses they were neglected, but when the miners were able to buy them they took pride in them and kept them painted. Both Lois Lenski, in *Coal Camp Girl,* and Annabel and Edgar Johnson, in *The Bearcat,* add a new dimension to this dreariness by creating a community in which all of the company houses look alike. While describing the warm, supportive family of David Moore in *Journey to Jericho,* Scott O'Dell notes that the family lived in a "very small house for so many people." Dareen Rappaport is not nearly so laconic. She has one of her characters announce on the eve of a strike: "Now this shack, flimsy and broken-down as it is, is the only home we've got. But it's owned by the company, and if the mine owners want us out, they can evict us."[13]

Company ownership of houses, eviction of coal mining families during strikes—these are subjects that younger readers do not easily comprehend. Although writers like Burton Egbert Stevenson and Francis Rolt-Wheeler in the first two decades of the twentieth century generally praised coal mine owners, Rappaport and others believed that children were ready by the fourth grade to examine the exploitative nature of the profession, which often stemmed from the practices of management. Her descriptions of management firing union activists during a strike, evicting widows from their homes, and refusing to negotiate are as vivid as those in adult fiction. Lois Lenski's condemnation of company practices is more implied than stated. She describes how mining families have to buy necessities in the company store for which they tender large deductions from their already meager paychecks. The company's giving of tawdry Christmas presents to miner's children in *Willie Pearl* may be glossed over by a generation who no longer remembers this practice. But they will not forget how management in *The Bearcat* fails to care for the safety of its workers. A young miner in the shower room hears several older workers talking about the quality of air in the mine and the company's obvious lack of concern for its men:

> "Yeah, the air got so bad down there," one was saying, "I was spittin' pure coal dust." . . .
>
> "Yep. We're a hundred feet and they ain't bothered to put in no ventilation yet."

> And the first added grimly, "I reckon the Company figures it's cheaper to bury a few of us than to give us something to breathe in there."[14]

In children's fiction, coal mining only occasionally brutalizes the miner to the extent that it does in adult literature, film, and theater. But the mining life undoubtedly causes tensions within the family in youth material. Whether or not family problems are simply the anticipated themes of the "problem novel" or directly related to family members working in mines is debatable. What is obvious, however, is that at least some family problems are directly linked to this profession. Writers such as Stevenson, Johnson, Lenski, Rappaport, and Green describe the continuing struggle of miners' wives to stretch their husbands' checks. De Angeli and Stevenson write about the family tensions that sometimes develop when children want to pursue careers outside of the mines. The Johnsons and Rylant analyze how parents handle their own frustrations in ways that can be detrimental to their children. Lenski and O'Dell suggest some of the difficulties children experience when parents—usually the fathers—leave families behind to look for work. Most dramatic of all is Rappaport's descriptions of how a prolonged strike can divide families and threaten friendships even among those on the same side. None of these situations is unique to coal mining, but in the young reader's mind they undoubtedly reiterate the problematic nature of this particular way of making a living.

Rylant, in *A Blue-Eyed Daisy,* suggests that going underground on a regular basis is more than most people can handle. She suggests as much by writing that "a lot of miners drank on the weekend to scare away the coming week." Even less subtle is Welch's *Danger at the Breaker.* What sets this book apart is its harsh portrayal of nineteenth-century mining life and the lack of warmth between father and son. As an eight year old, Andrew Pulaski knows little about coal mining, but what little he knows he does not like. "He thought his father's job must be awful. His father always came home with a rattling cough and covered with coal dust. His mother had to scrub his father's aching back every night." Much of the story is Andrew's initiation into the realities of life as a breaker boy, including an explosion in the mine that briefly traps his father. Andrew's father drops him in front of the tipple without any show of affection; he later stares into space with arms folded in front of him as his son's head rests on his shoulder. Totally absent from this book is the family warmth so much a part of other children's coal mining fiction. The little boy "never got used to the noise, the dust or the threat of danger. But it was something he had to do. Because that was life for a miner's son many years ago."[15]

The dangers of coal mining are also depicted in the books for older children. Accidents and disasters, as an intrinsic part of mining, are essential for a realistic picture. But as children's literature critic Nicholas Tucker argues, even younger children can appreciate a sense of danger that adds tension to the plot. Children do not like tragedy, however, and want to return to the routine once the danger has passed.[16] In many of the stories for younger children there are dangers, but not ones that lead to fatalities or permanent injury. The wall of coal that falls between the two little miners, for example, is treated as a temporary inconvenience. An injured miner on a stretcher, in *Mama Is a Miner,* reappears a few pages later laughing and joking during the lunch break. Mining accidents and disasters are more common in books targeted for older children and often shape the structure of the narratives. Rappaport's *Trouble at the Mines* begins with the sounding of the steam whistle, the frightening signal of disaster. Alvena Seckar's short narrative *Trapped in the Old Mine* focuses on a boy trapped in an abandoned mine. Lenski, Rolt-Wheeler, and Greene devote much of their books to accidental entombments in working mines and successful rescue efforts. A mining accident leads to the family's move to California in O'dell's *Journey to Jericho.* The death of a father in a mining accident plays an important role in both Byars's and Stevenson's novels. Finally, the slate fall that permanently cripples Okey Farley in *A Blue-Eyed Daisy* is the main cause of his alcoholism.

As accidents and death are muted but nonetheless present in children's coal mining fiction, a mixed message is also sent to young readers about whether or not digging coal is an acceptable way of making a living. Christina Wilson's father, in *Coal Camp Girl,* is thankful when he finally returns to work. "At least I have work again and I am thankful for that. Coal mining is a dog's life, but I guess I'm hardened to it. I'm a miner by trade and I never want to be anything else." Even though Tom Moore, in *Journey to Jericho,* leaves his family behind to work in a California saw mill, he remains a miner at heart. In his first letter home he writes, "I have a good job here in Jericho. I work at a mill on top of a mountain, sawing the bark off of big trees. I am saving money. When I have enough I'll send it along so you can come to Jericho. P.S. I like mining better than sawing logs." Like Scott O'Dell's narrative, the novels of Greene, De Angeli, and Rolt-Wheeler all reflect positive views of coal mining. The blind character, Bennie, in *The Blind Brother: A Story of the Pennsylvania Coal Mines* has two reoccurring dreams—regaining his sight and digging coal with his brother. Although coal mining is in the background of De Angeli's *Up the Hill,* the family patriarch, who earns a scant living as a music teacher, believes that his son will do much better than he financially by digging coal. Rolt-Wheeler's main character, Clem Swinton, tells a young companion that over the years miners have had to learn more about the job and, in doing so, have made the mines safer. "Don't you make the mistake of thinking that all a miner has to do is to use a pick! He's got to know his business thoroughly or he's useless to the mine boss and a danger to all his fellow-workmen." Swinton never denies that mining is dangerous but suggests that the prevention of hazard with know-how makes it exciting and satisfying work.[17]

Other writers are not so positive and maintain that the way up is the way out. Small boys, like the triplets in *Three Boys and a Mine,* want to be miners rather than firemen or policemen. These youthful dreams are not to be indulged; the authors have something else in mind for them. "If you boys want to be miners you must finish school," they are told, "go to college and study engineering." One wonders if the response would have been the same had they wanted to be cowboys or sailors. Early in his novel *Tommy Remington's Battle,* Stevenson writes about a teacher from Richmond, Bessie Andrews, who learns of the socially destructive impact of coal mining on people. She is determined to love the people in her community. She believes that years of labor in the mines has "marred their brains no less than their bodies; both, shut out from God's pure air, and blue sky, and beautiful, green-clad world, grew crooked and misshapen, just as everything must do that has life in it." Rappaport, in her more recent work_*Trouble at the Mines,* has Mother Jones tell the striking anthracite workers that "mining at its best is wretched work," whereas David Moore's mother, in *Journey to Jericho,* can no longer accept the daily suspense about her husband's safety. One evening at the supper table her anxiety boils over: "I've had all I can stand. Two men were killed in the mine last year and three so far this year. Besides all the men who have been badly hurt. We're going to leave this place, Tom. I can't stand it another day."[18]

What is truly unusual about these books and suggestive of an unconscious "othering" is the lack of fantasy. While fantasy is a traditional mainstay of children's literature, it is remarkably absent from coal mining literature for children. Granted, the vivid imagination of the grandfather in *Coal Mine Peaches* and Eliot's anthropomorphizing in *The Little Black Coal* suggest elements of the fantastic, but, for the most part, they are exceptions to the dominant trend in children's fiction dealing with coal mining.[19] This approach is puzzling. Children's reading interests between the ages of six and twelve dramatically change. Less infatuated by daily routine, they become more interested in the fantastic, the improbable.[20] Yet the coal mining novels intended for this age group do not seem to respond to the changing interests of their readers. As is the case with authors of adult mining fiction, it may be that the authors of children's books are simply unable to shed their preconceived beliefs about the mining life. To them the mining of coal is such a mundane, dirty, dangerous, and physically taxing job that it simply does not lend itself in fiction to the whimsical or fantastic.

There are certainly examples of coal mining fiction that allow the reader to escape into an unfamiliar, strange, even fantastic world. There are miles of passages below the ground, hundreds of rooms, railroads, first aid stations, ventilation devices, the bobbing lights on the hats of the miners, and everything is shrouded by the all-absorbing darkness. Above the ground is the "real" world, the one of villages, homes, wives, parents, children, and the usual bustle of daily life. This fictional mixing of the familiar with the unfamiliar might be labeled the "Heidi syndrome," for as critic James Steel Smith writes in *A Critical Approach to Children's Literature,* these elements are combined in *Heidi,* where "a familiar domestic situation and recognizable kinds of people are combined with a faraway land."[21] Smith argues that this motif is common in modern children's literature. The same is true in children's coal mining fiction except that the faraway land is one that exists underground. Yet the whimsical or fantastic ways in which the motif is presented in other genres has eluded the writers of children's coal mining fiction. Could it be that most view coal mining as inextricable from the reality of its limitations on people's lives?

The appeal of the unfamiliar can also be found in young adult literature. Although, as Janet Steel Smith reminds us, the interests of the thirteen or fourteen year old may well be closer to the concerns of the five or six year old than those of the somewhat older child. The adolescent reader can be consumed by issues related to growing up: school, family situations, or peer pressures. He or she enjoys reading about the world of immediate experiences.[22] In his essay "Adolescent Initiation: A Thematic Study in the Secondary School," Hugh Agee suggests that much adolescent fiction focuses on initiation into the adult world. This initiation involves a sense of loss associated with the ending of childhood, confusion related to physical changes, a feeling of isolation and loneliness that can breed a desire to flee the familiar, and the inevitable exploitation of many of these pressures within the family.[23]

Although young adult and adolescent coal mining fiction is as thematically varied as that intended for children or adults, with a few notable exceptions, it is less imaginative and entertaining. These coal mining novels for teenage readers have several common qualities. In addition to the aforementioned problem-oriented approach, most of the main characters in these novels are adolescents who, whether from mining backgrounds or not, share many of the same concerns with their readers' age group. Although mining is portrayed as an exploitative and, at times, brutalizing way of making a living, the immediate mortal dangers of the profession dominate the narratives. Mining disasters play significant roles in nearly half of the novels. In a third of the novels, the reader's introduction to the mining culture is through the terrifying, shrill cry of the company whistle. At its sounding, reader and characters rush to the mouth of the mine to find out what has happened. In many of the novels this disaster or one that occurs later is important to the plot. Writers of adolescent fiction believe that such events are essential to capture and sustain the interest of their young readers. Mining accidents or disasters are also useful ways of introducing another favorite theme of adolescent fiction, one that concerns the adjustment of teenagers to the death or severe injuring of a parent. In seven of the twenty novels examined here a father is either killed or permanently injured in a way that precludes his ever returning to mining. The family has to adjust personally and economically to his absence. Yet with mines so often seen as places of crippling injuries, deaths, and massive explosions, it is little wonder that in most adolescent novels the mining occupation is negatively portrayed. Would not a person who continued to work at a job that so often maimed and killed its workforce seem different from the rest of us? In this "othering," adolescent coal mining fiction is closely related to the ways mining is envisioned in adult literature, on the stage, and in films. This approach is especially true of earlier adolescent fiction, especially that written before the 1940s.

Like their counterparts in adult fiction, two earlier adolescent novels—Kirk Munroe's *Derick Sterling: A Story of the Mines* (1888) and R.P. Phelps's *Tom Martin the Breaker Boy* (1926)—are set in the anthracite coalfields of Pennsylvania. These two novels are somewhat longer than their modern counterparts, and both are didactically moralistic in upholding middle-class values. Derick Sterling's crippled friend's response to Sterling's promotion to door-keeper—"Oh goody, Derick! I'm so glad to get out of that hateful, back-aching breaker"—suggests how mining is viewed in each of these of novels.[24] From the perspective of these pre-1930s writers, if the mining of coal is a dangerous, dirty business, this is not the fault of management. Those who advocate radical change, like the Molly Maguires in *Derick Sterling,* are evil and not to be trusted. The ultimate goal is to learn the mine and work one's way up the ladder to a white collar position like that of a mining engineer. This is the plan of the protagonist in *Tom Martin the Breaker Boy.*

An aversion to a mining career may span the history of adolescent fiction, but, unlike the authors of the earlier adolescent novels, those of more recent works—N.A. Perez, *Breaker* (1988); Connie Jordan Green, *Emmy* (1992); Phyllis Reynolds Naylor, *Wrestle the Mountain* (1971); Robert T. Reilly, *Rebels in the Shadows* (1979); Juliette Ann Holley, *Jamie Lemme See* (1975); and James Forman, *A Ballad for Hogskin Hill* (1979)—are more openly critical of the exploitative nature of management and more sympathetic to the needs of miners and their families. Like Perez and Green, Mary Jo Stephens enthusiastically describes the organizing efforts of the UMWA in her own book, *Witch of the Cumberland* (1974). Even while condemning the violence of the Molly Maguires in his novel of that era, Reilly concludes that out of the ashes of their defeat there would emerge a more organized and democratic union that would correct the wrongs suffered by mining folk. Perez, Green, and Carol J. Scott, in her book *Kentucky Daughter* (1985), also confront similar class issues, while Holley, in her story of a six-year-old African American boy growing up in the coalfields of West Virginia, attempts to combine race with class. Race actually plays a relatively minor role in Holley's novel. When conflicts occur, they are too often settled through the Pollyannish good will and reasonableness of the opposing sides. Jay Parini, in *The Patch Boys* (1986), and Alvena Seckar, in *Zuska of the Burning Hills* (1952), explore the mining culture from the perspective of newly arrived immigrants, though neither the Czechoslovakian miners in Seckar's work nor the Italian ones in Parini's are miners at heart. In Seckar's novel the Stebinas dream of living on a farm like the one they own in the old country. The oldest of the Cantini brothers of *The Patch Boys,* even while working for the union, holds a jaundiced view of his new job. "What was mining after all," he asks, "but a worm's way of life?"[25] It is also a way of life filled with lingering aftereffects like black lung. Green, Naylor, Scott, Curry, and Holley all try to show that the health problems are as deadly as explosions, slate falls, and floods. Many of the novels written for adolescent readers also share a view of the coal mining family as a besieged yet enduring institution, parents and children joining together in helping one another confront and survive a dangerous and unpredictable way of life. This approach falls into the realm of problem fiction. More recent writers in this sub-genre also concentrate on broader environmental and historical themes.

Not surprisingly, writers of adolescent fiction interested in the environment tend to focus on strip mining. These novels usually show how mining and mountain families as well as concerned outsiders try to prevent the despoliation of the earth. James Forman's *A Ballad for Hogskin Hill* is perhaps the most unsparing in its attack on the unmitigated greed of strip miners and their lack of concern for the lives and the land they destroy. When the main character, David Kincaid, returns to his home in the Kentucky mountains from Detroit, all of the changes are negative. "The plateau belonged to the coal tsars and always had. First they'd punch it full of holes. Now they were skimming it off from the top. Wouldn't be a thing worth saving, once the strippers were through."[26] When protest fails, he dynamites the six- to eight-story earth-moving machine and has to flee the region, but his flight is as much from the mining culture as from the law.

Miners are treated as heroes rather than villains in Forman's novel, yet the author suggests, as do Munroe, Stoddard, Phelps, and Buck in older works and Parini, Scott, Curry, and Holley in more recent ones, that coal mining debilitates and destroys. If strip mining harms the land, underground mining harms the miners. Anxious to see his home again, David Kincaid is determined never to work in a mine. He tells his girlfriend that "smoking is about the worst thing for you, next to coal mining." He speaks from experience, having repeatedly observed that on the day the monthly relief checks arrive the sidewalks become cluttered with "motley gangs of damaged miners for the most part, walking in slightly disjoined fashion like puppets which had been broken, then glued back together." Fleeing the mountains, family, and home by novel's end, David is unsure of what lies ahead, but he is certain that his future will not be viewed from a coal mine.[27]

The way of life David Kincaid flees is placed in historical context by three other novels, each set in the anthracite coalfields of Pennsylvania. Robert T. Reilly's *Rebels in the Shadows* fictionalizes the Molly Maguire era and N.A. Perez's *Breaker* deals with later labor organization, while Jay Parini, the most lyrical of the three, is classic in his emphasis that no one digs coal if other opportunities are available. Parini's *The Patch Boys* is a novel of initiation. Sixteen-year-old Sammy di Cantini struggles with his father's death in a mining accident, his first love, the nature of friendship, and his own sense of identity—all during the summer of 1925. By summer's end he is more self-assured than at any other time in his life. He is convinced that he and his family have never really been miners in the true sense of the word. When his girlfriend asks if he plans to be a miner to continue the family tradition, he tries to explain that "we *wern't* really miners. Not at heart. Vincenzo should have been a ballplayer. Louis was in business. Jesse was a miner almost by accident, since there was nothing else for him, and Papa should have been a schoolteacher. He had been the smartest man in the patch."[28] For Sammy di Cantini, working in the mines was a temporary necessity in his family's history, and there were far more exciting opportunities for a meaningful life above ground.

Intended for a slightly younger audience than either Parini's or Reilly's novels, Perez's *Breaker* more or less takes up where *Rebels in the Shadows* ends. The novel follows the activities of a twelve year old, Pat McFarlane, and his family during the great anthracite strike at the turn of the century. As a result of his father's death in a slate fall and his older brother's obsessive fear of going underground, Pat provides most of the family's income through his work as a breaker boy and later as a mule driver in the mine. Pat is torn between his mother's hatred of everything associated with the coal business and the sense of pride that his father had in being a miner. Unlike his father, who never joined a union, Pat helps organize his fellow workers on the breaker and reminds them that even if their vote "doesn't count for much, we can at least tell the delegates how breaker boys feel. After all, we're a part of this, too!" By the novel's end Pat's commitment to organizing seems likely, though he is barely an adolescent. The strike has matured him. He has learned to accept his father's death and mother's remarriage. He also understands why his brother Cal needed to leave the coal regions to pursue a different career. But most important of all, he realizes how closely tied he is to the insignificant little mining patch that has always been home. "Scatter Patch was a poor, drab, ugly place. Hard things happened there. Yet Pat sensed he was connected to it in a way that Cal was not, to the good and the bad, the light and the dark."[29] Unlike so many of the characters in young adult, adolescent, and especially adult fiction, departure from the coalfields is not Pat's ultimate goal. Instead, he plans to remain a part of a way of life that he understands while working toward changes to dignify and improve it.

In adjusting to his father's death, mother's remarriage, and brother's leaving home, Pat McFarlane is involved in the kind of problem-solving predominant in young adult and adolescent fiction written since the end of World War II. Phyllis Reynolds Naylor's *Wrestle the Mountain,* a portrait of an artistically oriented young boy's relationship with his coal miner father, is a more sensitive representative of this category. If there is tension between father and son, there is also love and respect. This relationship is established early with Jed's ritualistic participation in pumping water for his father's bath after his return from the mine. Unlike the immigrant males in Seckar's and Parini's works, Samuel Tate, Jed's father, believes that mining offers a test of manhood and is also a lifestyle that links generations together in meaningful ways. "We're five generations, Jed," his father explains in one of their disagreements over Jed's future. "We're five generations in the mines, and you're the only son I got. If it ain't to be the mines, it's got to be somethin' awful good." Jed is neither contemptuous nor fearful of coal mining but simply more interested in wood carving, at which he is extremely gifted. His father initially is not enthusiastic. Samuel Tate's commitment to coal mining is as much a part of his emotional makeup as carving is of his son's. When his father's oldest brother, Caully, loses a leg in a slate fall, Jed anticipates his father's angry reaction. He calls the mine "a hell hole . . . not a fit place for a human creature." His reaction to the injury of any miner is always the same kind of spontaneous anger, but equally swift is his willingness to return to work. "Tomorrow he'd go back to the mine as always, and if the tunnels caved in and caught all the men but father, he'd be wanting to go back the next day."[30] If Samuel Tate loves what he does, it is not a fanatical, blinding kind of commitment. He gradually comes to understand the differences that exist between him and his son. These differences eventually lead Jed to Morgantown for a ten-week course in wood carving and a career that could mean leaving home and family for good. What is important in this novel is its portrait of a sensitive, caring parent who is also a coal miner—a miner deeply committed to a way of life but willing to accept a different one for his children. Samuel tells his son that he does not fully understand his gift for carving but he is nevertheless happy for him. His work as a miner is hard, often dangerous, but it does not brutalize him. He can appreciate the needs of a creative and talented son who loves his father but does not want to be exactly like him.

Naylor's novel compares favorably with some of the best adult works that deal with the mining experience. In length, character development, and narrative sophistication it stands apart from all the picture books for younger children. Yet, in many respects, these simpler books intended for younger children are the most intriguing, particularly in their efforts to portray the mining culture from a child's perspective. As in coal mining poetry, images are all-important, while specifics about the actual digging of coal or the dangers involved are scarcely mentioned. To the younger child, the mining of coal is simply something that happens, done without a great deal of fanfare. And even though dirt, darkness, and perhaps even danger are associated with it, there is nothing particularly demeaning or fatalistic about choosing it as a way of making a living. Young children might find it fun to crawl into exciting places, get dirty, and dig in the ground. In these books for younger age levels, mining children act like children everywhere. If Hendershot is at all accurate in her memories, they accept the good along with the bad. For the writers of these children's books, mining is a way of life that may well be more exciting than others. It certainly should not be feared or avoided. Only with increasing maturity comes an awareness of the dangers. Offered only a partial view of the job, younger children seem capable of confronting the mining way of life with less editorializing than older ones.

Young adult readers get to know characters of their own age who want to leave everything behind. A close identification with these fictional characters and especially their rejection of coal mining may be based on nothing more dramatic than the maturity level of the audience. A close identification with a character often stems from shared likes and dislikes, prejudices and assumptions. As with adult fiction, these characters may tell us more about the fears and prejudices of the authors than the miners they are writing about. The implied interpretation of the coal mining way of life in the early picture books is essentially a positive one. Evaluating a culture or an occupation is, of course, a difficult and complex undertaking, especially when the writer fears or misunderstands that which is under investigation. Many of the authors of books for older children as well as those writing for young adults and adolescents, like their counterparts with adult audiences, could not imagine why anyone would choose to dig coal. This inability to accept agency in the lives of miners and their families helps explain why didacticism as well as thematic departure are more common in works for older readers than in those intended merely to introduce a young child to coal mining. In the books intended for young readers, coal mining is a different but not inferior or degrading way of earning a living. It is different in the same way that being a policeman or fireman can differ from many other professions. Children are years away from making career choices but not young adults, who, it appears, need to be made aware of the "realities" of digging coal for a living. In describing these "realities," writers of young adult novels frequently create characters who, in spite of heroism and love of family, are so different from the rest of us that their lives take on a tragic "otherness," which limits and proscribes everything they do. Unlike Pinocchio they never come to life. Objects of authorial creation, they exhibit little or no real subjectivity. As a result they remain one-dimensional working-class "characters" who never become "personalities" or experience life to its fullest. How could these fictional coal miners be viewed as anything but "the other" by young and old alike?

Chapter 6

Coal Mining and the Poetic Imagination

One recent critic argues that poetry has become the "most private and least accessible" of the arts. Another critic, whose book title *Can Poetry Matter?* reflects a similar concern, notes that "outside the classroom—where society demands that the two groups interact—poets and the common reader are no longer on speaking terms."[1] Despite these observations, the apparent lack of public attention has not deterred poets in the modern era. The numbers are increasing at a remarkable rate.[2] A few modern poets have turned to coal mining as an appropriate subject for their creative efforts. Here they have followed in the footsteps of late nineteenth-century and twentieth-century writers who were also attracted to the mining experience. American poets who creatively embrace coal mining have done so for a variety of reasons. Some have merely used it metaphorically to vivify unrelated concerns or subjects and have only written an occasional poem about coal. Others have been motivated by the prospect of voicing their perceptions of a way of life that both repels and attracts. A few have burrowed more deeply. Whatever the extent of their fascination with the American coal mining experience, most of these poets better fit the mold of a writer like William Carlos Williams, who grappled with the realities of industrial America, than that of other such canonical figures as Pound, Eliot, and Stevens. In writing about the world of coal mining, poets have often tried to fill in the history of ordinary people, which, Bertolt Brecht argues in "A Worker Reads History," has been so often neglected.[3]

Like Brecht, many of the poets in this chapter describe and praise the labors of ordinary people. Yet the poetry often has more to say about the poet than the miner, and this is the primary focus of the chapter.[4] The analysis here is directed to the ways in which imagery reflects the mining experience and the ways language is used to induce the tone of a poem. What is the poet's notion of coal mining and miners? What is the creative attraction of the mining experience? How do poets compare to other creative writers like dramatists, script writers, novelists, and writers of children's and young adult literature in the use of coal mining in their works? This chapter deals less with the technical skills of the poets than with their thematic similarities to one another and to writers in other disciplines who, like themselves, enter the mines through literature as much to voice their fears as to stimulate their creativity.

Poets have approached coal mining in ways similar to other writers, though their creative range has been wider and their interpretation briefer and more personal. Since poets usually do not labor under the same commercial restraints as do playwrights, scriptwriters, or even novelists, they can give freer reign to their emotions and creative inclinations. Although some poets have devoted an entire work to mining culture, most are far more thematically eclectic. Their coal mining poetry often exists alongside poems that have nothing to do with this occupation. Interested as they are in images, compressed expression, and emotion, poets, like the patrons of a cafeteria, can sample freely rather than commit to a table d'hôte.

Nearly all of the poets studied here wrote after World War II.[5] But the work of two early nineteenth-century poets best symbolizes the ways that American writers have creatively approached coal mining as a subject for their verse. In a long and distinguished career spanning much of the nineteenth century, William Cullen Bryant was interested in many aspects of American life, but coal mining was not among them. In one of his rare efforts at humor he wrote "A Meditation on Rhode Island Coal," which versifies the trials and tribulations of anthracite coal before it was accepted as a domestic and industrial fuel. He glorifies its future in mock heroic terms that nonetheless avoid the manly versification of eighteenth-century English poets like William Cowper.

> Thou shalt make mighty engines swim the sea,
>   Like its own monsters—boats that for a guinea
> Will take a man to Havre—and shalt be
>   The moving soul of many a spinning-jenny,
> And ply thy shuttles, till a bard can wear
> As good a suit of broadcloth as the mayor.
>
> Then we will laugh at winter when we hear
>   The grim old churl about our dwellings rave:
> Thou, from that "ruler of the inverted year,"
>   Shalt pluck the knotty scepter Cowper gave,
> And pull him from his sledge, and drag him in
> And melt the icicles from off his chin.[6]

Living and writing in New York, Bryant had no interest in exploring the mining life further. In the Rhode Island piece, coal merely serves as a convenient vehicle for writing a humorous poem. A much lesser-known poet than Bryant, Samuel H. Daddow, was a mining engineer and pioneer in the early coal industry. In 1866 he co-authored an industrial manual, *Coal, Iron, and Oil.*[7] Thirteen years earlier, Daddow had published a book of verse, *Trevaro and Other Occasional Poems,* with a range of romantic themes from unrequited love to the beauty of the seasons. Several of the forty-four poems reflect on coal mining themes, mostly in a negative light. In "Old Mount Laffee, or the Home of Our Childhood," Daddow laments the fact that the name of the village of his birth in the mining region had been taken by another hamlet a short distance away that was as "notorious for its rudeness and strife as the former was for its picturesque beauty, rural sports, and charming quietness."[8] The poet considers it an act of audacity for the mining town to dare expropriate a name he associates with beauty and esteem. In two later poems that hint at the future costs of industry, "The Aspen or Tremble Tree" and its sequel "The Aspen—Continued," Daddow charges that a well of pure, cold water and the stately tree that shaded it were both destroyed by the waste from a coal mine.

When Daddow wrote about the miners, he emphasized only the heroic and civically vital aspects of their work. In "Miner's Song," their dangerous work is likened to that of soldiers and sailors, emphasizing that miners never receive the honors and accolades of their martial counterparts:

> Before the Miner pierced the field,
> The soldier had no sword to wield:
> To Sailors' Neptune would not yield,
> Old ocean like a parchment scaled:
>   Then ho, for Miners! Hey for Miners!
>   They who foremost pierced the field—
>   They that made old Neptune yield:
>   Sing ho! for Miners ho!

Half a dozen poems does not make Daddow a coal poet or even a poet with a consuming interest in the coal mining experience. Yet the range of his concerns was far greater than that of Bryant. His life and work in the anthracite region is reflected in his fascination with miners as well as his uncertainty about the social and environmental impact of mining. The handful of poems that Daddow has written about coal mining shows a psychological tension between his fear of and admiration for the rough but essential miner. Miners may have been different, but not more so than sailors and soldiers.[9] Daddow's ambiguity toward miners and mining is similar to an ambiguity found among twentieth-century American poets. While some, like their creative counterparts in other disciplines, focused primarily on the negative—thereby suggesting the "otherness" of anyone engaged in this kind of work—others like Settle, Giardina, Cizmar, and Naylor were willing to contemplate it as a difficult but not appalling way of making a living.

Other poets have followed the early example of Bryant and Daddow, using coal mining metaphorically and symbolically while showing little more than a passing interest in miners themselves. The African American feminist Audre Lorde writes "Coal" to describe her blackness in a way that inspires her imagination. Suzanne Matson's "Love in the Coal Mine" and Irene McKinney's "Six O'clock Mine Report" use mining imagery and allusion in a poetic depiction of making love. In an often quoted poem, "Caliban in the Coal Mines," Robert Untermeyer offers a whimsical creature who beseeches God to brighten the dreary mining environment:

God, if You had but the moon
  Stuck in Your cap for a lamp,
Even You'd tire of it soon,
  Down in the dark and the damp.

Nothing but blackness above
  And nothing that moves but the cars. . . .
God, if You wish for our love,
  Fling us a handful of stars!

Untermeyer's "Caliban" anticipates other twentieth-century poets' view of the mine as a dismal and uninviting place even for the radiance of the Almighty.[10]

A number of twentieth-century poets view the mine as not only unpleasant but exploitative, brutalizing, and dangerous, as do their creative counterparts in other genres. In a short poem, "Working the Face," Jay Parini describes miners, mole-like on their stomachs, digging coal in perilous places to earn higher wages for their work. Louise McNeil, in "The Company," writes about management's smothering domination of a company town. John Beecher, the radical activist, poet, and direct descendent of Harriet Beecher Stowe, in "Run of the Mine," shows that the miner's sense of loyalty and service was clearly not reciprocated:

I went into tight places for them (he said)
When the inspector had condemned a gallery
I went in and I got men to go with me

And we dug coal and kept our mouths shut
And I thought when the time came I needed it
They would go into a tight place for me
but because I had a foaming fit on the job
from high blood pressure and because I was old
and they thought I might cost them money
if I died at work in the mine
they fired me and put *unsatisfactory*
on my discharge slip and when I wanted to know
what unsatisfactory thing I had done
they said to come back next week for a statement

Sociologist and poet Mike Yarrow has been interviewing miners for years. He uses their experiences, along with his imagination and poetic license, to write what he calls "found poems." In "Laid-Off Miner," he describes the agonizing effects of enforced idleness on a furloughed miner. When finally rehired, the miner returns to a work environment that is more regimented and impersonal. The speaker had become a miner by following his father's example, and he undoubtedly benefitted from the previous generation's struggles for better working conditions. Yet, once rehired, he becomes a participant in what a critic for *The New York Review of Books* calls "The New, Ruthless Economy." Throughout much of the poem, Yarrow's miner describes the "new" conditions of his employment:

Working conditions now are so severe
I couldn't tolerate the stress,
not reading a book to my son at night.
Seeing him maybe on Sunday? Nooo!
You hear older miners talk how miners came home,
set their lunch buckets down, fell asleep beside the fire,
got up and went back to work, dirty and just so tired.
That history is repeating itself.
People working now in these hell holes—
I don't know how they handle it, be a father,
Hold their lives together.
I couldn't.

Work rules, respect, safety standards, and numerous other rights won through generations of struggle are now as much in decline as the industry itself. The miner in Yarrow's poem abandons what he truly loves because of the insanity of working in a world in which the market calls the shots:

Mingo County, McDowell, even Raleigh County [W. Va.]
are as much a part of the Third World as the Third World is itself.
The "global economy" gives you peasants next door.
They disperse the steel mills to Mexico, capitalist enterprise
to keep them from communist aspirations.
Capitalism can come to them,
but the price is we have to become part of the Third World.[11]

Strikes add to the profession's exploitative aspects, and Robert Wrigley's poem, "Diary of the Strike," based on a lesser-known work stoppage in Illinois, suggests that in most strikes miners were often the victims rather than the perpetrators of violence. "The strikebreakers, cleaning their teeth / near the pool hall, are rumored to spit- / shine their boots with miners blood." While the miners gear themselves for the next confrontation, "the goons / slice their steaks with the same knives / that cut off noses and thumbs." The chronic violence of labor-management confrontations in other regions of the country has also captured the imagination of poets. Just as Harlan County, Kentucky, fascinated and frightened writer's groups in the 1930s, creative interest continues in the modern era. Born in Harlan, Kentucky, social worker and poet Jenny Lind Cawood seems as convinced as Robert Schenkkan is in the *Kentucky Cycle* that feuding and violence are endemic to Appalachia, or at least to this part of it. She sets the mood of "Sundown Song—Harlan County" in the first stanza:

The hounds of hell
  heaven, and/or Harlan
are loose and ravenging [*sic*]
  in the sundown hills

She goes on to lament the strikes, the violence, the looting, the Battle of Evarts, the election killing. Cawood concludes the poem with a question.

"When will it end?"
  they ask, returning
blood once more
  unto these hills.

Blood for blood
  is how it stands,
until the song is struck
  from whippoorwills.[12]

What made matters even more difficult for miners is the way that their representatives, especially John L. Lewis, let them down. Billy Edd Wheeler, Ray Lee Harmond, Louise McNeill, Patricia Shirley, and John Beecher have all written poetry about Lewis. The poems of Wheeler, Harmond, and McNeill praise what the UMWA leader did for miners. Although not one attempts to evaluate his leadership, they all more or less agree with Wheeler's assessment:

> Somewhere something shorted out and times got bad
> After the war. They say
> John L. let us down. Sold us
> Down the creek to big machines.
> I wouldn't know.
> I love the old man.

Beecher and Shirley are far more critical. Beecher's "Like Judas, Wasn't It?" leaves little doubt where sympathies lie. Patricia Shirley, the most systematic in her analysis, devotes four poems under the overall heading "King Coal, 1933-1969," in *Mary Peal Kline,* to Lewis's leadership. Agreeing with those who praise him, Shirley's "God Bless John L. Lewis" and "Harmony" recount how the growth of the UMWA helped all miners. But in "Trust the Old Ways" and "The Devil Take John L. Lewis," the poet narrates how many of Lewis's defenders began to question his extravagant lifestyle, political break with the Roosevelt administration, and acceptance of automation in the mines. Most appalling of all, however, was the closing of the miners' hospitals that Lewis had opened with so much fanfare, which had failed because of his bankrupt leadership. "Well, when the final door was closed on them hospitals / Lewis built, Carl bowed his head and cried / over the shadowy ruin brought needlessly / by a cantankerous, unfit mind."[13]

Other poets are less concerned about whether or not the UMWA leadership misled the rank and file than about the ways mining blights everything with which it comes into contact. The poetry of Richard Hague reflects upon the present lives of parents and friends in the coalfields of Ohio and Kentucky. Hague, in "Watching Bison at the State Preserve, Noble County, Ohio," notes how man and animal try to exist in an inhospitable and coal-scarred landscape. A scarred landscape mirrors scarred lives:

> And as we turned to leave,
> To skid down coal-dust roads
> Toward evening in the hollows,
> Toward Hep's bitter whiskey, Brud's cold stove,

My own wind-drilled, temporary home,
Crows cawed from the pit,
And everywhere a sour wind was rising.

In another poem, "Sacks: A Folk Declension," Hague sees mining as so innately debilitating that bags of coal, like ancient ruins, contain hidden tales of sorrow and misfortune:

Sacks genitive,
the black of sacks
stained with the blood of wrecked men
wrestled up through rock—
uncles, brothers, bearded, once as sturdy
as the woods—
now snag-limbed, shattered,
made stumps of.
Sack accusative,
black as lungs of miners
or the sleep that blackdamp brings. . . .

Sacks accusative,
threadbare
as a winter evening's sorrow,
empty as starvation.

Mary Joe Coleman (*Take One Blood Red Rose*) believes that a miner's life can bring with it near-impossible physical and psychological demands. Whether the miner in "Floyd Coleman, My Grandfather" suffered mental problems as a result of his work is unknown, but his mangled body is a reminder of the dangers of working underground: "his right side dangled like a slack scarecrow / where the kettlebottom caught him / in the roof fall at the Lex mine." The namesake of "Noah Totten" endured a life of quiet desperation—too much work, the terror of union battles, too little love, the loss of children: "He grew to resemble a rocky cliff / where the sun seldom broke out / An old man who stalked barren fields in winter / looking for wasted fruits." For other poets, physical wounds outweigh the psychological ones. In George Ella Lyon's ironically titled "Salvation," the old miner, Virgil, after a lifetime of drudgery, suffers a heart attack because he is "wore out and give out and plumb used up Lord." Other miners feel depleted because of their exposure to coal dust. Don Johnson, the narrator in "Taking the Greyhound from Coaltown," like so many others before him, is fleeing the depressed mining area to which he is native. As the bus speeds by decaying miners' houses, the poet imagines that he can see inside, where "behind the doors the women bathe / their wheezing husbands toward death." The miner in Richard B. Patterson's "Black Lung Marriage" can scarcely breath at all:

An old coal miner
Rocks on his front porch
Talking to any who will listen
As he points to his oxygen machine.

"How do you like her?
She's a looker, eh?
Makes me breath real heavy, know what I
mean?"[14]

If black lung–related illnesses hung over the heads of all miners, so too did sudden and more terrifying kinds of death. Lillie B. Chaffin, for example, wonders if miners are inevitably fatalistic despite their religious convictions. In "Appalachian Deaths and Resurrections," a Pentecostal minister assures the survivors of five dead miners who were crushed in a cave-in that resurrection is as much alive in the present as in the past. He then asks the mourners at the graveside to kneel and pray with him that all miners be cleansed of their sins before facing the dangers of "poison gas, weak timbers, roof rot." In the last four lines, the voice of the minister recedes and that of the poet emerges to provide a coda far less reassuring than the funeral oration: "When the five accidents have been eased into the amber clay, / and duly marked with stone, / they return, these living brothers of the black earth-womb, / to await the lottery, and their numbers." A mother in Muriel Dressler's "What'll I do" finds it impossible to accept a son's death because of her inability to bury him.

What'll I do if they seal up the mine?
I can't hold no settin' up at driftmouths
That blasted shut, ner kin I understand
Why things like this have to happen, honey,
When our graveyard's laid out on our land.

Harvey Elliot, in the aptly titled poem "Numbers," suggests an overwhelming numbness that coal mining communities, facing multitudes of deaths, have too frequently endured:

Later commentators
will assure me
it was a day like all days.
I will have had another
cup of pale tea
drifting between what is common
in the black jeweled earth
of west virginia
and this grey sky

And at other times
I may stop
trying to understand the words
for a number of men
a number of feet deep
isolated as this
afternoon echo
of water falling in a sink

as the radio begins knowingly
dealing in numbers.

And finally, in his poetry as well as his plays, Lee Pennington suggests that to be a miner is to suffer. He finds expression for this suffering, which often ends in death, in the nocturnal imagery of "Dark Smell."

This night smells of Appalachia,
Dark Eden earth spilled in a coal dust sun
Seeping like the milk of your face into rains,
Counted tracks cracking from coal dust wheels
From coal truck wheels and two eyed dragon
Food rolling on the line, child of blackness
Whimpering at each curve, whispering sudden
Echoes on otherwise foreboding silence,
White silence of a baby's hand,
Green silence of a mother's eye.
Black silence of a father's misery,
And the dark bird, black bird, red-
Winged black bird silence inside
A coal miner's mind watching rats
Scampering on gray feet, pulling long

Grey hairless tails, silent rats dancing
From the pits
Before the final slatefall.[15]

While country singer Waylon Jennings warns mamas not to let their babies grow up to be cowboys, Patricia Shirley and a number of other poets offer a similar message about mining coal. In her book of Appalachian storytelling poems, *Mary Pearl Kline,* Shirley suggests that the decision to go underground comes as a last resort:

Outdone by tilted earth, worn thin,
we made our move, with silent dread,
to Smoot Creek and Consolidated's mining town,
squalored by black dust and the humanity
whose very breath belonged to "King Coal."
Ignoring seasons, soil and choice,
Carl faced the shiny seam to dig, and blast, and curse
the greedy schemes of coal operators never met.
Hapless, I endured the cheating store, the stench,
and pain to see my kids run wild in the grimy place.

From Shirley's perspective, to mine coal is to face a life of limited choices. A miner's wife in Louise McNeill's poem "Overheard On A Bus" would agree. While dreading her husband's daily descent beneath the earth's surface, she stoically acknowledges the inevitable: "But I reckon they pay him well, / And it's all he knows." In "A Pennsylvania Family," Anthony Petrosky recalls that his Lithuanian grandfather, who mined coal near Exeter, would not allow his sons to follow him into the mines even if they had to sell illegal whiskey instead. In Ann Cobb's "The Commitment," an injured miner near death leaves a warning to his sons. As his wife relates: "My man was killed in the mines last week. / You know—Rob Major's Bill—? He roused and spoke before he passed, / 'Keep them out from under the hill.'" In the "Ballad of Thomas Ratliff" (*The More Things Change the More They Stay the Same*), Kentucky poet Jim Wayne Miller ponders whether or not mining people can ever escape from the past. Stylistically and thematically the poem is one of Miller's most interesting, marked by its alternation between traditional verse and prose. The narrative is a simple but moving one in which an unemployed Kentucky miner leaves family and friends to work in the shipyards of Baltimore. Later, because of his age, he works as a night watchman in Columbus, Ohio. Unable to visit with the folks back home because of "workin holidays and Sundays," he finds himself painfully alone. He attempts to maintain family ties with the pictures of grandchildren on his bureau. Ultimately, he dies alone, but the deceased offers his own uniquely Appalachian benediction:

Well, boys, the way I figure it
A man ain't just a man,
Your young years and your muscle
They're a wide vein in a mine.

But when that vein begins to narrow
As you get along in years,
You're abandoned like a coal shaft
To sleep full of bitter tears.

Bury me in a mine shaft
In an east Kentucky hill,
Kentucky was my heaven
And coal mines my hell.

Let my body turn
To sandstone and slate,
For that's what is left behind
Where the coal mines operate.[16]

Although there is no clear cut dichotomy between poets writing in areas where coal mining is still a viable part of the economy and those writing in parts of the country where it is not, at least some of the coal poets in both regions were willing to explore aspects of the mining culture in ways that transcended the negative and allowed the voices of mining people to be heard. Historical and geographical distance may have had less to do with their perspectives than with personal and creative inclinations, but, like Goldsmith in the "Deserted Village," they often recalled the way of life with both a fondness and sense of remorse as it was ending.

West Virginia poet Arline R. Thorne discovers that her own creativity is enhanced by imagining how her grandfather worked, how he envisioned the flickering images that his lamp cast, like some subterranean dance troupe, along the tunnel's walls. Here the distinct lives of granddaughter and grandfather are symbolically joined together beneath the earth's surface as they create in their own unique ways. James Ballowe describes how his grandfather found religion underground ("C Remembers Grandparents"), while Kip Knott insures through poetic memory that he will never forget his grandfather's fellow miners in "Inheriting Sunday Creek." Knott's grandfather created another kind of memory and spent twelve years using his weekends to build a house on the hill above the mine shaft where he and his buddies dug coal. The building site was carefully chosen. The poet discusses how the house took on a special significance:

I think of him and other men
who tunneled the hills,
pulling out a living with each ton,
some never coming out again.

His house sits over the shafts
so he would never forget
where they were buried,
and a stand of pines blocks the mouth

hiding whatever drifts up from below.

The house was not intended as a mausoleum but a living symbol to a life filled with meaning. The mines in the area around Knott's grandfather's house had long since closed. Little remained of the coal towns as well, but the symbolic location of this particular house helps the poet understand not only the significance of his grandfather's life but also the lives of others who chose to work underground. While splitting wood for the old potbellied stove in the house, the poet accidentally disturbs a nest of ants in a log. This provides a final metaphorical celebration of his grandfather and of other lives well spent.

A colony of dormant ants
spills from a log like sawdust.
Their tunnels spiral deep
into the heart of wood.

Leaning back against the house,
I trace the patterns
they left behind, admiring
the geometry of their lives.

From a somewhat different perspective, Anthony Petrosky recalls how his Lithuanian grandfather, Jurgis Petraskas, led the first miner's strike in Exeter, Pennsylvania, and made up for what he lacked in saintliness with courage and vision:

Draped in khaki, Jurgis
who steals chickens

makes his way in the black dust
among the workers—so tired
and slow—trying to persuade them
that some abstraction is worth their jobs.
Jurgis with fireflies in his head.
The old women sipping from a little bottle
of whiskey shake their heads and pray
to Matka Boza, virgin of virgins,
to deliver us from this affliction,
this crazy man who tells everyone
God is not good enough to them.[17]

Another family memory, contributed by Scotty Lee Hamilton, describes a father returning from the Virginia coal mines. Hamilton's persona in "Pappa's Home" expresses jubilation with an imagined pre-arrival celebration that has become a tradition:

Lordy
mamma
yonder comes papa
bout a mile down the road.

I know it's him
mamma
by the two big sacks
of groceries
he always brings
with him
when he comes back
from the virginny mines.
. . . .
The way he stops now and then
though I bet you
he's got a pint
of peach brandy
or strong gin
and has to let down
one of the sacks
to free an arm
to take a drink.

Yessirreebob
mamma
we'll eat big tonight
and have a dandy time
cause daddy's back
from the virginny mines.

Other poets affirm how the mining life links one generation to the next. In his interviews, Mike Yarrow obviously encountered miners who electively dug coal, because the poem "Laid-Off Miner" includes descriptions of positive feelings associated with the work:

My father was a miner.
Going underground and digging coal had real meaning,
continuance of life, one generation to the next.
Once I got in the mines, I loved it, I really felt at home.
I enjoyed learning that skill.
When you go in the mines you turn that light on
and it's a whole different world, the danger of it,
the intimacy, everybody dependent on everybody else.
It brought back feelings I had in the war.
All that camaraderie.

In "Slate Fall," Ernest Kroll envisions a miner whose Ahabian defiance of fate keeps him alive in a dangerous job. After surviving a slate fall he cries out:

        "No slate
pit has lapped
me yet!"
        And,
meaner than
a bat from
Mammoth, I
shot the gap
the hell clean
out of there.

Just like that.

Even when a miner dies while working underground, songwriter and poet Billy Edd Wheeler believes that mining folk, like all human beings, are multidimensional and have more questions than answers when faced with death. In "Cooger Long," the poet speculates about what a dying miner might think about as he lies buried in a massive cave-in.

They say you're dying deep and dark,
  Old Cooger.
That was patriotic during the war, but now—
  Now what?
Who needs your dying now, now coal is dying?

Under the heavy haunch of darkness, do you think
  Of God?
I AM WHAT I AM . . . FORM YET UNFORMED, SHAPE
  STILL UNSHAPED.
Do you see any comfort in being blind?[18]

Catastrophic death is a common topic in all of the genres examined thus far, but as the industry and way of life disappears, a sense of decrement more frequently permeates coal mining poetry. Abandoned tipples, sealed mines, rusting machinery, deserted coal camps, and unemployed miners conjure up poetic images and memories, which frequently are all that remain of a once-vibrant culture. In poetry it is more often a lament than a celebration, which reaffirms that at least some people think the mining life should be commemorated rather than disparaged. Russell Marano, for example, writes from the perspective of a second-generation Italian immigrant growing up in Clarksburg, West Virginia. The community remembered in *Poems from a Mountain Ghetto* has all but disappeared, but Marano creates an impression of resiliency rather than resignation. Marano experienced plenty of hardship, but the solidarity of family members and neighbors was strong. Growing vegetable plots, discussed in "The Gardens," was a means by which local inhabitants helped one another during difficult times. While most of the working people were poor, not all were "respectable," but even these social lines were blurred by sorrow and catastrophe:

And when the coal mines
killed a miner,
sometimes whores,
not pension funds,
fed his family,
    and thus the spiraling ghetto
        parceled out its morsels.

Dream is meshed with needs in "Flora," "Policy," "Pettiness and Pride," "An Apology," and "Coal Miner's Fingers," as Marano suggests how the cruel uncertainties of coal mining were often tempered by the concern and mutual assistance found in mining communities. Flora, whose husband has been killed in a mining accident, is evicted from a company house and comes to the "mountain ghetto" with her five children. The situation is desperate. The family is divided, with the youngest children in orphanages. Finally, a whorehouse madam dreams that an angel tells her to sell her house to the family for half price with no down payment. Dreams of a different sort fuel the endurance of other ghetto dwellers whose "Policy," as the title indicates, is to play the numbers. This practice may have been "more a gamble than the stock market of the rich," but it encouraged fantasizing as a foundation for hope. Often Marano deals with the less optimistic side of mining communities. Two old-country buddies, "Pettiness and Pride," work side by side in the mines for years. When Tony fails to return a borrowed pot to Benito, Benito refuses to ask for it. Later, when Benito is killed in a cave-in, his friend feels a "sly triumph," though he cannot look at the mangled body in the coffin. "An Apology" is a similar reflection on the nature of relationships. A high school student loafing on a favorite street corner with his buddies turns his back in embarrassment when his coal-mining father passes by, covered with the grime of a day's work. Even though he is forgiven by an understanding parent, the narrator can never forget this supremely insensitive moment of his youth. In the shorter but equally poignant verse of "Coal Miner's Fingers," Marano shows that aesthetic sensitivity is limited by neither class nor occupation.

> I watched him tenderly
> pat
> dachshund-like ears of irises,
> hold
> tips of bleeding hearts
> with coal miner's fingers,
> then
> prune cascading roses
> until petals beckon neighbors.[19]

Much like Marano's poetic memories, Billy Edd Wheeler's *Songs of a Woods Colt* recall a coal camp of his youth. In "Silent Mountains," he laments the disappearance of this way of life and, even more so, the histories of the mining families all but forgotten in an impersonal landscape:

> Now the town itself is swept away.
> The gray and crumbling houses are the whey

Of three hundred lives, as near as many broods
Who had to bide the mountain and its moods.

The mountain stands
Silent now, biding other mountains.

Gone is the work on which the entire camp depended. For Barbara Smith, an abandoned baseball diamond is a fitting symbol of decay. For Joseph W. Caldwell, it is the rusting rails on an abandoned coal siding. Stanley Plumly envisions a similar sense of superfluousness. While writing about a coal town, he mirrors the lives of many in our postindustrial society:

In southeastern Ohio there are porches,
one to a hill, that lean into the calm
like the decks of ships too long, too far out.
The coal is gone and the children have nothing to say.
And in the leftover towns the men fall asleep in their
hands.
And the women stand on the porches in the evening
inside the deep eye of the sun,
listening for some kind of wind,
fixed utterly in any direction.[20]

None of the poets examined here have developed the theme of decrement or decline more forcefully and imaginatively than P.J. Laska. A resident of Morgantown, West Virginia, Laska has roamed the hills and towns of his state to see and write about what is left of days gone by. In *The Day the Eighties Began* he intermixes short, biographical sketches of community relics with other poems that speak of a fading era. "Lucille McDowell, the Oldest Widow on Coal Run" has lost none of her spunk and zest for life, as she still enjoys efforts at courtship:

I had to laugh the other day,
this retired miner called me up
and talked about the old mine.
I told him it was just his excuse
for callin' us old widder women.

"Burley Belcher's Warning" is a more plaintive description of the disappearance of a community birthright:

Coal Run once had a sign that said
Heart of the Bituminous Coal Field.
When this place died
they took it down.
I think the heart was transplanted
somewhere out West,
Wyoming, maybe.
The Government let's [sic] 'em strip
all the coal they want out there
on land owned by the Indians.
I'd like to know what happened [to]
that sign.
I think they should have
left it here as a warning.

In other poems like "Ancestral," "Extra Munction," "The Coal Field Passage," "Red Dirt Afternoon," "Song of Terry," "Epitaph for a Coal Camp," and "Song of the Old Layland Mine," Laska reflects on youthful memories of coal camps. He recalls out migration, the lives of those who remained behind, human and environmental decay, the symbolic meaning of discarded rubble. He fuses the past and present through images of abandoned mines, deserted mining camps, and prematurely retired or unemployed miners. No poem embraces the idea of decrement in such poignant images as those of "The Coal Poets." Old as well as "new and unused" coal miners gather in the antiseptic setting of a shopping mall, where the past and the present combine with the same chaotic configurations, as the fast food franchises replace the mine shafts for these idle men. The modern miner, like other industrial workers, is disabled by a market-driven corporate ethos. But now bureaucratic condescension and indifference have replaced the more overt coercion of the old coal barons.

"Listen, Consol's got it all, right.
Well, I went up 'ere and the sign said
for all applicants to go in the back door.
Now what's 'at tell you right off?"
"Then you go in and wait,
and the secretaries start bossin
        you around."
"Don't you know, that's how they teach
you red-caps the chain of command."[21]

The nostalgia that fills Laska's coal mining verse is marked by a barely concealed anger about the national rejection and neglect of a working people once valued in America. Like Burley Belcher, Laska would "like to know what happened" to the occupation, to the people and region. What has produced so much physical decay, environmental destruction, personal sorrow, and social dislocation?[22] Mining people from his perspective are not marginal "others" but, in their oppressed condition, harbingers of an insidious process that haunts working people throughout the entire country.

Don West is as angry as Laska and paints a far bleaker and more stereotypical portrait of the mining world. Yet, what sets his poetry apart from that of other poets who concentrate on the profession's negative side is that, like Laska, he sees miners as part of a larger process. Thus he avoids treating them as exploited "others," instead viewing their problems from a universal perspective.

"Miner's Widow," for example, focuses on the poet's youthful introduction to the mining scene during the Wilder Strike in Tennessee in the early 1930s, when he was a student. Industrial warfare was graphically demonstrated by the murder of labor organizer Barney Graham. The persona in the poem is Graham's widow, who, reminiscent of Wobbly songwriter Joe Hill, ridicules the religious message of the preachers who have come to conduct her husband's funeral:

> Preachers spout their platitudes
> To workers hard and lean
> Who toil with aching bodies
> For wealth they've never seen.
>
> Parsons who live in plenty
> And drive a limousine
> Say they bring a message
> From a toiling Nazarene . . .
> ....
> Say, we don't need you preachers
> Who rant and rave and yell
> About a poor man's sinning
> That sinks him down to hell.

Three other poems, "Harlan Portraits," "Harlan Coal Digger, 1934," and "I've Seen God," relate to West's relatively brief mining and organizing experiences in eastern Kentucky. The beauty of the countryside of Harlan County enthralls the poet in the first part of "Harlan Portraits," but a sense of guilt and anger quickly push aesthetic feelings aside:

But beauty
Never visits the coal diggers.
They live in the coal camps—
Dirty shanties,
Stinking privies,
Grunting pigs,
And slop buckets . . .

"I've Seen God" is thematically similar to "Miner's Widow," for just as Christ is portrayed as a working person, God is often found where least expected—even "in a Kentucky coal camp." The poem "Harlan Coal Digger, 1934," while calling for union solidarity, testifies to the poet's familiarity with the life of a miner and his "gummy clothes" and "aching body."

Although he never mined coal after the 1930s, West's interest in and activities on behalf of miners continued for the rest of his life. "Pineville, Kentucky, 1946" laments the death of twenty-four miners killed in a shaft that had been condemned by federal inspectors. "Hazard, Kentucky" sympathizes with a strike by miners in that county in 1963. In "Automated Miner," an unemployed coal miner from Cabin Creek, West Virginia, who has worked twenty years underground, despairs of losing his job to a machine and of his failure to find other work. Dependent on welfare while living on "molly-grub and gravy," this man's loss transcends the purely economic in the poem's last two lines: "No job, no home, / No place to go."

Finally, what makes Don West different from other coal poets who concentrated on the negative aspects of mining was his social vision. Undoubtedly influenced by a lifetime of activism on behalf of oppressed groups, West believed the roots of oppression to run deeply in history. In a long poem, "Something of America," he probes the entire span of the country's history but focuses on the struggles of mining people. Throughout the poem, personal memories blend with historical events. Courageous acts mingle with tragic failures in a pastiche of the country's history:

John Woody, a man I know of 48 years
waiting to die of black-lung,
never knew the school room,
went to the mine at nine.
. . . .
Blair Mountain, 1921
Ten thousand miners in struggle
bombs dropping from the air.
. . . .

Ludlow . . . !
Map makers leave it off now.
A stone-carved miner
with wife and slain child at foot
mark the spot to:
". . . the men, women and children
who died in freedom's cause
April 20, 1914."
. . . .
In 1934 in a Kentucky jail death cell
with three men sentenced to die
I learned the song:
"Shut up in the Mines at Coal Creek"
from one on his way to the Chair.
. . . .
Something of America I love
and cherish with warm pride
And something I intensely dislike.[23]

Don West's love-hate relationship with America was similar to his love-hate relationship with coal mining. He loved the miners, their courage and ability to endure but, at times, seemed to hate the industry—particularly those who controlled it—for the way it destroyed dreams and crippled lives.

The final poets to be analyzed exemplify the complexities and ambiguities that make coal mining poetry somewhat different from the other creative disciplines examined thus far. While Mike Yarrow, Billy Edd Wheeler, and Don West creatively mix positive and negative images in ways that avoid an us-versus-them mentality, others poets take a different approach. Growing up in a Kentucky coal-mining family, James B. Goode writes from the perspective of the present, whereas the contributors to *Coalseam: Poems from the Anthracite Region* are immersed in memories from the past. The poets of the anthracite region seem to distance themselves from their subject matter, while Goode is unable to do so.

Although James B. Goode reminisces about the passing of an era in several of his poems, it is primarily events within his own lifetime that haunt his imagination. In a recently published book of poetry, *Up from the Mines,* Goode collaborates with photographer Malcolm Wilson to produce the most comprehensive vision of coal mining of any poet examined here. Goode grew up in a coal camp in Benham, Kentucky. His paternal grandfather, a miner, died of pneumoconiosis. His father mined coal as well. A student of Lee Pennington at Southeast Community College, Goode most likely would have been a third-generation miner had he not continued his education at the University of Kentucky and become a teacher. Because Goode comes from a coal region, he has personally observed some of mining's most disastrous effects, including his grandfather's black lung illness and the accidental deaths of friends. Writing about mining rather than practicing it has led to what might be termed a "poetry of catharsis," as the poet wrestles with conflicting emotions and perspectives in trying to understand a way of making a living that, despite his professional distance from it, remains so much a part of his identity.

Up from the Mines is a compilation of coal-oriented poems from an earlier volume, *Poets of Darkness* (1981), and those he has written since. In the preface, he promises to challenge the negative, stereotypical images of miners and their communities:

> The negative images of the coal miner have overshadowed the positive ones for too long. Where are the accounts of his sensitive, artistic side? Many of the coal miners I knew in the International Harvester coal camp at Benham, Kentucky were different than those images I read about when I started college at the University of Kentucky. They were coal miners first, but they were also poets, lyricists, sculptors, musicians, story tellers, horticulturists, conservationists, and independent thinkers.[24]

He intends to explore their complexities and diversities with the kind of creative honesty they deserve. Goode keeps his promise. Many of the poems suggest not only an insider's familiarity with a way of life not widely understood but also a respect for those who have endured the perilous work involved. In the preface to *Poets of Darkness,* Goode writes that while he was completing the manuscript, the Scotia mine explosion occurred in Oven Fork, Kentucky. Twenty-six miners died, three of whom were his highschool classmates. Soon after, one of his closest childhood friends was killed in another mining accident. Goode revisits memories of not only his grandfather's sickness but the overall suffering that was the daily fare for any mining camp.[25] There is an element of catharsis in his work. He mourns those who have been lost while praising those who have survived the mining experience.

In many of the shorter poems, such as "The Miner and the Land," "Coal Miner Falls for Azure Eyes in a Dream," and "Cold Beer on Hot Harlan County Nights," Goode intends for the reader to understand that the rhythms of existence in coal mining communities are much like those in communities elsewhere. They reveal the same uneven mixture of good and evil that characterizes the human condition. Other poems explore the unique aspects of life that can only be found in communities of mining folk. In "Like the Last Good-By," for example, Goode deals with the anxiety felt by mining wives as their men go off to work. In "Coal Miners Come Home," he describes the welcomed sounds of a returning miner, sounds that calm the anxiety until the next shift. In "For Those Who Sleep," Goode expands on Hemingway's assertion that a man's scars tell his story to illustrate how a miner's body details his own personal history. "Boom Town Boys," "Boom Town Poolroom," and "Roadhouses" show how miners try to escape the burdens of their work. As their titles suggest, "Pentecost in Coal Town," "Appalachian Snake Handlers," and "Funeral for Five" suggest somewhat different forms of relief. "Ballad for a Union Man" and "Pug-Uglies in Harlan" recount older struggles for social justice and union organization, while "100 Days and Counting . . ." concerns a more recent Harlan County strike during the Carter administration.

The poems that set the tone for both *Poets of Darkness* and *Up from the Mines* are longer ones exploring the impact of losing friends and loved ones in mining accidents. In an effort to confront the death of the poet's best friend, the fellow miner who speaks in "Late Afternoon" is unable to find the words to express either solace or understanding:

> "It was his time to die.
> If he'd a been six inches to the left or right
> It would've missed his chest
> And probably only have broken his legs.
> But he was in the right spot at the right time."

These meaningless deaths continue to haunt the poet. In a later poem, "Coal Miner's Graveyard," Goode compares the remains of miners, many of whom died violent deaths, with seeds randomly blown into the graveyard:

> Searching for a place to rest—
> A place where they will uncoil
> In a miner's dust
> And stretch an aching for new life
> Slowly toward the sun.

The poet understands this stretching for new life, which he has achieved through education. There is a sense in much of his work that friends would have done the same had they the opportunity. Like a war veteran who feels guilty for surviving, Goode knows that only his exit from Benham has saved him. No matter how careful, skilled, or even lucky a miner might be, Goode knows that harm may nonetheless come to him. What infuriates the poet even more, he believes that brave men and women work underground for the "whims" and "pleasures" of a civilization of consumption:

I have been to their funerals.
Sometimes in the coal camp houses
Caskets wet with tears
Roll from the detached steel hands of morticians
Through the vision of innocent children
Who wonder? And Why?
About a world of such sadistic appetites.
And What For?
About such games of chance.
They become wiser among the screams of grief.
Callouses form and thicken
As hundreds of pallid faces pass the motionless head
In the open casket.
Some pause in awkward silence,
Some in frenzied tears
Over the men who never look like themselves,
Were never taken because they wanted to be—
Never because God wanted them to be.

There are no explanations offered for the tragedies in this poem. The beginning provides the only conclusion, which, although biblical in origin, is still more existential than enlightening:

Who from darkness came into the world
To toil in darkness
And to darkness
Shall return.[26]

For all of his knowledge of coal mining and his compassion for miners, Goode sees the work as something one does if other options fail. The men he knew who went underground had lives that were as full and creative as any. It is not the way they lived but the senseless way they suffered and died that infuriates the poet. Goode questions if any work should demand so much and return so little. There is no way of determining whether Goode's mentor, Lee Pennington, influenced his bleak view of the mining life or whether personal experiences were more than enough. Goode never stereotypes miners or treats them as working-class curiosities, but there is, as with Pennington, an overwhelming bleakness in his mining poetry, which suggests an insurmountable conceptual gulf separating those who toil underground from the rest of us. It is this gulf that transforms mining people in Goode's poetry into "others," however sympathetically.

Whereas *Poets of Darkness* and *Up from the Mines* are the most important collections of coal-related verse written by any individual in the modern era, *Coalseam: Poems from the Anthracite Region* is the most comprehensive anthology of modern-day coal poets. Although not all of the thirteen contributors have provided poems that directly relate to mining, without exception the verse touches life in the anthracite region. Frank MacShane discusses this thematic coherence in the foreword. He argues that the people of this region overcame extreme hardship by creating a heritage and history that reflects "the strength of human spirit and their own determination." MacShane begins the discussion, however, with a negative tone. He notes that the "very names that mark the settlements of Port Carbon, Minersville and Coaldale reflect the grim lives of the men and women who over the years have worked the anthracite mines and managed to raise families in a hostile and remorseless setting."[27] In several instances, MacShane clearly wants to praise the tenacity of the human spirit. This foreword does not precisely reflect the tone of many of the *Coalseam* contributions. These poems praise the human spirit by showing that life in this region is not innately grim and the inhabitants are no different from the rest of us. The perception of mining folk as "the other" through focusing on their suffering is not the mood in this anthology. The difference may have something to do with the poets' personal and historical distance from the mining of coal. As Karen Blomain points out in her introduction, deep mining for anthracite was ending by the early 1950s.[28] Although small illegal operations still existed and strip mining was still being done, the way of life was facing an overall decline in America and, for all practical purposes, ended in Pennsylvania. The last poem in *Coalseam,* written by Thomas Kielty Blomain, "So the Coal Was Gone," provides an appropriate ending to both a book and an era:

> So black lung is a pension
> coughing in the streets
> where nurses walk and watch their feet
> past the bars that still for a dime
> offer the past
> and various ways to forget
>
> So kids know anthracite by its name
> and throw chunks of it at passersby,
> laughing on the railroad tracks

and at the caboose going by
the city
slower than the rest of the world.

For the anthracite poets, mining as a way of life has been over for almost half a century. There are no friends still dying in the mines, no struggles with rapacious mining companies, fewer individuals like Miller's Thomas Ratliff who are too old to learn a new skill and too young to die. Anger is not lacking in this anthology—anger often surges to the surface when the suffering of parents, grandparents, and older generations is remembered. Yet most of the poets are less interested in relating the inhumanity of the work than in describing how ordinary men and women went about making a living.

The daily lives of people in this volume are no different from those of characters in Thornton Wilder's *Our Town* or Edgar Lee Masters's *Spoon River Anthology.* Blomain is particularly effective in her descriptions of how women and children respond to the routines and quirks of daily life. Though a teacher ridicules the town's children for their imaginative use of language, Blomain explains in "Mango" why they give this name to common green or red peppers: "There was nothing exotic to name / In the coal town, still / We found words we liked the taste of / And used them as we chose." Marital difficulties are described in "The Miner's Wife Leaves Home"; the passing of youth and its freedom from responsibilities, in "The Dancers"; and of course, the inevitability of death, in "Sickness." If Vincent D. Balitas describes a desolate, coal-scarred landscape in "Paynes Patch," he also shows a sense of resiliency as the people in this small mining community go about their daily routines. In these poems the comic and tragic are often inextricably linked, as exemplified by Anthony Petrosky's "Father and Mother." This poem relates the pain of children caught in the midst of an unworkable marriage, but there is also a moment of comic relief when the father tells his son about the time that his coal miner grandfather discovered the family's cat urinating in the pickle jar.[29]

Harry Humes has more pleasant visions of family life than Petrosky and, in "My Mother at Evening," imagines a young woman eagerly awaiting the return of her coal miner husband. The mine is five miles away. He often hops a train while she sits by the tracks, waiting "for him to swing down, smiling, / out of the dark." Reflecting on other memories while viewing "The Photograph" of his father holding him and his brother in his arms, Humes cannot find in his father's expression any sign of his black lung or any concern about working below ground: "he seems like a man thinking of nothing / but holding his two small sons." Humes never tries to romanticize the dangers of mining. If the black lung of the previous poem is not reminder enough, the kaleidoscopic thoughts of a miner engaged in one of the most dangerous of jobs, "Robbing the Pillars," is proof of the deep anxieties miners face every day. Humes may have hoped to understand coal mining lives by reading abandoned company records. In "At the Counting House of Buck Run Mine," he finds no clues to explain why men worked in such danger or why the entire industry eventually shut down. In the world of his memory and imagination people lived and died, fought and made up, suffered and enjoyed. They left the ultimate meaning of their lives as elusive as the forgotten company records. There was much that Humes, as a poet, could never understand, but he could creatively build bridges linking past to present. He could feel a sense of belonging and reassurance when a son, like his father before him, began "Walking the Anthracite":

> There used to be a man here, a father
> with bad lungs and scar-blue knees.
> I imagine him standing at his pit, the earth
> thick on him, eyes gathering
> all the light before he went down.
> This ground could be my darkest blood,
> its hot veins place I must crawl.
> I think of my pregnant wife, her pregnant shape.
> I am minded by fatherhood; I have broken my carbons,
> dynamited my flesh, walked alone into these hills for days.
> At night, by an old carbine lamp,
> drinking the bitter hill water,
> I feel the tunnels rising like charms to my flesh,
> calming me, offering the lost pale face like long sleep.[30]

Like Humes, many of the poets examined in this chapter have written about coal mining because of personal and regional ties. But as Terrence Des Pres notes in *Praises & Dispraises: Poetry and Politics, the 20th Century,* all modern writers are confronted with the wretchedness of other people throughout the world. The revolution in communications has created a "technological expansion of consciousness."[31] If events in Mogadishu and Sarajevo can be brought into our living rooms, so too can the mine explosions, trapped miners, victims of black lung, and the bitter strikes. All are dramatic reminders of the human cost of our postindustrial way of life. So it is often the most dramatic and frightening aspects of coal mining that capture the imagination of those writing about it. Goethe once claimed that he nurtured his creative abilities by imagining himself committing every crime.[32] Many of the poets analyzed here have nurtured their creativity through envisioning only the most fearful aspects of coal mining. Wallace Stevens reminds us that poetry is the most intensely personal literary genre. At its best, poetry reflects the despair and hope that compose the nobility of the human condition. "It is a violence from within that protects us from a violence without. It is the imagination pressing back against the pressure of reality. It seems," Stevens adds, "in the last analysis, to have something to do with our self-preservation; and that, no doubt, is why the expression of it, the sound of its words, helps us to live our lives."[33] For some writers, coal mining poetry has served as a kind of creative catharsis helping them to confront unimaginable danger and suffering, while for others it is an expression of their interest in a way of life that is different but not uniquely tragic. Within this creative diversity, a number of poets have taken the perspective of the crippled World War II veteran speaking to a person of color: "Resign yourself to your color the way I got used to my stump; we're both victims."[34] Such privileging of one's own position while defining another is as arbitrary as it is naïve.

Chapter 7

Voices from within the Mining Community

In an article that first appeared in the *Pittsburgh Press* and later in a 1900 issue of *The United Mine Workers Journal,* journalist W.S. Applegate quotes a mine superintendent's Emersonian heralding of long-awaited literature that would finally reflect the coal mining experience. "Some day," predicted the gray-haired superintendent, miners "will have their place in literature, just as have the sea toilers, the factory people, the soldiers and their life at the army post and the railroad men." He believed that "down in the underworld of Pennsylvania there is material for a hundred books that all the world would stop to read. Tales of adventure and brave deeds, of men whose names are not on tablets of brass, but who lived and worked and proved themselves heroes when they died of engineering feats which have made the scientific world wonder, and of the many unsolvable mysteries of those vast underground chambers." Not just anyone could write about mining coal. That special individual "who will write of the life properly must have the soul of the poet, the mind of the story-writer and the experience of a miner, but having all these he will not be greater than his work."[1]

The writers examined thus far have most often drawn on their imaginations rather than their experiences. But coal mining communities have also produced men and women who write about what they know firsthand. Few of them would see themselves as writers in the popular sense of the term. Some, such as the protagonist of a poem in a 1904 issue of the *UMWJ,* are determined to write the great mining epic. The author of this poem uses the 1902 Anthracite Strike as background. The protagonist shuts himself up in his room each evening to write:

> Alone in a room where the sun seldom shines
> Sits a strong, brawny youth, a son of the mines;
> His evenings in writing he spends at a stand,

With his paper before him and pencil in hand.
We glance at the title, the name, "Richard Lee,"
Are the first words of writing our eyes chance to see.

This strong, brawny youth, whose name is Robert Moore,
Has visions of fame and of laurels galore;
Has visions of lines when we'll herald his name
Across the two continents with immeasurable fame;
Has visions of times when we'll go far to see
The noted young author of the book, "Richard Lee."

By writing at evenings after work in the mine
(He writes from four-thirty 'till fifteen to nine),
He hopes to conclude his small manuscript,
And have his good name with fame's laurels typed,
And have for his labors, on the large scroll of fame,
His (Robert Moore's) as the first honored name.

Robert Moore spent a dollar to send the manuscript to a publisher only to have it returned with the message "Unaccepted, the world doesn't know you."[2] Like Mark Twain's poet of the morbid, Evaline Grangerford, who pined away when the undertaker beat her to a death scene, Moore was shattered by his failure. He died within a year, perhaps, like Grangerford, of a broken heart. The number of Robert Moores within the mining community must have been small. James F. Murphy, in his revisionist study of 1930s proletarian writing, reminds us that even during this heyday of working-class writing, the vast majority of these novelists wrote for a living.[3]

With obvious occupational time constraints, most worker/writers prefer shorter works. Often these shorter works are poems. George Korson, in *Coal Dust on the Fiddle,* identifies a tradition of poetry that stretches back into the Scottish and English mining communities long before the transfer of these cultures to the United States. The recitation of long poems from memory was common in many working-class homes around the turn of the century. A former miner and the country's first Secretary of Labor, William B. Wilson, reasons that "my parents being both fond of poetry and having read so much of it myself, it was natural that as a boy I should drift into the composition of rhymes."[4] Wilson never developed into a major poet, though he did publish a small book of verse, *Memories,* which was reviewed in a 1904 edition of the *United Mine Workers Journal.* The reviewer insists that Wilson "does not lay claim to the name of poet," and in the book's preface the Secretary of Labor belittles his creative efforts by quoting a friend who contends that "no man ever writes poetry except when his liver is out of order."[5] Disclaimers aside, Wilson is among a group of poets who have written short pieces about their lives, hopes, and dreams that relate, in one way or another, to the mining experience. From its inception in 1891 through the present day, the *UMWJ* has acknowledged the creative efforts of its rank-and-file membership by publishing their poetry, stories, anecdotes, vignettes, and other literary efforts. These pieces represent the efforts of ordinary men and women to define their own experiences while adding meaning to their lives. As poet and critic Jim Wayne Miller reminds us:

> Individually and collectively, people have a story to tell. Literature consists of different parts of that story, or different versions of it. When people tell their story, a peculiar thing happens. People present themselves—to themselves and to others—as they know themselves to be, as they want to be. Literature helps people write their own script rather than be actors in somebody else's play; helps people define themselves. Literature helps people make up another self if they don't like the one they have. Literature helps people get control over their own image. People have always needed to tell their own story.[6]

Biographer Douglas Wixson argues that most of the miner/writers who contributed to the *UMWJ* never found their own voices. Their writing, he attests, was limited by the artificiality of the genteel tradition.[7] There is some truth to Wixson's analysis. In-house publications like the *UMWJ* do not encourage criticism of the union or its leadership. Nor do they encourage stylistic experimentation, which can cloud rather than clarify issues. Nevertheless, the poems in these journals are conscious efforts of mining people to define themselves and their work. They are writing their own scripts—the message is far more important than the medium. In his study of radical poetry that has not made it into the modern literary canon, Cary Nelson argues that even the most straightforward verse can transmit electrifying messages. "In part because of its long historical links with song and with the speaking voice, and in part because we are especially aware of its formal properties," he writes in *Repression and Recovery,* "poetry offers us subject positions we can take up consciously and with a paradoxically self-conscious sense of personal identification. Compared to prose, and certainly in contrast to many forms of public rhetoric, poetry is perhaps less likely to write itself out on our tongues unawares."[8] To suggest, then, that the traditional stylistic orientation of these miner/writers somehow mutes their concerns is to undermine their creative agency. It also serves to trivialize their lives and their efforts to define them. If on occasion a *UMWJ* contributor is not identified, this omission may have more to do with fear of managerial reprisal or community ridicule than with any sense of writing in a folk tradition. In any case, these contributors to the *UMWJ* (none of whom would be considered professional writers) and the handful of other miner/writers evaluated here are much closer in their analysis of mining culture to the poets anthologized in *Coalseam* than to the majority of writers, who have envisioned the coal mine as an industrial hell populated by working-class "others."

This chapter joins the voices of miner/writers with those of the professional writers examined in previous chapters.[9] Before the advent of radio and television, the *UMWJ* tried to entertain as well as inform its readers. A number of the early stories published have little or nothing to do with coal mining. The authors probably viewed the *UMWJ* as a vehicle for publication. They used the mining experience, as have so many other writers, to fuel their plots or to add a sense of danger or adventure to their narratives.

Although the Horatio Alger motif occasionally surfaces, melodramas and romance between middle-class characters in a mining backdrop are more common. No author is named for "The Adventures of 'Jock' Pitbreeks," the episodic, twenty-two-part Civil War saga first published in a 1909 issue of the *UMWJ*. Coal mining is included only parenthetically rather than as a major concern in this long, rambling narrative, which typifies many of the fictional pieces in the journal during this period. A number of these early contributors predictably envision mining as a job to escape. Life in a mining town is usually an ordeal. "If I can only dispel that terrible feeling of despair, of utter hopelessness and bring that vision of a better time which is surely dawning into that town, and among those people," reasons a youthful middle-class minister who finds himself in the middle of a strike, "I shall feel my soul honored in its mission."[10]

To some extent the miner/writers reflect the racial and nativistic intolerance of their era, though the journal editors tried to temper extremist views. Editors used less restraint when strikebreakers were the object of attack, as this contribution during the 1902 Anthracite Strike suggests: "You have heard about the trouble / Out in the anthracite. / They are working imported labor / Instead of the honest whites." A West Virginia miner writing in the same year more openly condemns management's use of foreign workers:

> The company looks after NUMBER ONE.
> The life of a man is no account—
> There's carloads of Dagos his place to fill.
> The combine can contract for any amount
> Of Europe's rubbish to be dumped at will.

As an 1895 piece demonstrates, racist language was not relegated to immigrants, though the author may well have been suggesting that racial scapegoating is counterproductive:

> There's too many of us diggers,
> Treat blacklisted men as strangers;
> We should never talk of "niggers,"
> We're the source of our own dangers;

Other contributors used the slave analogy, quite common in a variety of literary works, in a fundamentally different way. Professional writers were struck by the slave-like appearance of miners, the chain-like clanging of their lunch pails, the drudgery of their lives, the brutality of their work environment. Miner/writers did not necessarily perceive themselves as slaves but used the slave analogy to describe the treatment of workers by management. One miner wrote in 1895:

> We sign then a contract
> As agreed between men;
> Though it holds us like slaves,
> It never holds them;
> And when they've exhausted
> The old contract score,
> Thep [They] capped the climax
> With the company store.

To use the analogy was not to acquiesce or openly acknowledge that miners were becoming slaves. Rather, it was more of a warning about what could happen if they and their union were not vigilant. It was less an issue of a flawed occupation than of the rapacious way management tried to manipulate the workers' lives.

> Those aliens that were hither brought
> From distant countries now are taught
> Our laws and right of ways.
> Those barons thought they had a slave,
> But tutored in Columbia brave
> They basked 'neath freedom's rays.

A poet writing in the *Progressive Miner,* a journal opposed to the leadership of John L. Lewis, in 1932 claims that in opposing both management and the

UMWA, the Progressive Mine Workers of America "have broken our slave chains." The slave allusion appears well into the 1960s. A 1940 poem best captures how the miners and their unions have combated enslavement to ensure the freedom of all working people:

> Ever keeping in mind John Mitchell's gain,
> Strong men have labored, enduring the pain
> Of seeing their friends, and foes alike,
> Against them turn when they called a strike
> To break the high walls of greed and hate,
> The slavery of men in the mines to abate.
> They have fought unafraid 'til the union stands
> Upholding mine workers with mighty hands;
> A living memorial to ever proclaim,
> Security and union is an American aim.[11]

Seldom do contributors suggest that the union is enslaving the rank and file. Some miner/writers complain that pensions and disability payments are too low. Others are critical of the union but nonetheless hint that miners bring some problems on themselves. In 1904, for example, one poet praised the courage of the union's leadership in avoiding a strike by accepting a compromise wage in spite of considerable opposition. At the same time, another miner chastised his fellow workers for failing to feed the mules during a strike, which, he believed, showed their inability to think beyond the present. A number of years later, a West Virginian lamented that during the hurried working conditions of the World War II era, some miners stole coal by switching tags on mine cars. Finally, using a short story rather than a poem to vent his concerns, a miner in the 1990s condemned a fellow union member for advocating wildcat strikes instead of thinking about the long-term needs of the rank and file.[12] For the most part, these were isolated criticisms. Miner/writers typically directed their creative anger toward management and others outside the coal mining community.

While convinced that they were exploited, these writers never insinuated that such exploitation was different from that faced by workers in other professions. Exploitation by management or other outside sources was seen as simply another obstacle to earning a decent living. The courts, automation, redbaiters, critics like farm groups, and postwar antilabor legislation like the Taft-Hartley Act were all attacked at one time or another. During World War II, when the UMWA received increasing criticism because of its bargaining position, Congress was a favorite target for several miner/writers. In December 1944, a miner from Kacking, Ohio, compared miners' contributions in helping win the war with those of Congressional representatives. In a poem entitled "The Audacious Coal Miner," he writes,

> Work, miners, work! Your all must be given!
> Wield that pick and shovel with lightning stroke;
> For at our next election, if you are still living,
> You'll be classed as men good enough to vote.
>
> When completely exhausted load a few more tons!
> Remember! Congress of our United States
> Worked overtime with blistered tongues
> Crushing the enemy with long and stupid debates!

Another worker/poet reminds his readers that mining families had to survive while contributing to the war effort: "Some writers said they were unpatriotic / And gave them many unfair and cruel blows; / But they just wanted fair wages so their families / Could have shelter, food, shoes and clothes." Contributions to past wars were likewise not to be forgotten, a Jasonville, Indiana, miner admonishes his readers:

> So, brother, when you're knocking
> on the man that digs the coal,
> Just stop and think he's human
> and has a heart and soul,
> And don't forget the millions
> of tons he loaded out
> When the Kaiser tried to smear on us
> his lager, beer and kraut.[13]

If the bulk of creative contributions to the *UMWJ* is any indication, the greatest sources of anger for the miner/writers were the traditional grievances—scabbing, inadequate wages, and the greed and arrogance of management. The scabbing poems and stories, which are most common by far, are usually descriptive, didactic, and unimaginative. An 1891 poem submitted by a "fallen brother" summarizes, in spite of its first-person perspective, what would become an archetype of the miner consciousness:

> I'm not ashamed my mining friends
> To thus address you so,
> And swear an oath for all I'm worth
> I'll never stoop so low

As try to burst a noble cause
  Or give it such a stab,
For I never more will court the name
  Of an accursed scab.

A deep-seated anger over inadequate wages permeates many of the poems. Some poems attribute the widespread use of child labor to the fact that wages are so low families must send their children into the mines. Others point to inadequate wages as the reason behind older miners' inability to retire. The belief that current wages failed to compensate for the dangers of coal mining also found its outlet in verse. As an Indiana poet phrased it, "Just view one of the many scenes the miners undergo, / And then I think you'll agree with me / Their wages are too low."[14]

Writers also attacked what they saw as the insatiable greed and exploitative agenda of management. More than anything else, managerial practices gave coal mining a bad reputation, encouraging the view that it was a degrading way of earning a living. No miner doubted that digging coal was hard, dangerous work. What made it seem unbearable was a host of problems: low wages often paid in script, dead work (work for which miners were not paid), company deductions, arbitrary layoffs, company stores, armed mine guards, inadequate housing, wretched schools, poor medical care, and disregard for safety precautions.[15] It seemed as if the mining regions were located in some third world country, dominated and exploited by foreign capitalists. As a Colorado poet wrote:

Talk of freedom! Why, the freedom
that the workingmen enjoyed,
In the mines of Colorado, was the
brand that is employed
In such countries as the Congo, or be-
neath a tyrant's rule
Where each horny-handed victim is to
Capital a tool—
Just a tool—a thing with reason, but
without the right to think
Just a sort of human critter born to
work, sleep, eat and drink

The power of the coal owners was bad enough, but the paternalistic arrogance of superintendents and other managerial personnel within the mine was especially galling to workers who saw themselves as independent laborers rather than subservient lackeys. A retired miner mimicked management's self-perception in the late 1920s:

I am divine, I own the mine,
  So I must have full sway;
'Tis my desire to never hire
  One union man today.
I dictate when both boys and men,
  Shall loaf or work or play;
Now don't forget, no cash you'll get,
  Old scrip is what I pay.

Unless I shave what ev'ry slave
  Does earn by night or day;
Men must agree to bow the knee,
  And use my scrip to pay.
No one shall bring a friend to sing,
  No one shall kneel to pray;
I must decide what groom or bride
  Shall wed in camp today.[16]

While many miner/writers merely satirized managerial injustice, some tried to generate change. Their poems and stories fall within two general categories. They either describe and comment on specific strikes and related events in the past or justify the use of strikes in broader terms as a necessary and legitimate weapon of labor. These writers seeking change produced poems and stories focusing on local strikes or major ones like Lattimer, Ludlow, the great anthracite strike of 1902, and Pittston. In a short story written in 1915, entitled "A Woman's Influence," for example, a miner's wife shames her husband into staying with his fellow workers during the 1902 walkout. The author, who may have been a sympathetic supporter rather than a miner, editorializes that the world learned a lesson from the courage of the men and women who participated in this titanic struggle:

> Talk about fields of battle—wherein lies the bravery in the maddened conflict of guns and bayonets, when we compare it with the unsurrendering disposition in the brain of a striker? While, perhaps, the dear wife and children suffer for the necessaries of life, he still holds out against the greed and cruelty, perhaps blandishments, of the employers and, at last, snatches a positive victory from the unholy talons of despair. 'Tis to such men that the world owes much, and 'tis to the women who help them that the world owes equally much, if not more.

Eight years later a poet in Hazleton, Pennsylvania, suggests that in 1902, and perhaps again in 1917, the miners had been struggling for the rights of all working people:

And yet when LABOR fought its greatest fight,
  Yours were the troops that held the foe at bay—
Shock troops sent in to save the workers' right
  To living wage and hope of better day.

Well have you earned a place out in the Sun,
  You did your bit as on life's way you trod,
Unselfishly you fought with pick or gun—
  For country, home, your fellow-man and God.[17]

As the strike poems suggest, only through the solidarity of collective struggle could miners hope to combat degrading circumstances. The battle was constant, though the issues changed over the years, whether centered on the defense of John L. Lewis or Tony Boyle, the need for higher wages, opposition to the Taft-Hartley Act, legal attacks on the union's organizing efforts, or the need for black lung legislation and compensation. The mood of these poems is as varied as the authors. One poet, for example, pleaded with his fellow workers not to be vindictive after the 1902 strike victory. Ralph Chaplin, a poet, miner, songwriter, and close associate of Big Bill Haywood, reflected the attitude of many striking West Virginia miners during the Paint and Cabin Creek strikes of 1912-1913.

The hills are very bare and cold and lonely;
I wonder what the future months will bring.
The strike is on—our strength would win, if only—
Oh, Buddy, how I'm longing for the spring.
. . . .
I will not watch the floating clouds that hover
Above the birds that warble on the wing;
I want to use this gun from under cover—
Oh, Buddy, how I'm longing for the spring.

While miner/writers disagree on some issues, most seem to concur that a monumental struggle, both justified and unavoidable, lay ahead. To succeed, a campaign would have to cut across ethnic lines.

There's Russian, Slavish, Polish and Jew,
Italians, Dutchmen and English a few,

With Irishmen, Scotchmen and Welshmen, too.
In the organized camp at Ellsworth.
. . . .
We now are a unit if we haven't been long,
Of a union, the finest ever formed by man;
Unite them [in] strength, and you'll ever be strong
To strengthen the cause in Ellsworth.[18]

The message that unity is necessary in the struggle for change resonates throughout the poems. Solidarity usually means joining or supporting the United Mine Workers of America. Some poets use biblical analogies. One Colorado miner compares the forces set against the miners in his state to Goliath. A day of reckoning would come when David, in the form of the UMWA, would end the tyrannical collusion between management and government. An older West Virginia miner writing in the 1960s recalls what it was like before he and other miners stood shoulder to shoulder in the union:

I came to this world without my consent,
  I will leave it against my will.
I worked in the mine that came to an end,
  Now the Welfare Fund is my very best
    friend.
I started in the mine in 1909,
  To earn a decent living you had a hard
    time.
. . . .
No compensation, no two weeks pay,
  No mine inspection, once a month pay.
No union to back you, no man your brother,
  Kill a mule buy another, kill a man hire
    another.
That's all in the past, that's come to an end.
  Yes, the Welfare Fund is my last best
    friend.

Written in a more didactic tone, a 1930s poem argues that the union was only as good as its membership. Several years later a West Virginia bard details in free verse how to keep a union in operation. He emphasizes a level of solidarity that places the good of the whole before all. "To be loyal to the union one must be willing to do, dare and endure for the good of mankind." For the wife of a Progressive miner, the prescription is simpler:

Three cheers for the P.M.A., we
know they will win,
When we all work together and
cheerfulness lend;
For after all, down life's shorten-
ing miles
The people who smile are the ones
worth while.[19]

These pro-union poems are not the musings of an industrial underclass who thought they were cut off from other workers, but a call to arms by those who believed they were the vanguard of the American labor movement.

Some worker/poets wondered whether the problems that mining people faced were fully understood outside the coalfields. Unions were coming under attack by both the public and the government during the late 1940s, though miners were only asking for a decent standard of living.

We, too, crave cleanliness and light,
And life in the upper air;
Let us change places with some of you—
Some of you come down here.

Lay hold of the pick, and the shovel and spade,
With your two white hands, you men
Who draw your thousands sitting aloof
In some bright and cheerful den.
....
You will not lower your dividends
To give us a dollar more;
You claim a director's salary plus
Your dividends and some more.

We need more of the things you have
To make our lives less grim.
Do you every [*sic*] think of the miner's lot?
Do you ever think of him?

Another writer contrasts the unattractive houses of the mining families with the palatial ones "Frequented only part of the year / When company directors visit here." When World War II ended it seemed to some miners that they had become the enemy. A Kentucky poet, refusing to be ashamed of his work and his union, proudly trumpets them in these lines:

I'm not ashamed of filth and dirt—
It's never done me harm;
For someone has to dig the coal
That keeps you nice and warm.

It's true I have big calluses
And corns upon my feet;
It's true my shirt is not so white
And my collar not so neat.

But I have love of my fellow man—
On this I place my stand.
I'm mighty glad that God made me
A red-blooded union man.
. . . .
I'm proud that all are not like you—
An operator's plum—
Trying to take our honest pay
When our work is done.

So now I've told my story,
There's nothing more to tell.
You string along with stuffed shirts,
We'll stick to old John L.[20]

Miner/writers clearly believed that supporting the union and maintaining class solidarity were proven ways to deal with the workers' plight. Historian David Corbin and film director John Sayles argue that class solidarity in mining communities also helped overcome ethnic and racial divides.[21] There is ample evidence that miners in both the anthracite and soft coal regions could put many of their ethnic antagonisms behind them. They were able to unite on a common front before management. Evidence in poetry of any permanent racial solidarity among miners is rarer.[22] Even a radical poet like Stanley Kimmel, who in *Kingdom Of Smoke* (1932) tries to "defamiliarize" racial epithets by overusing them, still writes in a stereotypical style.[23]

Niggers dream of nigger love.
Niggers dream of watermelon moon.

Overhead are great slabs of coal.
Is there never an end to toil?
Swing low, shovel hands, banjo hands . . .

In the *UMWJ,* the racial concern expressed by Kimmel—as flawed as it may be—is the exception rather than the rule. Miner/writers just did not delve into racial issues. One poet, signing himself "Huber Joe" from Wilkes-Barre, Pennsylvania, stands virtually alone in his celebration of racial solidarity:

There's sweat that's shed in the mine,
And bodies that show labor's sign
there's youth and aged there,
With skin dark and fair;
Amid miners there is no race line.[24]

The silence of miner/writers on racial issues is revealing. African American miners and their families do not voice their concerns about racism in the union's journal. Whether this is because of individual choice or editorial censorship is unknown. In any case, as students of power and power relationships from Foucault to Gaventa point out, what does not occur can be more important than what does. The lack of a union dialogue about racism in the coalfields speaks volumes. Why most of the miner/writer contributors to the *UMWJ,* the *Huntington Labor Star,* the *New Masses,* or the *Progressive Miner* skirted racial issues is difficult to say. But they were passionately interested in writing about their demanding jobs and the special kind of character needed for them.

They wrote about what they did with a sense of pride—not as browbeaten workers in a degraded profession. Often, poems detail with rhyme and wit the jobs of mule drivers, breaker boys, shuttle-car drivers, timbermen, mechanics, operators of Joy loading machines, coal scoops, and fire bosses. They explain such processes as robbing the pillars, long-wall mining, and the safety preparations made at the beginning of each shift. Other poems, more didactic than descriptive in nature, deal with various aspects of mining safety. During the hand-loading era, miners worked in separate chambers of the shaft. In matters of safety, as this 1914 poem suggests, the group was more important than individuals:

In the next place to yours the top is
loose,
Take Safety First,
"I'm not his keeper" is no excuse,
But Safety First.

He may be green, don't know the way
To protect himself or again, he may
Be old and foolish enough to say:
"What's Safety First?"

Miner/writers also instruct their coworkers to avoid horseplay, pranks, smoking, and disobeying rules. Otherwise, they would endanger the common good and give management a way to be lax about safety.

If the machinery isn't safe, they want you
to run it just the same,
And then if you go and get yourself hurt
who do you think they blame! (YOU!)
As sure as day to dusk, dusk to night, and
a rainy day is long,
If you're a miner and want to live, you'd
better know right from wrong.[25]

Knowing right from wrong kept miners alive, and these writers never disguise the dangers of their work. Yet, like most people who work in dangerous jobs for either psychological or practical reasons, they do not dwell on the risks. Some of the writers say they avoid thinking about what could happen to them, while others redirect their thoughts to home. The persona in the following poem simply refuses to be cowed:

As this mole-man toils in the earth's dank
womb
The phantom of danger follows fast on his
heels;
Is hunched to spring on his every track.
But he laughs or voices a song or a curse,
And he stops for a moment to ease his
back.

The author of this poem captures the matter-of-fact way that miners go about their work without being immobilized by fear. Other writers say that miners need a stoic fatalism to return to the mine day after day. All would agree with a West Virginia miner's assertion that digging coal requires a special kind of courage: "There's a stamp they can't erase. / They fought death, conquered and gone / And lived to see the face." This is the voice of a miner who, like a Hemingway hero, has the skills and nerve to remain cool under pressure.

In a short poem entitled "Courage Within," a miner from Prenter, West Virginia, describes the heroic grace in the face of danger that marks a good miner:

To keep his head while in fright,
And find his way without a light;
To know his job from bottom to top
And beware the dangerous falling rock;
To administer first-aid to a dying buddy
Whether he be scratched or soakingly
  bloody;
To light the fuse and handle the worst
Knowing not when the seam will burst.
Though his face may be dirty
And his clothes all wet,
Not a more courageous man is found
Than under that dirt and sweat.[26]

Miners also share an acute sense of responsibility for one another in times of crisis. Mining lore is filled with stories of the heroic efforts of miners who lose their lives while trying to rescue trapped comrades. The wife of a Pennsylvania miner describes the courage of the rescue teams who battled a fire at the Mathies Mine in the fall of 1990:

Burns, scrapes and bruises,
You all had a few,
Off to the hospital; Oh, what a
  long ride!
Praying for teammates not at
  your side.

Your [*sic*] were not just a team,
A family you all became,
Worrying about each other,
You all felt the same.

Checked, taken care, wrapped
  burns,
And then you rested,
Picked, probed and your lungs
Were then tested.

Discharged and then given a
choice,
What did you do then?
Back to the mine,
They may need you again.

This concern for fellow workers carries over into the community and beyond. Miners feel responsible for the families of the injured and killed. As one Tennessee writer praises in an early 1950s poem, miners would "give their last dime to help you along."[27] When management exploits and the government neglects, a mining community provides its own safety net for those in need.

Despite the hardships of their lives, some contributors to the journal exhibit a willingness to laugh not only at themselves and their employers but also at the most frightening aspects of mining work. Few doubted that management's only real concern was production. No one felt the pressure more than the section boss.

"Coal!" the section boss cried,
As he ran through the crosscut, fit to be
tied.
"Coal!" he cried, as off he ran,
Going so fast he looked like a fan.
His face and shirt were wet with water,
He wobbled like a duck escaping the
slaughter.
His coattail sailed like a flag in the wind,
He passed everything on the section, his
face was grim,
His eyes looked wild, his nerves strung
tight,
He looked like a bull before the fight.
....
Down the runway he came and I stepped
aside,
In a cloud of dust he passed me by;
I wonder if he'll ever stop to rest,
His legs must be two of the best.
Off he traveled, for coal he had greed,
And he went out of sight picking up more
speed.

On some days nothing seems to go right. Recriminations become as thick as coal dust as everyone tries to "pass the buck" to explain the slowed production:

The coal's not movin' fast enough
So "knocks" come down the line;
The boss chews out the foreman
He passes it to the mine.

The foreman "knocks" the motorman
Who chides the switchman's pace;
The switchman blames the trackman
An' he says check the face.

Someone at the top finally works out the only conceivable solution to such a mess:

Some smart guy solved the problem
The man up at the top;
He blew the quittin' whistle
An' made the whole mine stop.

When management is not making things worse, the miners themselves are capable of such. In a poem from the coalfields of Utah, a new shift comes to work and discovers that the preceding one before it has left the mine in such disarray that no work can be done. The day shift curses the night shift. They complain that it is made up of farmers and other riffraff who know absolutely nothing about mining coal. The poem then ends with an O. Henry–like twist:

About that other shift that worked—
What's that?—You're sure you're
right?
The heck you say, how could that be?
There was no shift last night????

Even average days can be filled with inconveniences that, at the time, appear overwhelming:

The belt it broke and the splice it flew,
It hit my arm and I swallowed my chew.
I'm deep in pain, and really get sore,
And I tell the boss I won't fix it no more.
SORE KNEES, HEADACHE, PAIN IN
THE CHEST.

The boss, he's sore cause we bit a roll,
And he'll get hell if we don't load some
coal.
But it can't be done cause the Mole is
broke,
The armature grounded and started to
smoke.
COUGHIN', BOSS HOLLERIN', BOILIN'
MAD.

We spitter and sputter and finish the shift,
To get back in the mantrip is a heavenly
gift.
We put out our lights and hang down our
head,
Never felt better not even in bed.
GOIN' HOME, HUNGRY, FEELIN' GOOD.[28]

The above miner somehow survives his improbable day and is looking forward to going home. Other events in the mine are not so easily surmounted, but even these could be faced when blending humor with a sense of the absurd.

Accidental death was an everyday reality, but for Bob Fowler the best way of dealing with it was to satirize human frailties. In an eight-stanza poem, "Safety Slips," seven miners die because of their own carelessness:

Here lies the body
Of Johnny Blair,
Who stepped for the cage
But it wasn't there.

Beneath this stone
Lies Billy Hopp,
Might have been here yet
If he'd set a prop.
. . . .
Here lies the body
Of Freddie Bar,
Who wasn't afraid
Of the trolley wire.

Another poet, using a traditional form of humor associated with wakes, writes about the incredulous widow of a miner, who has heard so much blarney about her deceased husband that she believes her mind to be playing tricks on her. She asks for a second opinion:

> So to her son she does direct—
> "Look to that box without neglect,
> And please report, I do declare—
> If it's really your father lyin' there!"

Another miner finds humor in the absurd lengths that management will go to in avoiding government coal dust regulation. The poet first describes a pump designed by The Mine Safety and Health Administration that accurately measures the level of dust in a mine. He then reveals how management uses it:

> So the company comes down on the faceboss, and I
> swear this story is true.
> They tell him, "You'll get a good sample or you'll
> carry this pump till you do."
> So the operator signs for the dust pump, and some-
> times it sure makes him sore,
> When he finds it was out in the lamphouse, hidden
> behind the door.

Sometimes air samples are taken when nothing in the mine is running. These samples are free of dust.

> So now as my steps get much slower and I find that
> it's harder to breathe,
> I'll know that it's not from the coal dust as others
> have led me to believe.
> I'll not listen to what others have told me. Their
> theories are not worth a dime.
> Our government's little dust pump will prove there's
> no dust in the mine.

Just as miner/writers can laugh at themselves, at times they are intent on showing the unique character of miners. Numerous portraits of mining fathers by their children, for example, recall moments of tenderness. Some remember playing games with their fathers or learning important life lessons. The daughter of an Illinois miner writes, "He always told me to have / Respect, concern and love for others." A poet in Pennsylvania summarizes his father's personality as an incongruous mixture of opposing characteristics:

He is rough and yet he is gentle,
He is tough and yet sentimental.
He is the man I call father
And I am proud to say he is a miner.[29]

The poems capture how children admire and love a parent who, while engaged in the most demanding kind of work, still finds time for them.

Generosity and affection are not limited to family members in mining communities but, some contributors suggest, to anyone in need. According to one Alabama writer, a miner is not perfect but will always lend a helping hand:

In religion he isn't a saint,
He is seldom known to pray;
But with each brother he finds in need
He gladly shares what comes his way.

Not surprisingly, miners have great pride in themselves, each other, and their work. Poets express this special quality in verse.

His mighty muscles strain,
Superbly strong he walks along,
This man of unsung fame.
He battles bravely underground
Great danger, dampness, cold,
Rewarded for his faithfulness
With a nobler gain than gold.
So pity not the miner,
He possesses boundless wealth,
Contentment born of honest toil
And deep faith in himself.

In an unsigned poem entitled "The Coal Miner—The Rare Breed," the poet asks more probing questions about the direction and meaning of his life. What is most interesting about the poem is not so much the poet's quiet confidence that he has lived a useful life. Rather it is his belief that his work is the unifying framework for his exploration of the human condition:

If I strive for things that I value but others hold
with disdain, will it be said that I did not know?

If, after a lifetime of searching the total of my thoughts
contains no grand revelations, will I have failed?

At the end of my roaming, if there are two or three friends
who knew me let me ask of them—
Refer to me as one who never lost faith and tested that
faith against living.

Let them say of me: weak, strong, laughing, crying, loving,
rejoicing he was so real he seemed unreal—
He was the coal miner—the rare breed.[30]

Some of the poetry that tries to define the character of coal miners also offers the perspective of the mining wife. Carol Giesen, in *Coal Miners' Wives: Portraits of Endurance,* finds that shift work is nearly always a major concern. Wives also struggle with the dangers of their husbands' jobs and with the hardships resulting from strikes and layoffs.[31] Shift changes invariably cause family problems and force husbands to alter their sleep patterns and go to work exhausted. One Pennsylvania poet recalls her family's anxiety when her father worked the "hoot owl" shift:

When Dad works all night
   the next day fills us with dread
If someone yells - - - or even breathes
   it's, "Sh-h-h-h! Your Dad's in bed."
....
When Dad wakes up
   he's "Crab of the Day"
If we're using our heads
   we keep out of his way.

Our hearts fill with relief
   when third shift is gone
Because Dad is himself
   and the hassle is done.

Everyone is happy
   but we sure will be down
For we know that in two weeks
   third shift comes around.[32]

Economic problems plague mining families too, especially during strikes. The wife of a miner in Ohio's Hocking Valley writes:

Have you felt the need of bread, butter,
  And potatoes, too?
Did you ever live on bread and gravy
  For a full nine months through?

Did you ever have your children
  Come home from school at night,
Begging you for something
  That was simply out of sight[?]
. . . .
It takes a stouted [*sic*] hearted woman to be a
  miner's wife,
For to stand the ups and downs and the
  ills of life.
For to stand the strikes, the stops and stands
Which come to us every year in Hocking
  Valley lands.

Some miners' wives envy their husbands because they seem too busy to worry. But one sympathetic husband praises his wife as the true heroine in a poetic tribute. She stands alone to face the creditors:

When the store bill came due,
And other bills, too,
The wife always answered the door:
. . . .
Her face turned red
And she wished she were dead,
But she smiled even though she was sad.

But her husband could see
It was she and not he
Who had courage when life seemed so bad.[33]

Among the worries of miners' wives, first and foremost was the daily anxiety for the safe return of loved ones from the mines. A miner expresses these fears in a 1940 poem:

She lives a life of constant fear,
Believing death is ever near;
She hides a deep intensive fright
At sounds of blasting dynamite;
Almost every day that comes to pass
She reads of falls or deadly gas;
. . . .
Concealing feeling as best she can,
The life of the wife of the Miner Man.

This constant waiting fostered a special kind of bonding within the mining community. Wives of coal miners usually found the deepest friendships with each other. Among this group of friends was always someone who had lost a loved one in the mines.

The watching world
Sorrows with her for a spell, and then
Forgets, and she must bear her loneliness
Alone, save for those others who have
Also tasted grief, the ones the coal deep
In the earth has robbed of life.[34]

While children in coal towns did not necessarily brood about the dangers of the mine, they still lived in its shadow. Columbus Ratliff, who grew up in eastern Kentucky, describes in a short poem how children of miners were not used to seeing their fathers around the house. One day when the tipple breaks down and their father is home, the children, barely able to contain their glee, "gathered around and they all begin to grin, / George said, 'Mommy, who is that man?'" A poem by a miner's wife suggests that the closeness of her family helped to compensate for the absence of the material comforts:

Fried 'taters and beans, biscuits and gravy,
Family reunions and such,
Mama would sing gospel songs as we swung on the
grapevines
We had fun though we didn't have much.

The daughter of a West Virginia miner recalls walking home from the mine with her father. Each day he would save her something from his dinner bucket.

Thinking back I now wonder what it was I loved most,
The food or the talk with my Dad, so I could boast.
Was there really something different about the food he saved,
Or was it just that he would listen to what I had to say?
Did that little bit of food he save mean more than I could know,
Was that Daddy's way of telling me, Honey, I love you so!

Another daughter understood later in life the depth of her father's affection. Here she writes about his patience at the end of a hard day's work:

He worked in dust and coughed and choked
Other men might not even bother.
Though tired and worn he sat me on his knee
I'm proud he is my father.[35]

As much as black lung was feared in mining communities, fatal accidents in the mine were dreaded even more.[36] There is little indication that children had an inordinate fear for the safety of their fathers. Daughters may have felt the underlying tension more than sons, given their closeness to worried mothers. The daughter of a Pennsylvania miner, for example, recalls the prayer she offered that her father would be safe and that his days would be brightened in an unusual way.

Lord, watch o'er my daddy today,
Let me see his happy, dirty face
At the closing of this day.
Let it be a good day for him,
Right from the very start;
Let a little sunshine in,
At least into his heart.

The daughter of a Kentucky miner, who eventually followed her father into the mines, is more pessimistic: "It's like we're in another world / and survival is our aim."[37]

Although the primary concern of most children was the safety of their parents, they also understood economic problems. Low wages affected all family members, but none more so than young males. A retired miner who spent forty-six years underground recalls,

When I was twelve-and-a-half years old
My folks were mighty poor.

So my dad took me in the mine
To help keep the wolf from the door.

Now when we worked a full week
And both worked mighty hard.
We could keep the wolf away from the door,
But couldn't keep it out of the yard.

The sixteen-year-old daughter of an Indiana strip miner, in a 1974 poem, warns of the dangers of a new contract and a likely strike:

We don't have a cost of living provision
like most other industries do.
This will be an important part
of the contract we'll try to put through.
. . . .
We are thankful for our medical insurance,
we think it's a really good thing.
But we'd like to have a sick pay plan
for the peace of mind it will bring.

The wives and the children of miners
know that November 12 brings.
A tightening of belts and doing odd jobs
and hopes that it ends by spring.

Forty years earlier, a West Virginian, possibly a school teacher in a coal mining area, claims in "Children of the Mines" that the children of unemployed miners suffer the most. A child cannot understand the abrupt end to the family's happiness when a father is out of work. The daughter of a Pennsylvania miner recalls that everyone in her family dreaded the periodic closing of the mine:

They're always hoping
There will be work again tomorrow;
Sometimes there is, but sometimes
There's a home left in sorrow.
They have to earn a living though
They cannot live on "borrow,"
So they keep on hoping
There will be work on the morrow.

Ironically, while mining families regarded a busy coal tipple as a welcome sight, literature and film give it a sinister cast. Coal tipples darken the afternoon sky or serve as a kind of garish Walpurgis Night. But one West Virginia daughter of a miner, who grew up surrounded by two generations of a mining family, remembers their joy when they knew that the tipple was running:

> The humming tipple is a day of life,
> To a miner, his children and his wife.
> It is humming we feel secure.
> This means prosperity is at our door.[38]

Another common topic of coal mining poetry, not surprisingly, is the death of miners. Twenty thousand have been killed in the modern era.[39] Some of the literary pieces are memorials. They are for the living, a reminder that no mining death will be forgotten. One miner's wife dedicates her poem to the wives of coal miners all over America. The author describes an explosion in Mannington, West Virginia, one so devastating that the bodies of the dead had to be sealed in the mine. The poet confronts the tragedy in the only way that makes any sense to her:

> I am the wife of a miner, too,
> And I can understand.
> These men who are miners
> Are the bravest in the land.

While this poet believed that to memorialize the dead was to encourage the living, others blamed greedy management or simply accepted mining fatalities as inevitable. Still others fell back on their Christian faith.[40] Whatever the response, it was always filled with a complex range of emotions.

Some of these worker/poets seem to distribute the blame for mining disasters among management and labor. A more common belief, expressed by a miner in mid-1940, is that mining safety increases proportionally with union strength. An Oklahoma miner, writing during the Progressive Era, was angered by how the press, often in collusion with management, misled the public:

> Another explosion rends the air,
>   "Some miner with open lamp,"
> Wires reporter to his editor,
>   "Has fired a body of black damp."
> ....

The public reads and shudders for days
  As to work and homeward they tramp,
And wonder why miners will suicide
  By lighting this "deadly black damp."

....

But reporters see strange things every day
  As seeking the news they tramp.
They are the only ones who ever saw
An explosion caused by black damp.

Miner-writers tended to focus their creative protest on the one group they believed most responsible. Time and again in poems and stories, production demands lead to the bending of safety rules, to unnecessary risks, and, ultimately, to putting dollars ahead of lives. Another target was the public's insatiable demand for coal. State governments could also be blamed, with West Virginia leading the way. After the 1907 Monongah mine fire, in which 361 men lost their lives, one poet wrote,

Let us ask of West Virginia,
Is it right to kill wholesale?
And if she has got mining laws,
If so, why do they fail?
Have them repealed, you should.
Make ones that will not fail;
Don't enchore [*sic*], we do implore
Such scenes as Monongah.[41]

Many miner/writers tried to face tragedy by relying on traditional religious beliefs. These beliefs often evoked poetic testimonies that only God knows why tragedies occur and that the bereaved must ask for the strength to endure. Doing so is not always possible. Three years after Carrie Comper lost her husband to an Illinois mine, she still questions his death:

Three years have come and passed
Since our loved ones were lost in the terrible blast
That took the lives of one hundred eleven
Brave men, good, kind and true,
Who loved life the same as you and I.
We still ask the same old question—why?
Why did they have to be taken
From wives, mothers, fathers and children

Who loved them and missed them so?
And why did God choose to take them this way?
Maybe some day He will tell us
So we can understand.

Other writers hoped to comfort those left behind. They explain that God has a special place in his heart for all those who suffer, especially those killed underground. Writes Garland Vaiers from Peince Hill, West Virginia,

When a miner's life is snuffed out like that
the Lord knows he was doing his best;
He will say, come on, old boys,
And take your eternal rest.[42]

A miner's religion did more than help him deal with tragedy. One poet reaffirmed his faith daily by viewing the three commanding towers in his town: the coal tipple, the church spire, and the natural towers of the trees. Each pointed toward heaven and the Almighty. Another poet believed that managers would face a final reckoning in which they would have to account for their treatment of the workforce. Other miner/writers proclaim, with Old Testament certainty, that righteousness is on the side of the union and its supporters. The two most popular themes within the religious continuum, if the number of *UMWJ* contributions is any indication, point to the special way mining people will be judged in the final reckoning. There was a considerable difference of opinion on whether or not mining exists in heaven. The adage that miners will have a special place in heaven because they have known enough hell on earth has been quoted so often that it has become a part of mining folklore. Writers reason that their fellow workers can expect a special role in the hereafter since only God truly understands what they have been through on earth. The sentiment that God is partial to miners is clear in the West Virginia poem "Coal Miner's Final Exams."

I heard a reverend say one day,
"You will be judged by the deeds you have done,
When He adds your score and gets the total,
He will judge you lost or won."

I was wondering about the miner:
Will he be judged the same way as the rest,
Or will some credits be given him
When he goes up to take the test?

The exams for him should be easy,
If credit is given for hardships and toil,
For those who were crippled, those who were killed,
For just plain labor and those who were skilled.

In the following poem a miner's widow consoles herself with the thought that no one holds a privileged place in heaven.

In Heaven the miner and rich folk
Shall all be as one without doubt;
If a miner is ready for Heaven
That is one place the rich can't keep him out.

Miners would have their place in heaven, but the writers could not agree on whether they would find a coal mine there; those widowed by mine accidents hoped they would not. A poet memorializing her husband offers words of assurance: "But trust in God and be glad / There is no coal mine in heaven." Another writer, at the turn of the century, fondly reminisces about his working buddies and his family, who often walked with him to coal mine "Number Three." He says that there will be no coal mines in heaven since all manner of toil is left behind for those remaining on earth. Yet a heaven without mines is not what a West Virginia miner from Big Creek has in mind. As the last two stanzas of his poem suggest, heaven will have a kind of mining that exists nowhere on earth:

We will have a good local up there
Where the password is rest;
The contract up there is eternal
And no scabs ever come to molest.

No strikes ever happen in heaven;
The boss loves the men I declare.
The house is in order in Heaven
And some day I hope to meet you there.

A poet from Dupont, Pennsylvania, not only sees coal mining in heaven but believes that it adds to heaven's celestial beauty:

They gather strong at heaven's door
With all pick miners gone before;
God knew they had a talent proud—
So He signed them to cut a cloud.

They're workin' on those high plateaus
And singin' songs of heigh-heigh-ho's;
Just look at all the clever ways
Those old pick miners pass their days![43]

A number of miner/writers looked to the past with a clear appreciation for the struggles of those who had gone before them. The events at Lattimer and Ludlow and the West Virginia mine wars were reminders of past sacrifices. The praise directed toward such mining heroes as Mitchell, Lewis, and the UMWA is often hagiographic in tone. Others such as Mother Jones, FDR, Tony Boyle, and Richard Trumka are also singled out for special attention in the poems.[44] Mitchell, not surprisingly, is often remembered for his efforts during the 1902 Anthracite Strike; Lewis is praised for his confrontations with management and government over union recognition and contracts as well as his campaigns for paid vacations, hospitals, and pensions. Only occasionally does a poem of this type transcend the obvious. For example, Mother Jones is compared to John Brown, Mitchell to Daniel in the lion's den, and Lewis to a kind of Nietzschean *ubermensch* in his taming of coal barons:

Yes, my poor heart is broken for what used to be
Before John L. Lewis finally caught up with me.
But he comes along when everything's fine
And bellows, "Come in the union or close down your mine."
Now what in all Hades is a fellow to do
But get down and crawl when Lewis comes through.
That man's not a man but an arsenal of brains
That ties up non-union like convicts in chains.
That fellows won't work and I can't turn a wheel;
He's a confounded superman made of pure steel.

To the National Progressive Union of Miners, Lewis was anything but a saint. Using the extended metaphor of Lewis as the commander of a sinking ship, "Captain John's Gun Boat," this disgruntled worker/poet announces:

We've organized it's ten to one
The Progressive Union is a Moses'
son.
It broke the bands that enslaved our
lives.
And organized our daughters and
wives.

We know you heard that we were
Reds.
But no we're not! We want our
bread!
We're the same old bunch, we've
been for years.
We've changed our name, from the
Racketeers.

They cut our wages, they cut our
voice
They cut our hearts, they cut our
choice
Not satisfied when we were broke,
They turned around and cut our
throats.

Now John stands on the burning
deck,
Grabbing dollars by the peck.
Along came a Progressive brave and
true,
And said "John L., to hell with you."

By the 1940s Lewis had solidified his power and the Progressive miners had disappeared. The rank and file praised Lewis during the 1940s as much as the rest of the country maligned him.[45] Worker/poets struggled to address the negative popular image of miners and their union frequently throughout American history, but especially during World War II. Wartime demands, they believed, were justified. Despite hostile public opinion, miners were more patriotic than any other group of workers in the country. The secretary of a local in Chrichton, West Virginia, for example, argued in 1943 that since young miners had conquered their fears underground, they were better prepared than other recruits to face the enemy. Another poet points out that many mining families were actually fighting a war on two fronts:

Their sons were fighting over yonder
bearing their part of the brunt.
These fathers were also brave soldiers
And were fighting on the black diamond front.

Writing near the end of the war, a poet in Adena, Ohio, notes that the soldiers' work is done, "But the miner must still load his car— / The need for coal did not end with the war."[46]

In the 1940s, although the nation still depended heavily on coal, the traditional mining life was already becoming a thing of the past. This reality is apparent in two poems of the late 1940s. In "Do You Remember?" the poet nostalgically links together memories of what it was like to grow up in a coal camp during the hand-loading era. He probably did not realize that his elegy of times past hinted of things to come. A former anthracite miner concludes his piece with a stanza that foreshadows for the bituminous fields what has already come to pass in the hard coal region of Pennsylvania:

> The mine is gone, and the breaker's clatter
> The mules and the slopes and the miners'
>   chatter,
> But we still remember and always will
> The mine that stood there on the hill.

By the 1990s, the passing of a way of life was well underway. The sister of two retired miners recognizes this cessation in a poem reminiscent of Oliver Goldsmith's "The Deserted Village."

> I pause to look and listen
>   At this place once filled with life,
> Where are all the men who worked here,
>   Their children and their wives?
>
> The poplars still are standing
>   With ivy intertwined,
> Around the rock foundations
>   Of the houses, stores and mines.
>
> All that's left are rock foundations
>   Of the towns that lined the hills,
> Now the tipples and the bath houses
>   Stand deserted and quite still.[47]

Other mining poets were not content to describe a bygone era. They analyzed the impact of a dying industry on individual lives and communities. A poet from MacArthur, West Virginia, asks his readers to understand the loathing of unemployed miners for the machines that replace them. A Pennsylvanian tries to explain what it felt like to be part of a community without a future:

> Her days are bitter yesterdays,
> the people torn by sorrows;
> Her legends now are history,
> A town with no tomorrow.

This Utah miner from District 22 more elegantly describes his own sense of loss:

> Day after day
> I sit by the window
> Searching for memories
> To keep me alive
> How many times can I look
> On the same view
> And hold to the madness
> That helps me survive
>
> Lord can't you see it
> You sit right beside me
> And stare at the winter
> That keeps me inside
> Lord can't you feel it
> That desperate emotion
> Of a coal town in trouble
> And a working man's pride?
> ....
> Day after day
> There's no use in praying
> That things will get better
> So why even try
> Who really cares
> That this family's decaying
> Or a good man goes begging
> While this old coal town dies?[48]

To describe the passing of a way of life is one thing. To understand the reasons for it is quite another. In the works of miner/writers, economic explanations generally overshadow environmental ones. There are occasional laments about mining's impact. But these writers show no sustained interest in environmental issues. A short story published in the 1991 edition of *Tell It to the World,* the creative issue of the *United Mine Workers Journal,* suggests nonetheless that some within the mining community believe that economic issues cannot be separated from environmental ones. William B. Gamblin of Madisonville, Kentucky, writes about an unemployed miner, Billy Joe Simon, who worked twenty-four years in the mines, never graduated from high school, and found himself unemployed at age fifty. In a final act of frustration he carries into town a handmade sign: "I didn't cause acid rain!" With an elegance he never knew he had, he addresses the gathering crowd. A heckler calls out that high-sulfur Kentucky coal endangers every living species on earth. Simon reminds him that farm chemicals filter into the soil and rain and that the space shuttle put holes in the ozone layer; yet the miners are usually singled out for blame. Miners are easy targets, he argues, because they lack political power. "The only reason they want to do away with my job is that I hurt them the least," he explains. "I'm too young to retire, but too old to get a job. . . . All of you better worry, since you could join me tomorrow." As the crowd warms to Billy Joe's message, local law enforcers arrest him and charge him with disturbing the peace. He realizes that his message, so obvious to all, is the kind that inspires fear.[49]

Given the myriad hardships of the mining life and its potentially destructive impact, it is no surprise that a few miner/writers hoped to leave that life behind. Some could not overcome their fear of working underground. One Pennsylvania poet explains how he tried mining for a while but was terrified that the roof of the mine would fall. Some writers attacked the industry and the periodic closing of the mines. Others hated the monotony of daily work. Some poets complained about the cramped positions underground, while others felt like slaves. In a poem entitled "The Coal Miner's Widow," a dying miner tells his wife not to let their son follow him into the mines:

> The last thing John said was:
> "Anne, sell the old cook stove and bed,
> Go to your Ma.
> Tell Johnnie not to mine the coal,
> It doesn't pay at all.
> Good-bye, all my love to you—
> Tell Ma—
> Kiss Johnnie hard for me.
> Good-bye Anne, my darling,
> I'm a-goin' now."[50]

Worker/poet Jock Wilson never forgot why he became a miner. He interrupted his education at age thirteen to follow his father into the mines when his family needed money for his sister's operation. Though he had little choice in the matter, years later his anger is tempered by pride:

> Yet I was proud to bear the torch of brawn,
> Despite the fact I curse such dead-end means
> Of sustenance; to grope the fog-banked dawn
> And sweat eight hours for grits and black-eyed beans.[51]

Ed Falkowski, a radical former miner who often contributed to the *New Masses,* was, like Wilson, so exasperated by management that he saw anything associated with coal in the worst possible light. In poems such as "Coal Town," Falkowski describes the bleakness of mining life. In a short sketch, "A Miner's Good Morning," he writes of a miner who has lost hope: "He hates the life. Whenever he thinks of it, he must cry. Or drink and get crazy. There's no way out for him. The world is a locked place. The mountains—grimy culm banks—close him in. His whole life is lived inside a mine." Another poet of the 1930s, Stanley Kimmel, portrays a coal town minister in "Reverend Spilman." The poet sympathetically describes the grief this eighty year old carries after years of administering to a flock beset by tragedy:

> He leaned a little as he walked,
> Leaned as a tall tree leans with too much wind
>   against it.
> He must have gotten mighty tired trying to justify
> God's actions underground.[52]

Most miner/writers did not need to justify God's actions underground. Instead, they expressed pride in and satisfaction with their work. Three broad themes in the works of miners reflect these feelings. First is the belief that coal is essential to the economic well-being of modern-day society and that miners have played a special role in the country's industrial growth. Second is the focus on manliness, a quality miners believed to be essential to their work (which helps to explain the resentment toward female miners). The third broad theme suggests a sense of agency as miner/writers creatively reflect on the skill and imagination that go into mining coal, which adds dignity to their profession and purpose to their lives.

Coal generated much of the country's wealth, keeping its factories running and its people warm. In times of war, miners served their country both at home and abroad. But miners were often unappreciated and misunderstood. As a retired miner's wife explained in the 1970s,

Miners are humans and not rats
Going in and out of holes.
But men who helped make our Nation free
and beautiful.
For coal runs factories and big ships, even in
roads
Where everyone travels on,
The rich and poor and the humble ones
To church or maybe to work and to the
Stores.
Why it even makes plastic
That makes all kinds of things
From a big dish pan
To a bobby pin.
For all these we can be thankful to coal
mines and to its men.[53]

If most miner/writers acknowledged coal's importance to the nation, a few universalized its benefits. In a 1949 piece, one West Virginian suggests that even though miners seem forgotten in history, God keeps track of their many contributions. Another poet succinctly describes the importance of his work by concluding, "I blast from the innards of this world / the 'essential' of this age." An Illinois contributor to the *UMWJ* anticipated in 1960 that energy needs would still be filled by mining in the future. The modern world might depend on oil and atomic energy, but there would always be a need for coal:

Coal will be needed to power and light
To drive and heat our industrial might.
So continue to mine and work the seams,
For coal will be used to fulfill our dreams.[54]

Carol Giesen, in the book *Coal Miners' Wives,* concludes that these women felt society did not appreciate the importance of coal miners. "They, their parents, their children, and grandchildren were all part of a society in which those who produced materials to meet the basic needs of the society were devalued because of the nature of their service and often put at a disadvantage by those who received both the service and the profits."[55] Giesen is accurate in assessing the anger that mining families feel when their contributions are devalued, but many contributors to the *UMWJ* make it clear that mining people do not accept these social attitudes. Miner/writers reiterate that outsiders will never define them and that they will never allow the world to forget what they do.

Again and again they praise themselves and their work. They do not wait for others to do it for them.

At times this praise takes a masculine tone. Digging coal contributes to a miner's personal sense of manhood. Within mining communities this concept bears only slight resemblance to the middle-class view of masculine ideals that was popular at the turn of the century. The middle-class view emphasized the strong bodies of the working class, the pursuit of the strenuous life, and the latent primitivism of the masculine mystique.[56] Still, as Michael Kimmel writes, manhood is infinitely eclectic. It has always meant different things to different groups at different times.[57] To miner/writers, it has rarely meant the brute strength or "he-man" qualities of a Charles Atlas.[58] Instead, these working-class poets emphasize a kind of holistic manhood.

The earliest example of miners exploring the meaning of manhood is their insistence that "true men" stand up for their rights. To do otherwise was to be unmanly and subservient. The following poem translates a communal kind of manliness into active support of the union:

> Let our manhood parade in solid battalions;
> Organize, brother miners, and do all you can,
> Let reason and justice co-operate wisely
> Proclaim the American miner's a man.
> Range in battle array 'neath an organized emblem,
> Demand living wages, dodge it not, never shirk;
> It is better by far to starve going idle
> Then [*sic*] work for the idler and starve while we work.

Forces like owners, management, and state governments made it difficult at times for miners to stand by their beliefs. The following worker/poet suggests that these forces, egregiously united in some cases, threatened to strip a miner's sense of manhood.

> In West Virginia a man's like a mouse—
> Afraid to be seen in the light of day.
> A five year's lease in a company house
> And the frown of the boss makes him sneak
>   away.
> Why does he sneak to his hole in the mine,
> Or the wretched soap-box he calls his home?
> It's because the tyrants are a combine
> Chartered to crush him wherever he'll roam.

Another poet blames the work itself for undermining his manhood. "It takes away your manhood / And it's tiresome to your soul."[59]

Most miner/writers felt no damage to their manhood. In spite of all the dangers and hardships, the American coal miner prevailed because he was a "man among men." Poets hailed older miners who were tested throughout their lives but never succumbed. "You could take the dollar the bossman paid / And walk home proud—a man to be praised." John L. Lewis, who led his union against an angry nation, was "a brother, a man among men." One turn-of-the-century story features the heroic efforts of an engineer, Sheppard, who operates a lift in the midst of a raging fire until all miners are carried to safety:

> To-day tries the manhood of Sheppard;
> "To die for one's fellows is grand
> I'll hoist ev'ry miner that signals,
> Or burn to a crisp where I stand!"

During the era of World War II, there was some concern that the manliness of miners as well as their important role in society might be overlooked.

> The man who burrows far beneath the earth,
> What manner of man is he?
> Supplying the fuel for factory and hearth,
> A real man I'd say is he.
> ....
> A stern man yet noble and just,
> I've often heard is he;
> An honest man whom you can trust,
> A manly man is he.
>
> A man who asks no favor of life,
> In this man we can see;
> A man who can smile through hardship and strife,
> A man among men is he.

An Alabama writer expressed a similar concern for the miner's image. In "No Saint the Miner, But Every Inch a Man," he attests that although there are many easier ways to earn a living, "For me I'll choose to toil and die / With the lads who mine the coal."[60]

No miner/writer was Pollyannish about his job. All acknowledged the hardships and dangers of working underground. At times some hold management responsible for union busting, low pay, and lack of steady work.

Others complain about missing the seasons, living in darkness, or eating their meals in an atmosphere filled with dust. Some writers even claim to have become miners against their own wishes. Far more profess, however, a sense of agency in their work and pride in their connection to a mining community. Even as he notes that mining takes a fearsome toll on his body, a writer during the hand-loading era asserts that he "had a pride to make a living there." Over half a century later, a miner from Alabama proclaims his pride in a poem entitled "Old King Coal" by listing the many ways coal could be used. A contributor from Virginia explains that in a profession filled with contingencies, knowing when and how to use one's skills gives the most satisfaction:

> But a miner must mine the coal
> That challenges from the pit;
> For mining is what he knows
> What he has mastered
> What he must do.
> Coal-mining is his livelihood
> His peculiar independence
> His fierce pride
> His life.

Finally, a Pennsylvania miner who lengthily details how hard he works during the week is more succinct in describing what happens on payday—he could relax, have a drink or two, and take the time to think "Of my good wife and my good life / I owe to coal, body and soul!"[61]

A number of miner/writers were satisfied in knowing that they did a difficult job well. Others emphasized the challenges they faced. Sandy Stiltner Coleman, who followed her father into the mines, was proud of doing a job that few women had ever considered.

> I never dreamed I'd go this far
> To keep food on our table
> But the money I earn is honest and clean
> And I'm proud of my coal miner label.

Other miners simply liked being important players in a larger picture. They were proud to help provide the many coal-based products of a consumer society and the power that ran industry around the world. A contributor from Coal City, West Virginia, tries to explain what it is about mining that he believes miners find the most appealing:

It isn't the pay, tho it's better now,
It is not that they love the work
There's a challenge there to meet each day,
And this they never shirk.[62]

Coal mining was so embedded in the heritage of some families that pursuing another career was almost unthinkable. While some parents hesitated to allow their children to enter the mines, others were eager for them to do so. Wartime poems anticipate sons returning home safely from overseas to resume the work their grandfathers and fathers have always done. For one poet writing in the 1950s, the decision to enter the mines is as much a matter of genetics as a career decision: "There's coal in their blood, coal in their talk." Ted Verbitsky, the former head of a local in Suffolk, Pennsylvania, recalls how immigrant coal diggers fought for all mining people's rights at a time when the union was trying to solidify its right to bargain collectively. These immigrant miners viewed the miner's lamp as a kind of Olympian torch to be passed down from one generation to the next:

"From our heads," I heard them cry,
"Take the burning lamp before we die.

"Harken! Let it not darken, harken!
But hold it high.

"So that we may see
Our way to dig to eternity.

By the time Verbitsky composed his poem, most of the men he wrote about were dead. Several poets, perhaps hoping to preserve their own memories, praised the mining life after having retired.

These former miners, who hoped to justify their work, instead explain the pure joy they had in doing it. Writers from Fairmont and Charleston, West Virginia, agree that as retired miners they could always hold their heads high. More typical is the response of an elderly West Virginian. Although reconciled that his prayers will not be answered, he wants nothing more than to do what he has always done:

Though we pray and we pine till we're weary and sick,
Fate never will answer our prayer:
To feel the old thrill, of the shovel and pick,
And to be with the gang that was there.[63]

Although, like most writers in this chapter, Barbara Angle was a worker before she was a writer, her case is exceptional because much of her writing has been published outside the pages of the *UMWJ.* The choice to create fiction rather than poetry also sets Angle apart from other miner/writers. Yet much of her work is autobiographically based. Like her protagonist in *Those That Matter,* she too lost the use of an arm in a mining accident. But this is not why her work provides a fitting coda to miner/writers' perspectives. In a short story entitled "Any Man: Kate's Story," a novelette entitled *Rinker* (1979), and her most recent novel, *Those That Mattered* (1994), Angle has produced a more sustained body of work than any other writer who held a coal shovel.[64] All three works, but especially her novel, examine in greater depth than any other creative writer the experiences of women miners. Although she is a devoted supporter of the union, her support is member oriented. She dedicates *Those That Mattered* to the rank and file of the UMWA, whose voices she is most interested in capturing. With an insider's perspective similar to that of Denise Giardina and others, she tries to portray mining folk as intricate, contradictory, and often fascinating human beings rather than heroic or tragic symbols of oppression.

Her first work, *Rinker,* is similar to Alexander Solzhenitzyn's *One Day in the Life of Ivan Denisovich* in that it is intended to provide the reader with insights into an unique way of life. In this early work Angle is, at times, as guilty as other writers in generalizing about West Virginia coal miners. Many of their interests may well involve the out-of-doors, but her claim that "they trust instinct over reason, custom over innovation, union over management, and most of them, hell over an uncertain heaven" belies the social complexity that she develops in later work.[65]

Angle subtly explores the feelings of comradeship, solidarity, and even love that many miners feel for their comrades underground. The novel's main character, Rinker, who started working in the mines when he was twenty, has a wife and young children who are still living at home. The heart and soul of the miners' local, a six-foot-four committee member known as the Dutchman, in his gruffness and sardonic humor, commands respect but not necessarily affection from those around him. Rinker and the Dutchman have known and appreciated one another long enough to feel something more than friendship. "Now Rinker eyes him, appreciatively. Dutch catches the look. For a moment the facade slips, and they half-grin at each other, a look of mutual respect and love. It is a powerfully good feeling. Both look away hurriedly; these are emotions not to be confronted."[66]

The characters in *Rinker* engage in a never-ending war between management and labor on a daily basis. Regardless of union and government regulations, dozens of years of hostility are not easily forgotten—nor is the feeling that the two invariably are working toward opposing objectives. It is an undeclared war with no resolution. If Rinker has little faith in the company's concern for its workers, he is just as skeptical of the labor bureaucrats in his own union. Management in both company and union is concerned primarily with its own well-being. The rank-and-file workers must depend on themselves. Such sentiments help explain the affection and trust that miners like Rinker and the Dutchman feel for one another, and the sense of pride they have in their work.

Angle tries to show why men like Rinker not only choose to become miners but, more importantly, stick with the profession. She develops a kind of dialogic tension that is both intriguing and inconclusive. The author editorializes about mining in the book's first paragraph: "They say it's a hell of a life. It's a good life. But only for someone with a calling to work the coal."[67] Rinker becomes more relaxed and aware in the total blackness underground. His senses become more acute, similar to the volunteer camion drivers described by Malcolm Cowley in *Exile's Return*: "The underground coal miner has a heightened sense of life and of his ability to deal with it: an intimacy. If there is a sense of manliness and pride among coal miners it is with good reason."[68] A large part of Rinker's manliness is his acceptance of who he is and the decisions he makes, particularly those choices that have led him to mining. His life is by no means perfect. As he approaches middle age he is torn between trying to act responsibly as a family man and dealing with the expectations of younger miners who, because of his experience, anticipate that he will always be the voice of opposition toward management. Rinker becomes angry, for example, when his younger partner wants him to deal with the foreman's daily abuse. Feeling guilty about his temper, Rinker struggles to explain his anger as a product of their work: "This place . . . ah, this place just gets to a man . . . I guess. It ain't human nature to work in a . . . hole." With the end of the day in sight and a warm shower awaiting him, however, Rinker reflects, "not such a bad life. Hell sometimes but not so bad." As he begins his drive home, Rinker addresses the miner he carpools with:

> He turns to Blue, whose eyes are still ringed black with coal, same as his own eyes.
>
> "Say, Blue,"
>
> "Ummm?"
>
> "Did you ever seriously think about getting out of mining?"[69]

Here the novel ends. Angle is content to close the conversation, the workday, and the novel with a question.

Female miners are virtually invisible in Angle's novelette. This is not the case in *Those That Mattered,* which was published fifteen years later. Angle follows the youngest child in a West Virginia mining family from early adolescence to her mid-thirties, when an accident ends her work underground. Portia is reminded daily that she is not accepted underground, that she is depriving a man of a job, and that she could make more money by putting a cot up at the pit mouth. She tries her best to ignore it all. Early on, the abuse goes far beyond traditional initiation rites: "the physical assaults in dark crosscuts; the stalking when she attempts to relieve herself, the excrement in her lunch box, the grabs for her ass, and the constant drilling of new peepholes in the bathhouse." Verbal assaults are even worse. Not surprisingly, women seem to resent her as much as men. Wives of miners call her a whore. The younger generation of women denigrates her for accepting the abuse. Portia comes to see herself and the one other female miner as "aliens in the world of the underground and freaks to those outside."[70] Yet she learns that many of the older miners are helpful and supportive. A grudging respect even emerges among the younger men, especially when they are not in groups. In the last chapter, when the buggy in which Portia is riding overturns and severs her arm, the men respond as they would to any fallen comrade. In the throes of agony, Portia realizes that she is finally accepted and that the crew will protect her. As the miner leading the rescue finally removes his hand from her artery, leaving Portia to await an ambulance, she puts the past behind her. Her "gaze follows the man as he leaves, trying to say . . . maybe thanks. . . . Maybe that she loves him for his caring."[71] In a chapter from an early draft of the novel, excerpted in *Rank-And-File Voices,* Kate (Portia in the novel) slowly recovers in a Baltimore hospital with a crippled arm. Those at the hospital attribute the healing to her "stamina and toughness," while Angle's third-person-omniscient narration suggests that it is more a matter of the needs of Kate's one-year-old son and "the union men's sympathy." Portia's character is complex in a different way. Angle endured much of the same kinds of abuse as her character, but she still dedicated the novel to her fellow miners. Having Portia's recovery helped along by "the union men's sympathy" would be too much like the conclusion of a formalistic 1930s novel, in which all problems are resolved through the union or the Communist Party. The hospital staff still praises Portia's toughness in the later version, but her recovery is more personal in its relationship to "a confused little boy who only understands that his mother has left him."[72]

The life of a female miner provides the narrative structure of *Those That Matter.* As she follows the history of the Crowe family and its most recalcitrant member, Angle weaves together such universal concepts as love, death, birth, betrayal, friendship, and the relationship between parents and children. Angle also explores, more than most in the genre, why an educated person such as Portia would choose to be a miner.

A child of the coalfields, Portia has a greater sense of place than does Mary Alice in *Death of a Miner*. Her sense of place is similar to that of characters in Giardina's and Settle's works. Her decision to work in a mine is closely tied to family relationships and to how she views herself. When her future husband, a Pentecostal minister named Saul O'Brien, tells her that divinity school will at least temporarily take him away from the coalfields, she cannot understand why anyone would want to leave. She shares a love of the region with her father, Daniel. "You have to be of the mountains to know," he points out; "born and bred, a piece of them." Ironically, Daniel's job is the cause of marriage problems, arthritis, black lung, and alcoholism. After one particularly demoralizing exchange with his wife, Ida, he exclaims within Portia's hearing, "I always said I'd shovel shit before I'd shovel coal. Now it just seems I do both." Portia learns, however, that what Daniel says is not always what he feels. Shortly after she turns fifteen, she asks her father to take her into the mine as a special Christmas present. Against company rules, the two slip into the closed mine. Daniel takes her to see the huge cutting machine that he operates. "Pops, you really handle that thing?" she asks. "Child I love it. She's part of me. I talk to her, coax her into cuttin' like she should. Nothin' else I'd rather be doin', despite my bitching."[73]

Portia is as rebellious as her father. She refuses to adopt the typical role of a woman, a minister's wife, or even a member of the Crowe family. Her revolt encompasses an extra-marital affair, single motherhood, and a job mining coal. When her father dies in a mine accident, Portia blames the company rather than the job itself. She learns quickly that mining is not for everyone. "Portia will learn that the mine affects men differently. To some, as to her, it seems strangely soothing, belying its reported vindictiveness. Others find it threatening and become bitter at being forced to work in a hellhole to maintain a life that doesn't seem worth it." Unlike her father, Portia cannot focus solely on her job. She has to fend off the blatant sexism of the miners below ground and the townspeople above. Despite this abuse and the challenges brought by a divorce, she is still content with her life. Shortly before the accident that will end her mining life, she thinks about where she is and how she has gotten there. "She is contented. *Happy* is too extreme a word, but things aren't bad: with the baby, the job, the life."[74] Her future is unclear, but she does not try to escape the mining world. The beauty of Angle's book is that it shows that men and women who dig coal dwell in a world unto themselves. They are like the rest of us in the mutuality of their humanness but different in how they perceive their lives. This difference does not suggest a limiting sense of "otherness" but instead a subjective awareness that agency is a fragile ideal that holds the promise of adding direction and purpose to our lives while knowing full well that the odds are often against us.

The other writers analyzed in this chapter also describe aspects of this working-class culture as diverse, contradictory, fascinating, ambiguous, and engaging as those in Angle's novel. Undoubtedly the filters of writing in a union journal influenced the ways stories were told, but it is also obvious that these mining people were describing the one thing that they knew better than anyone else: their lives and their work. All discourses are problematical, assumptive, and differently accented, but it should be clear that mining people and communities are not the imaginative creations of writers and intellectuals. They have lives, interests, and concerns of their own making, and although no attempt is made here to fully define the nature of mining culture, it should be obvious by now that many of those who have aspired to do so have done little more than construct artificial moats separating "us" from "them."

Conclusion

While some writers actively assisted miners, others merely wrote about them. Nearly all, however, envisioned mining people as "the other." Like Proteus, "othering" takes various forms. Some writers are driven by creative ambition, others by ideology or politics. Most hold a myopic view of mining people. They sympathize with them over their hard work but nonetheless portray them in limiting and stereotypical ways. In fiction, theater, film, literature for older children, and poetry, mining people are portrayed as one-dimensional working-class character types. Their creators regard them as objects without subjectivity. But not all writers try to simplify life in the coalfields. Giardina and West, Settle and Angle, Cizmar, authors of books for early age levels, Perez and Naylor, and contributors to *Coalseam* as well as the *UMWJ* try to depict mining people in more sophisticated and creative ways. In doing so they distinguish themselves from the majority of writers in the genre.

Except for the miner/writers in chapter eight, the authors examined here are professionals who made a living with their craft. Reed, Sinclair, Dreiser, Dos Passos, Frank, and Vorse were also hoping to find the good story in the good cause. They were willing to go to the coalfields and help the striking miners, but they did not allow those experiences to interfere with their writing. Paulo Freire, an educational theorist, explains that volunteers and investigators must frequently visit the area they are helping or studying if a dialogical process is to emerge between outsiders and those being helped.[1] Most of the writer/activists offered nothing more than token gestures of support. Their work in the coalfields was short, symbolic, and often unresponsive to what the miners really needed. The miners' struggle was buried beneath agendas addressing larger issues. Whether it was rapacious monopoly, class war, free speech, international fascism, or Dreiser's treatment in Kentucky, no one consulted the miners to ask: "What direction should our activism take?" The miners' struggle assumed a conceptual "otherness" and was confronted by these advocates on their own terms. Lloyd, for example, was dismayed when the miner's wife he had prepped rejected his plan to publicly discuss her family's suffering.

West and Giardina stand apart from other writers in that their activism was diffuse, persistent, and locally rooted. Yet neither should be viewed in strictly parochial or regional terms. Many of West's poems touch on themes that have nothing to do with Appalachia. Though West located his Folklife Center in a region in which he felt most comfortable, his concern for the poor knew no geographical boundaries. Giardina's spiritual beliefs were equally universal. Her interest in Bonhoeffer reflects the interplay between deeply felt moral issues and matters of social justice, which have always attracted her. In any case, West and Giardina worked best with people they knew and understood. Their activism reflects a humility and coherence that is absent from writers who are well-intentioned but ill-informed. They were less inclined to view mining people as "the other." While Giardina was a writer who found time for her activism and West was an activist who found time to write, each of them acknowledged that mining people had voices of their own.

Most writers are closer to Stephen Crane than West and Giardina in their creative responses to coal mining culture. Like Crane they were both attracted to and repulsed by that culture, but not to such an extent that it became a consuming literary passion or social concern. They wrote about it and moved on to other issues that fascinated or perplexed them even more. Yet the real question is not why so much literature exploring this culture lacks depth and creativity but why so many writers approached the topic in the first place. Why have authors written about coal mining more than any other kind of industrial work? Perhaps Crane's initial reaction upon entering a mine for the first time has something to do with it. Beyond Tzevtan Todorov's impressive study about the fantastic, there must be something primordial and thus creatively compelling about entering an underground world each day to make a living.[2] The darkness, the dangers, the uncertainties, the camaraderie, the anxieties, the daily return to the surface, the ritualistic cleansing—it all offers unlimited imaginative opportunities. Yet interestingly enough, most of the novels, plays, films, children's fiction, and poems are creatively lacking in fantasy—even in imagination. Many writers, directors, and playwrights never get far from violent strikes, hideous disasters, and grieving families in their imagined coal mining communities.

The coal mining culture can elicit fear and dread, two creatively compelling emotions. As Harry Levin posits in *The Power of Blackness,* the optimistic individualism of American life has a dark side that accepts the isolation of the human soul and questions the benevolence of the universe.[3] Crane pitied the breaker boys for their limited aspirations, for their failure to pursue the American dream. The myth of American exceptionalism implies that working-class status should be temporary. No worker should spend a lifetime digging coal. The breaker boys knew no better. In ascribing this limited world view to all miners, writers imply "otherness." The character of working people is defined by what they do, not who they are.

Like Native Americans and communists, miners were viewed as dangerous impediments to national progress.[4] If as Roger Cunningham suggests America has used Appalachia as a "projection-screen" for its own failings, writers have used miners to symbolize their fear of the working classes.[5] This negative view of miners may be related to our cultural attitude toward work itself. Just as working-class life is to be temporary, work itself is associated with indentured servants, slaves, "new" immigrants and—in our own time—the foreign born. According to Julia Kristeva, throughout much of the modern western world

> The foreigner is the one who works. While natives of the civilized world, of developed countries, think that work is vulgar and display aristocratic manners of offhandedness and whim (when they can . . .), you will recognize the foreigner in that he *still* considers work as value. A vital necessity, to be sure, his sole means of survival, on which he does not necessarily place a halo of glory but simply claims as a primary right, the zero degree of dignity.[6]

Writers, directors, and playwrights, especially in the last thirty years, have at times engaged in a kind of reverse reading of history. No one better reflects this trend than Robert Schenkkan, who after a brief visit to eastern Kentucky painted its history with panoramic stereotypes. He and other writers interpret the poverty of an area where coal is no longer mined as representative of the mining way of life. Unlike P.J. Laska, who sees decaying coal towns and unemployed miners as symbols of postindustrial America, some writers imply that these ecological, sociological, and economic wastelands of today differ little from their condition a hundred years ago.

However writers may approach the mining culture, their work usually reveals more about themselves than anything else. Labor historian Leon Fink's analysis of intellectuals who try to articulate the attitudes and beliefs of workers applies to those writing about mining folk. No matter how sympathetic the effort may be, "when 'intellectuals' propose to speak for 'workers' . . . their own self-image plays a large (and usually unexplored) role in the histories the intellectuals 'discover.'"[7] Sociologist Dorothy E. Smith shows how the value-laden assumptions associated with sociological inquiry can help explain how writers relate to their subjects:

> Riding a train not long ago in Ontario I saw a family of Indians: woman, man, and three children standing together on a spur above a river watching the train go by. There was (for me) that moment—the train, those five people seen on the other side of the glass. I saw first that I could tell this incident as it was, but that telling as a description built in my position and my interpretations. I have called them a family; I have said they were watching the train. My understanding has already subsumed theirs. Everything may have been quite other for them. My description is privileged to stand as what actually happened, because theirs is not heard in the contexts in which I may speak.[8]

Filthy working conditions, dreary and blighted towns, accounts of terrifying explosions underground—the incontestable realities of mining life translate into fictional narratives about broken bodies and stunted lives. Yet, most of the writers who have creatively reacted to this way of life have not ventured far beyond it. Essentially they have been one-dimensional in assuming that anyone doing this kind of work has to be different from the rest of us. From a slightly different perspective, Gayatri Spivak reiterates that "the unrecognized contradiction within a position that valorizes the concrete experience of the oppressed, while being so uncritical about the historical role of the intellectual, is maintained by a verbal slippage."[9] There is no doubt that coal miners were exploited and their struggles with management were real. They could not have achieved what they did without a struggle. Using Spivak's analytical model, however, it can be argued that when writers describe the exploitation of coal miners they are projecting their own fears and values rather than those of the miners. Like the slaves in Stanley Elkins's bleak depiction, miners do little more than respond to a controlling institution. They are brave, determined, and resourceful, but the odds are too often stacked against them. Their work rather than their humanity propels their lives. Mining is so alien to the typical work experience that a conceptual gulf separates "us" from "them." Surface images become total realities. Perceptions become truth. What is different becomes "the other."

A handful of creative individuals venture beyond the "othering" of mining people to invite a conversation among themselves, their characters, and their readers. This dialogue assumes the uncertainty and psychological groping of all human relationships as well as the provisional understanding and acceptance that may grow from them. Whether or not writers describe miners realistically seems unimportant. What matters more is how writers, their characters, and their readers confront the human condition within the framework of coal mining culture. Whether examining the tensions of class injustices and misunderstandings, the inability to reconcile personal needs with social responsibilities, or the inevitable incompatibility of anger and reconciliation, writers such as Giardina, Settle, and Cizmar have engaged in discourse rather than resolution. In the imaginative landscapes of their creations, both author and reader are "located in a real unitary and as yet incomplete historical world, which is to say, a world that is unfinalizable and in which the activity of writing and reading is shaped by presentness."[10] This sense of "presentness" emanates from imagination, humility, and compassion, enticing the reader to become a part of the dialogical process. The character in the play, poem, or novel is not "the other" but simply "another" who interacts with writer and reader alike.

While writers have creatively approached the coal mining culture from varying perspectives, most are essentially voyeuristic, compelled to look from one world into another.[11] For Barbara Angle and the miner/writers examined in chapter seven there was less distance between the world of their imaginations and the world in which they lived. Unlike Angle, most of the miner/writers wrote poetry, a form of expression closer to song, which is an intrinsic part of many working-class cultures. The steady flow of poetic contributions to the *United Mine Worker's Journal* through to the present day suggests that poetry continues to be a popular genre for workers.[12] Poets in the mining community were writing about their work and life experiences from the inside out. Their lives and creative outlets differed considerably from those of writers such as Settle, Giardina, Cizmar, and Still. Yet both groups nurtured a dialogical exploration of the diverse American coal mining experience. They neither defined nor limited its boundaries. Instead, they accepted its retelling as a process that is as uniquely personal and unpredictable as it is unending. This may not have insured the dialogical or even reflected the "truth," but at least, to use Richard Rorty's expression, it kept the conversation going. It also insured a resounding acknowledgment of Frantz Fanon's impassioned plea at the end of *Black Skin, White Masks:* "I want the world to recognize, with me, the open door of every consciousness."[13] Mines may continue to close. Coal may eventually be replaced as a key energy source. But as poet Howard Nemerov tells us, "The world is a very deep place, no matter how much of it we explain, and explain away, and the end of a particular form of experience does not mean the end of experience."[14] Knowing that the past can never be completely unlocked, a lesser-known poet also writing in the modern period hikes through an abandoned mining village and wonders about the people who lived there:

Walking this deserted canyon
In my mind I try to recall

Where is the company store, the post office
And the school that stood so tall?

I pause to look and listen
At this place once filled with life,
Where are all the men who worked here,
Their children and their wives?[15]

The more American coal mining recedes into the past, the more we may try to recapture it in our imaginations and memories. Let us hope that it will continue to be told in ways that uphold the dignity of the men and women of the coalfields. Let us hope that mining people will no longer be viewed as "the other" but as human beings engaged in a different but not dehumanizing kind of work. Perhaps it is time for us to reach the same conclusion that Homer Hickam did in his reminiscence of the West Virginia mining community in which he grew up: "The stars were complex and deeply mysterious. Coalwood and its people, it often seemed to me, were vastly more so."[16]

Notes

Introduction

1. John Grisham, *The Firm* (New York, 1991), 5, 133.

2. Elmore Leonard, *Pronto* (New York, 1993), 200-201.

3. Leonard, *Riding the Rap* (New York, 1995), 173.

4. Ibid., 320.

5. James Jones, *From Here to Eternity* (New York, 1998), 93.

6. Over the years I have had a number of informal conversations with Frances Hensley about growing up in Oceana, West Virginia. Hensley is the Associate Provost and Senior Vice President for Academic Affairs at Marshall University in Huntington, West Virginia.

7. Tzvetan Todorov, *The Conquest of America: The Question of the Other* (New York, 1992); Todorov, *On Human Diversity: Nationalism, Racism and Exoticism in French Thought* (Cambridge, Mass., 1993); Edward Said, *Orientalism* (New York, 1979).

8. Gayatri Chakravorty Spivak, *A Critique of Postcolonial Reason* (Cambridge, Mass., 1999), 171.

9. Spivak, "Can the Subaltern Speak?" in *Colonial Discourse and Post-Colonial Theory,* ed. Patrick Williams and Laura Chrisman (New York, 1994), 75.

10. Robert F. Berkhofer, *The White Man's Indian* (New York, 1978), 3-31; Chandra Talpade Mohanty, "Under Western Eyes: Feminist Scholarship and Colonial Discourse," in *Colonial Discourse and Post-Colonial Theory,* 200, 196, 220; Allen Batteau argues in *The Invention of Appalachia* (Tucson, 1990), 16-17, 56-58, 81-82, 127-44, that politics, commerce, and industry help shape the concept of Appalachia and Appalachians.

11. Todorov, *Conquest of America,* 132.

12. Abdul R. JanMohamed, "The Economy of Manichean Allegory," in *The Post-Colonial Studies Reader,* ed. Bill Ashcroft, Gareth Griffiths, and Helen Tiffin (New York, 1995), 18.

13. Said, *Orientalism,* 231.

14. Philip Rahv, "The Cult of Experience in American Writing," in *Essays on Literature and Politics* (Boston, 1978), 8-22; Shelly Fisher Fiskin, *From Fact to Fiction*

(New York, 1985), 3-10; Leo Braudy, "Realists, Naturalists and Novelists of Manners," in *Harvard Guide to Contemporary American Writing,* ed. Daniel Hoffman (New York, 1979), 84-152.

15. David S. Reynolds, *Beneath the American Renaissance: The Subversive Imagination in the Age of Emerson and Melville* (New York, 1988).

16. Eric J. Leed, *The Mind of the Traveler from Gilgamesh to Global Tourism* (New York, 1991), 3.

17. Ralph Ellison and Eugene Walter, "Interview with Robert Penn Warren," in *Writers at Work: The Paris Review Interviews,* ed. Malcolm Cowley (New York, 1965), 196-97.

18. David Sanders, "Interview with John Dos Passos," *Writers at Work,* 4th ser., ed. George Plimpton (New York, 1977), 84.

19. Mary Gordon, "The Angle of Malignity: The Cold Beauty of Katherine Anne Porter," *New York Times Book Review,* April 16, 1995, 17.

20. "No. 154, In the Depths of a Coal Mine," *Tales, Sketches, and Reports,* vol. 8, *The University of Virginia Edition of the Works of Stephen Crane,* ed. Fredson Bowers (Charlottesville, 1973), 923-24.

21. Tzvetan Todorov, *The Fantastic: A Structural Approach to a Literary Genre* (Ithaca, 1975), 24-40.

22. Crane, "In the Depths of a Coal Mine," 591, 593-94.

23. Ibid., 595.

24. Ibid., 599, 596-97.

25. Ibid., 592.

26. Jack B. Reese, *Grubbing the Bowels of the Earth* (Smithfield, Pa., 1988), 9, 170.

27. Bruce Chatwin, *The Songlines* (New York, 1988), 2.

Chapter One: Idiosyncratic Activism while Assisting "The Other"

1. Daniel Aaron, *Men of Good Hope* (New York, 1961), 136-53; Chester Destler, *Henry Demarest Lloyd and the Empire of Reform* (Philadelphia, 1963), chapters 7, 9, 10, and 13; E.J. Jernigan, *Henry Demarest Lloyd* (Boston, 1976), 21; John L. Thomas, *Alternative America: Henry George, Edward Bellamy, Henry Demarest Lloyd and the Adversary Tradition* (Cambridge, 1983), 135.

2. Henry Demarest Lloyd, "The Story of a Great Monopoly," in *The Lords of Industry* (New York, 1910), 14; *Wealth Against Commonwealth* (New York, 1984), 510.

3. Henry Demarest Lloyd, *A Strike of Millionaires against Miners* (New York, 1970), 9, 51, 55-56; Destler, *Henry Demarest Lloyd and the Empire of Reform,* 227.

4. John. F. Power to Dear Friend, Spring Valley, Illinois, January 3, 1889. Microfilm edition of Henry Demarest Lloyd Papers, State Historical Society of Wisconsin (hereafter cited as Lloyd Papers).

5. John Foley to Henry Demarest Lloyd, Chicago, September 20, 1889; L.M.P. Brady to H.D. Lloyd, Spring Valley, Illinois, October 7, 1889, Lloyd Papers.

6. John McBride to Henry Demarest Lloyd, Massilion, [Ohio], September 23, 1889, Lloyd Papers.

7. James O'Hare to H.D. Lloyd, n.p., October 11, 1889, Lloyd Papers.

8. H.D. Lloyd to *Chicago Tribune,* n.p., October 11, 1889; H.D. to Father Power, *Chicago Tribune,* October 17, 1889, Lloyd Papers.

9. H.D. Lloyd to Father Power, *Chicago Tribune,* November 2, 1889, Lloyd Papers.

10. H.D. Lloyd to Father Power, *Chicago Tribune,* November 3d, 1889, Lloyd Papers.

11. Aaron, *Men of Good Hope,* 143.

12. Lloyd, *A Strike of Millionaires against Miners,* 125-67.

13. Ibid., 199

14. Material pertaining to the 1902 strike has been obtained from Robert J. Cornell, *The Anthracite Coal Strike of 1902* (New York, 1957); Elsie Gluck, *John Mitchell: Miner: Labor's Bargain With The Gilded Age* (New York, 1969); Perry K. Blatz, *Democratic Miners: Work and Work Relations in the Anthracite Coal Industry, 1875-1925* (New York, 1994), 121-69. Related studies examining the entire anthracite region include Donald L. Miller and Richard E. Sharpless, *The Kingdom of Coal: Work, Enterprise and Ethnic Communities in the Mine Fields* (Philadelphia, 1985); Anthony F.C. Wallace, *St. Clair: A Nineteenth Century Coal Town's Experience with a Disaster-Prone Industry* (New York, 1987); John Bodnar, *Anthracite People: Families, Unions and Work, 1900-1940* (Harrisburg, 1983); *Hard Coal, Hard Times: Ethnicity and Labor in the Anthracite Region,* ed. David L. Salay (Scranton, 1984).

15. Cornell, *Anthracite Coal Strike of 1902,* 170.

16. H.D. Lloyd to Dr. Haynes, Little Compton, R.I., 1902, Lloyd Papers.

17. H.D. Lloyd to John F. Power, Little Compton, R.I., September 17, 1902, Lloyd Papers.

18 Charles Forcey, *The Crossroads of Liberalism and the Progressive Era, 1900-1925* (New York, 1971), passim; *Walter Weyl: An Appreciation* (Philadelphia, 1922), passim. Not all writers supported the striking miners. Ray Stannard Baker, *American Chronicle: The Autobiography of Ray Stannard Baker* (New York, 1945), 166-67, was angered by the way he believed members of the UMWA prevented miners who did not sympathize with the strike from working.

19. Examples of the kind of research and writing that he was doing are found in the *United States Bureau of Labor Bulletin* 11 (November 1950), 723-856; 6 (January 1902), 1-94.

20. Walter Weyl to John Mitchell, 9 West 68th Street, New York, September 5, 1902. Microfilm edition of John Mitchell Papers held at West Virginia University (hereafter cited as Mitchell Papers). James Marwick to Walter E. Weyl, New York, November 5, 1902, Mitchell Papers. H.D. Lloyd to Jessie Bross Lloyd, Wilkes-Barre, Pa., October 17, 1902, Lloyd Papers; H.D. Lloyd to Jessie Bross Lloyd, October 18, 1902, Lloyd Papers; H.D.L. to J.B.L., October 19, 1902, Lloyd Papers; H.D.L. to J.B.L., October 22, 1902, Lloyd Papers; H.D.L. to J.B.L., November 12, 1902, Lloyd Papers. Charles Destler has edited the most important of Lloyd's letters during this period of his stay in the coalfields: "On the Eve of the Anthracite Coal Strike: Henry D. Lloyd at United Mine-Workers Headquarters, October-November 1902," *Labor*

History 13 (1972), 279-95. The only discrepancy is that the letter from Lloyd to his wife dated October 20, 1902, in the Destler article is October 19, 1902, in the Lloyd Papers. John Mitchell to John R. Commons, Hotel Hart, Wilkes-Barre, Pa., October 29, 1902, Mitchell Papers. There is a disappointing lack of material pertaining to the strike in the Weyl Papers in the Special Collection and Archives, Rutgers University Libraries. Harold W. Aurand, in "Do Your Duty," *Hard Coal, Hard Times,* 153-62, attempts to gauge the editorial perspectives of some of the country's newspapers during the strike.

21. J.A. Horwick to Walter W. Weyl, Washington, D.C., October 30, 1902, Mitchell Papers; Walter W. Weyl, "John Mitchell: The Man The Miners Trust," *Outlook* 82 (March 24, 1906), 657-62; H.D. Lloyd to Jessie Bross Lloyd, Wilkes-Barre, Pa., October 22, 1902, Lloyd Papers; H.D.L. to J.B.L., November 7, 1902, Lloyd Papers.

22. H.D.L. to J.B.L., New York, December 4, 1902, Lloyd Papers.

23. H.D.L. to J.B.L., December 5, 1902, Lloyd Papers.

24. H.D.L. to J.B.L., December 9, 1902, Lloyd Papers.

25. H.D. Lloyd, *Men, the Workers* (New York, 1909), 251-252.

26. H.D. Lloyd to Jessie Bross Lloyd, Wilkes-Barre, Pa., October 7, 1902, Lloyd Papers.

27. Forcey, *Crossroads of Liberalism,* 67-70.

28. H.D. Lloyd to John Mitchell, Winnetka, Ill., February 27, 1903, Lloyd Papers. Since Weyl did not have the financial resources to pay his way, it can be assumed that his expenses were covered by the UMWA.

29. H.D. Lloyd to Father John F. Power, Little Compton, R.I., August 18, 1890, Lloyd Papers.

30. Czeslaw Milosz, *Native Realm: A Search for Self-Definition* (Berkeley, 1981), 80.

31. H.M. Gitelman, *Legacy of the Ludlow Massacre: A Chapter in Industrial Relations* (Philadelphia, 1988), 4-10; H. Lee Scamehorn, *Mill and Mine: The CF & I in the Twentieth Century* (Lincoln, 1992), 1-37.

32. George S. McGovern and Leonard F. Guttridge, *The Great Coalfield War* (Boston, 1972), passim; Priscilla Long, *Where the Sun Never Shines: A History of America's Bloody Coal Industry* (New York, 1988), 167-331; Gitelman, *Legacy of the Ludlow Massacre,* passim; Barron D. Beshoar, *Out of the Depths: The Story of John R. Lawson* (Denver, 1942), passim; Zeese Papanikilas, *Buried Unsung: Lous Tikas and the Ludlow Massacre* (Salt Lake City, 1982), passim,; John Graham, introduction to *The Coal War: A Sequel to "King Coal"* by Upton Sinclair (Boulder, 1976), vii-ix; Priscilla Long, "The Voice of the Gun: Colorado's Great Coalfield War of 1913-1914," *Labor's Heritage* 1, no. 4 (October 1989), 4-23. H. Lee Scamehorn, in *Mill and Mine,* 38-55, bases his examination of the strike entirely upon company records and thus provides a one-sided managerial perspective of the conflict; Melvyn Dubosky, in "The Origins of Western Working-Class Radicalism, 1890-1905," *Labor History* 7 (spring 1966), 131-154, offers an interpretative analysis of the entire region.

33. See *The Masses* 4 (July 1913) for Eastman's editorial and a cartoon by Art Young about the Associated Press. Max Eastman, *Enjoyment of Living* (New York, 1948), 464-65, 467-73; Art Young, *His Life and Times* (New York, 1939), 295-300.

34. Granville Hicks, *John Reed: The Making of a Revolutionary* (New York, 1937), 139-44; Robert A. Rosenstone, *Romantic Revolutionary: A Biography of John Reed* (New York, 1975), 170-79.

35. Eastman, *Enjoyment of Living,* 449-52.

36. Eastman, "Class War in Colorado," *The Masses* 5 (June 1914), 5-8; "The Nice People of Trinidad," *The Masses* 5 (July 1914), 5-8. John Reed, "The Colorado War," *Metropolitan* 40 (July 1914), passim.

37. Eastman, *Enjoyment of Living,* 452.

38. Eastman, "Class War in Colorado," *Masses* 5 (June 1914), 5-8.

39. Rosenstone, *Romantic Revolutionary,* 174.

40. Eric Homberger, *Americans Writers and Radical Politics, 1900-39* (New York, 1986), 72.

41. Reed, "Colorado War," 11.

42. Eastman, *Love and Revolution* (New York, 1964), 452.

43. George Creel, *Rebel at Large* (New York, 1947), 127-28. Edwin Markham, Benjamin B. Lindsey, and George Creel published *Children in Bondage* (New York, 1914) the same year as the Ludlow massacre. The chapter on child labor in coal mining, "The Cost of Coal," 94-113, was written by Markham and deals exclusively with the Pennsylvania anthracite region as does the material in the introductory chapter, 28-30.

44. Unidentified newspaper clipping in George Creel Papers, Manuscript Division, Library of Congress. (The collection is cited hereafter as Creel Papers.)

45. Ibid.

46. *Rocky Mountain News,* April 27, 1914.

47. George Creel, *Rebel at Large,* 128.

48. From unidentified but dated newspaper clippings in a scrapbook in the Creel Papers.

49. George Creel, "The High Cost of Hate," *Everybody's* 30 (June 1914), 770.

50. *New York Times,* April 30, 1914. In 1908 Sinclair visited Denver, met Judge Ben Lindsey, and visited a gold mine; there is no evidence that he was aware of the problems of the Colorado coal miners at the time. Leon Harris, *Upton Sinclair: American Rebel* (New York, 1975), 111-112; John Graham, "Upton Sinclair and the Ludlow Massacre," *The Colorado Quarterly* 21 (summer 1972), 55-67.

51. Upton Sinclair, *The Brass Check: A Study of American Journalism* (Pasadena, 1919), 143.

52. *New York Times,* April 30, 1914.

53. Ibid.

54. Ibid., May 2, 1914.

55. Ibid., May 4, 1914.

56. Graham, introduction to *The Coal War,* by Upton Sinclair, xii.

57. Upton Sinclair to Fred D. Warren, [Girard, Kansas], October 22, 1914, in the Upton Sinclair Papers, Manuscript Department, Lilly Library, Indiana University. (The collection is cited hereafter as Sinclair Papers.)

58. *Appeal to Reason,* May 16, 1914; May 30, 1914.

59. *Rocky Mountain News,* May 14, 1914; Sinclair, *The Brass Check,* 150.

60. Sinclair, *The Brass Check,* 154-60; *Appeal to Reason,* May 30, 1914.

61. Sinclair, *The Brass Check,* 181.

62. John Reed to Upton Sinclair, Provincetown, Mass., June 4, 1914, Sinclair Papers.

63. Untitled typescript in Sinclair Papers on which Sinclair wrote in pencil at the top: "I wrote this and Lawson read it at the Committee's hearing in N.Y."

64. Senate, 64th Cong., 1st sess., Dec. 6, 1915–Sept. 8, 1916, S. Doc. 415, vol. 26, *Industrial Relations Final Report and Testimony Submitted to Congress by the Commission on Industrial Relations;* vol. 8, *The Colorado Coal Miner's Strike Testimony, Jan. 29, 1915,* 8004-8008.

65. *New York Times,* February 13, 1932.

66. John W. Hevener, *Which Side Are You On?: The Harlan County Coal Miners, 1931-39* (Urbana, 1978); John Gaventa, *Power and Powerlessness: Quiescence and Rebellion in an Appalachian Valley* (Urbana, 1980); Theodore Draper, "Communists and Miners, 1928-1933," *Dissent* 19 (spring 1972), 371-92; Rony Bubka, "The Harlan County Coal Strike of 1931," *Labor History* 11 (winter 1970), 41-57; Alessandro Portelli, *The Death of Luigi Trastulli* (Albany, 1991), 195-238; Shaunna L. Scott, *Two Sides to Everything: The Cultural Construction of Class Consciousness in Harlan County Kentucky* (Albany, 1995), 39-66.

67. Hevener, *Which Side Are You On?,* 14, 34.

68. Gaventa, *Power and Powerlessness,* 96-104.

69. Ibid.

70. Draper, "Communists and Miners," 371-380.

71. Harvey Klehr, *The Heyday of American Communism: The Depression Decade* (New York, 1984), 74-75; Richard Lingeman, *Theodore Dreiser: An American Journey, 1908-1945* vol. 2 (New York, 1990), 347-48; Malcolm Cowley, *The Dream of the Golden Mountains* (New York, 1980), 55-58.

72. Lingeman, *Theodore Dreiser,* 335; Daniel Aaron, *Writers on the Left* (New York, 1961), 178.

73. *New York Herald Tribune,* December 22, 1931; Lester Cohen, "Theodore Dreiser: A Personal Memoir," *Discovery* 4 (1954), 119.

74. Murray Kempton, *Part of Our Time* (New York, 1967), 108.

75. Draper, "Communists and Miners," 377-380.

76. *Pittsburgh Press,* June 26, 1931.

77. National Committee for the Defense of Political Prisoners (hereafter NCDPP), *Harlan Miners Speak: Terrorism in the Kentucky Coal Fields* (New York, 1970), 3-6; Theodore Dreiser to President of Transylvania College Dr. Arthur Braden, New York, October 29, 1931; William J. Hutchins to Theodore Dreiser, Berea, Kentucky, November 2, 1931, Theodore Dreiser Papers (hereafter Dreiser Papers), Charles Patterson Van Pelt Library, University of Pennsylvania.

78. Lester Cohen, "Theodore Dreiser, A Personal Memoir," 106-08.

79. Theodore Dresier to Roy W. Howard, New York, October 29, 1931. A trip itinerary is also found in the Samuel Ornitz Papers (hereafter Ornitz Papers), The State Historical Society of Wisconsin, University of Wisconsin.

80. *Knoxville News Sentinel,* November 9, 1931; Lingeman, *Theodore Dreiser,* 359-60.

81. NCDPP, *Harlan Miners Speak,* 187-88.

82. *New York Herald Tribune,* November 17, 1931.

83. NCDPP, *Harlan Miners Speak,* 101-102; John Dos Passos, *The Theme Is Freedom* (New York, 1956), 75, 80, 84; Townsend Luddington, *John Dos Passos: A Twentieth Century Odyssey* (New York, 1980), 298-299; Lingeman, *Theodore Dreiser,* 358; *Lexington Herald,* November 9, 1931; *New York Times,* November 9, 1931; *Middlesboro Daily News,* November 1931. Lester Cohen, in "Theodore Dreiser, A Personal Memoir," claims that he and Dreiser went to Coal Creek where they interviewed miners while other committee members went elsewhere.

84. James Agee, *Let Us Now Praise Famous Men* (New York, 1960), 54.

85. John Dos Passos, *The Theme Is Freedom,* 73-87; *In All Countries* (New York, 1934), 194.

86. "A Letter from Samuel Ornitz," n.p. [1915], Ornitz Papers.

87. Samuel Ornitz, "Bleeding Bowels in Kentucky," *New Masses* 7 (October 1931), 3-4.

88. Theodore Dreiser to Marion Foster Wetherspoon, New York, November 22, 1932, Dreiser Papers.

89. NCDPP, *Harlan Miners Speak,* 10.

90. Ibid., 91-93, 101-02, 130-31, 199, 229, 277-78, 285-86, 288-89, 292-94.

91. Ibid., 17-27.

92. William Stott, *Documentary Expressionism and Thirties America* (New York, 1973), 202.

93. NCDPP, *Harlan Miners Speak,* 285.

94. Ibid., 102-129; Dos Passos, *The Theme is Freedom,* 75.

95. NCDPP, *Harlan Miners Speak,* 321.

96. Hickerson co-authored a play with Maxwell Anderson based on the Sacco-Vanzetti trial, but throughout a busy life he devoted most of his creative energies to a musical career. For Boynden, the wife of a Chicago lawyer, writing was more of a hobby than a profession and her one novel, *The Pink Egg,* was read only by friends. Quincy Howe, on the other hand, was multitalented but is best remembered as a pioneer radio broadcaster who helped establish the field of news commentary and analysis as well as a founder and editor of *Atlas.* Edmund Wilson, *The Thirties,* ed. Leon Edel (New York, 1980), 162.

97. Waldo Frank, *Memoirs of Waldo Frank* (Boston, 1973), 180.

98. Cowley, *Dream of the Golden Mountains,* 67-68.

99. Mary Heaton Vorse, Daily Summaries, 1932; Charles and Adelaide Walker to Mary Heaton Vorse, New York, January 29, [1932], Mary Heaton Vorse Papers (hereafter Vorse Papers), Walter Ruther Library, Wayne State University.

100. Edmund Wilson's letter to John Dos Passos dated February 29, 1932, appears in Edmund Wilson's book *Letters on Literature and Politics, 1912-1972,* ed. Elena Wilson (New York, 1977), 221. Wilson, *The Thirties,* 184-86.

101. Malcolm Cowley, "Kentucky Coal Town," *New Republic* 60 (March 2, 1932), 67.

102. *Pineville Sun,* February 10, 1932.

103. Malcolm Cowley, "Cumberland Gap," seven-page typescript, n.d., in Malcolm Cowley Papers (hereafter Cowley Papers), Newberry Library, Chicago.

104. Ibid.; Cowley, *Dream of the Golden Mountains,* 69.

105. Cowley, *Dream of the Golden Mountains,* 69; Wilson, *The Thirties,* 169-70.

106. Wilson, *The Thirties,* 171-78; Frank, *Memoirs,* 181.

107. *New York Times,* February 17, 1932; February 22, 1932; Cowley, *Dream of the Golden Mountains,* 75.

108. Senate, *Conditions in Coal Fields in Harlan and Bell Counties, Kentucky. Hearings before a Subcommittee of the Committee on Manufactures,* 77th Cong, 1st sess., on S. Res. 178. May 11, 12, 13, and 19, 1932. Cowley testimony 56-61.

109. Paul J. Carter, *Waldo Frank* (New Haven, 1967), 70.

110. William Bittner, *The Novels of Waldo Frank* (Philadelphia, 1955), 120-48.

111. Unless otherwise stated, indications of Frank's concern about his writing come from Waldo Frank's Notebook, January 1929–July 1932, Waldo Frank Papers, Van Pelt Library, University of Pennsylvania.

112. Aaron, *Writers on the Left,* 355.

113. Cowley, "Kentucky Coal Town," 68.

114. Ibid.; Cowley, "Cumberland Gap," 4, Cowley Papers.

115. Cowley, "Cumberland Gap," 7.

116. Ibid., 5; The same material slightly changed is found in *Dream of the Golden Mountains,* 69-71.

117. Wilson, *The Thirties,* 160.

118. Edmund Wilson, *The American Jitters* (New York, 1932), 303.

119. Ibid., 150-69; This same material is found in a two-part article in the *New Republic* issues of July 8th and 15th, 1931.

120. Edmund Wilson, "An Open Letter to Walter Lippmann," *New Republic* 68 (November 11, 1931), 345.

121. Edmund Wilson's letter to John Dos Passos dated February 29, 1932, appears in Wilson's *Letters on Literature and Politics,* 222.

122. Charles and Adelaide Walker to Mary Heaton Vorse, New York, January 29, [1932], Vorse Papers.

123. Vorse, Daily Notes, December 1931, Vorse Papers.

124. Ibid.; Vorse, Daily Summaries, 1932, Vorse Papers.

125. Vorse, Daily Notes, December 1931, Vorse Papers.

126. Vorse, Daily Notes, January 1932.

127. Ibid.

128. Ibid., February 1932

129. Wilson, *The Thirties,* 171-72; Mary Heaton Vorse, *Rebel Pen: The Writing of Mary Heaton Vorse* (New York, 1985), 43-47.

130. Vorse, Daily Notes, November 1932, Vorse Papers.

131. Ibid., April 1932; May 1932.

132. Mary Heaton Vorse, "Rendezvous," Vorse Papers.

133. Gaventa, *Power and Powerlessness,* 96-116.

134. John Dos Passos, "In Defense of Kentucky," *New Republic* 69 (December 16, 1931), 137.

135. Spivak, *A Critique of Postcolonial Reason,* 171.

Chapter Two: Two Appalachians: Don West and Denise Giardina

1. Unless otherwise indicated, the biographical material on Don West has been obtained from: FBI Files on Don West (File No. 100-20396, Sections 3, 7, 8, Series 46-61, 120-155) in the Personal Papers of Don West, Cabin Creek, West Virginia (hereafter cited as West Papers); Interviews with West by author, Cabin Creek, West Virginia, May 6, May 22, May 29, July 3, July 10, 1992 (hereafter cited as Interviews with West); Talk by Don West, January 21, 1975, Chapel Hill, N.C., transcribed by Linda Killen for the University of North Carolina at Chapel Hill Southern Oral History Program: Labor History Series, original transcript on deposit at the Southern Historical Collection, Louis Round Wilson Library, Chapel Hill, N.C. (hereafter cited as Talk by Don West, Labor History Series Transcript); Jessie Stuart, "Portrait of a Mountain Boy," in *In a Land of Plenty: A Don West Reader,* by Don West (Los Angeles, 1982), 9-12; Don West, "Harry Harrison Kroll," a four-page typescript in West Papers.

2. David E. Whisnant, *All That Is Native and Fine* (Chapel Hill, 1983), 109-110. Don West, "Life at Berry," clipping from unnamed newspaper dated October 17, 1924, in West Papers. West claims that his feelings about Berry and its missionary efforts have changed considerably since he wrote the article. Interviews with West, May 29, 1992. Tracy Byers, "The Berry Schools of Georgia," *Missionary Review of the World* 56 (January 1933), 33-36.

3. Stanley Lincoln Harrison, "The Social Gospel Career of Alva Wilmot Taylor" (Ph.D. diss., Vanderbilt University, 1975); David E. Whisnant, *Modernizing the Mountaineer: People, Power, and Planning in Appalachia* (Knoxville, 1994), 14-17.

4. Don West, "Alva Taylor—Man for Humanity," *The New Southerner* 1 (April 1956), 4.

5. The best description and analysis of the strike is Anthony P. Dunbar, *Against the Grain: Southern Radicals and Prophets, 1929-1959* (Charlottesville, 1981), 1-15. See also Fount F. Crabtree, "The Wilder Coal Strike of 1932-33" (master's thesis, George Peabody College for Teachers, 1937).

6. Dunbar, *Against the Grain,* 4-8.

7. Interviews with West, May 6, 1992; May 22, 1992.

8. Ibid.

9. Dunbar, *Against the Grain,* 9-10.

10. Interviews with West, May 6, 1992.

11. Antonio Gramsci, "The Intellectuals," in *Selections from Prison Notebooks* (London, 1971), 3-23; Harold Entwistle, *Antonio Gramsci: Conservative Schooling for Conservative Politics* (London, 1979), 118, 124-27.

12. Interviews with West, May 22, 1992.

13. Untitled and undated thirty-two-page (pp. 35-67) typescript of portions of an interview fragment with West, 48, 53, West Papers.

14. Interviews with West, May 6, 1992; May 22, 1992.

15. For an insightful, brief discussion of the Danish schools, see Whisnant, *All That Is Native and Fine,* 128-33.

16. Interviews with West, May 29, 1992.

17. John M. Glen, *Highlander: No Ordinary School 1932-62* (Lexington, Ky., 1988), 16-17; Frank Adams, *Unearthing Seeds of Fire: The Idea of Highlander* (Winston-Salem, 1975), 26-30. West has always insisted that he founded Highlander and then, and only then, invited Horton on board.

18. Alva M. Taylor, "Building Gains over the South," *Christian Century* 49 (September 21, 1932), 148.

19. Glen, *Highlander,* 26.

20. According to West, "Reinhold Niebuhr was Horton's man, Alva Taylor more my man." Too often the Northerners that Horton brought with him to Highlander were reminiscent of the missionary types who taught at the Hindman school in Whitesburg, Kentucky. Both Don and Constance West had been associated with the school during the Vanderbilt period and immediately after, Constance having taught there for about two years. Interviews with West, May 22, 1992; Untitled and undated thirty-page typescript of interview fragment, West Papers.

21. Thirty-page typescript of interview fragment.

22. FBI File on Don West, File No. 100-20396, Section 7, 1, Serials 120-155, 11-12, West Papers.

23. Dunbar, *Against the Grain,* 54-56; Interviews with West, July 10, 1992.

24. Richard J. Altenbaugh, *Education for Struggle: The American Labor Colleges of the 1920s and 1930s* (Philadelphia, 1990), 189-90.

25. Dunbar, *Against the Grain,* 56-59; Charles H. Martin, *The Angelo Herndon Case and Southern Justice* (Baton Rouge, 1976), 110-113; Thirty-page typescript of interview fragment; Talk by Don West, Labor History Series Transcript, p. 12; Interviews with West, May 6, 1992.

26. Interviews with West, May 6, 29, 1992. The Kayjay Mine mentioned by West may have been the Arjay Mine described by Jim Garland, who claims that West replaced him as an NMU organizer in the winter of 1933, *Welcome the Traveler Home: Jim Garland's Story of the Kentucky Mountains* (Lexington, Ky., 1983), 180.

27. Interviews with West, May 6, May 22, May 29, July 3, 1992; Archie Green, *Only a Miner: Studies in Recorded Coal-Mining Songs* (Urbana, 1972), 84-86. Dunbar, in *Against the Grain,* 142-43, claims that the Wests were arrested in the spring of 1936, but articles in the *Daily Worker,* October 29, November 1, 1935, suggest that West and a fellow organizer were arrested in October 1935. West reportedly said while testifying: "Certainly, I'm a Communist. . . . I was born and raised in these mountains. My people have always been crushed down in poverty. I'm a Communist because the Communist Party is leading the workers out of poverty and fighting for better conditions every day." Whether West spoke these precise words is unknown,

but the claim that he had his upbringing in "these mountains" is stretching the imagination, though the Appalachians do stretch from Kentucky to Georgia. In a later article for the *Daily Worker,* November 8, 1935, he described the crimes of several of his fellow cellmates as common examples of the "unorganized struggle of the poor against the rich."

28. Talk by Don West, Labor History Series Transcript, p. 10.

29. Don West, "Something of America," in *In a Land of Plenty,* 177; Mike Gold, editor of the *New Masses,* in an unidentified newspaper clipping, claims that the poet was released after "Kentucky friends" posted a five thousand dollar peace bond, West Papers.

30. Ken Sullivan, "Don West, Poet and Preacher," *Golden Seal* 5 (October-December 1979), 56.

31. Interviews with West, May 29, 1992.

32. Dunbar, *Against the Grain,* 143-144, 197.

33. Interviews with West, May 22, 1992. In 1967 West published a sermon entitled "Jesus the Quiet Revolutionary," which he had been preaching, in one form or another, all of his life. *In a Land of Plenty,* 186-89.

34. FBI File on West, no. 100-20396, Section 8.

35. Interviews with West, May 22, 1992. For an interesting discussion of the Hindman school *mentalité,* see Whisnant, *All That Is Native and Fine,* 19-101. Allen W. Batteau, in *The Invention of Appalachia* (Tuscon, 1990), 80-81, briefly analyzes the Berea College image.

36. Whisnant, *All That Is Native and Fine,* 260-61; T.J. Jackson Lears, *No Place of Grace: Antimodernism and the Transformation of American Culture 1880-1920* (New York, 1981), 60-96, analyzes therapeutic aspects of the nineteenth-century folk art movements in the United States.

37. Interviews with West, May 6, 1992.

38. Don West, "We Move to Pipestem," *The Appalachian South: Cultural Heritage—Folklore, Song, History, People* 2 (fall and winter 1967), 3-4.

39. Interviews with West, May 22, 1992.

40. Ibid., May 6, 1992; May 22, 1992; May 29, 1992; July 10, 1992.

41. *The Charleston Gazette,* May 25, 1978.

42. I am indebted to the McCreary County Public Library for providing me with valuable information about the strike. They were especially kind to send me Richard A. Couto's *Redemptive Justice: Church-Based Intervention in the Pursuit of Justice* (Whitesburg, Ky., 1979). Additional information was obtained from the *McCreary County Record,* March 1, 8, 15, 22, 29, April 5, 19, May 3, 10, June 2, 28, July 12, August 23, 1977; April 25, May 2, 30, July 11, September 12, November 7, 1978. *Louisville Courier Journal & Times,* June 19, 1977.

43. Unless otherwise indicated, material on the Appalachian South Folklife Center has been obtained from the following sources: Interviews with West; Sullivan, "Don West: Poet and Preacher,"; "The Appalachian South Folklife Center" and "Report to Our Friends," both reprinted by permission from *Gamaliel Magazine* (spring 1976) in West Papers; West, "We Move to Pipestem"; Peggy Perterman, "A Haven for

Mountain Heritage," reprinted from the *St. Petersburg Times,* December 30, 1976, in West Papers; *The Atlanta Constitution,* August 20, 1989; *Beckley Post-Herald,* July 1, 1982; *Bluefield Daily Telegraph,* January 23, 1974; *Hinton News,* August 10, 1978. The following clippings were found in the Don West Clipping File, West Virginia Archives, Charleston, West Virginia: *Beckley Newspapers Inc.,* October 16, 1984; clipping entitled "Folklife Center Is Emerging as a Living Memorial" from unidentified periodical; *Charleston Gazette,* June 17, 1967; "Don West," *West Virginia Hillbilly,* July 27, 1989, 16.

44. *Charleston Gazette,* May 25, 1978.

45. Bryan Hodgson, "Mountain Voices, Mountain Days," *National Geographic* 142 (July 1972), 118-46.

46. Unless otherwise indicated, the biographical material pertaining to Denise Giardina has been obtained from: George Brosi, "Denise Giardina: A Biographical Essay," *Appalachian Mountain Books* 3 (1987), 4-6; Interview with Giardina by author, Whitesburg, Kentucky, June 26, 1992 (hereafter cited as Interview with Giardina); Thomas E. Douglas, "Interview: Denise Giardina," *Appalachian Journal* 20, no. 4 (summer 1993), 384-93; Denise Giardina, "Appalachian Images: A Personal History," in *Confronting Appalachian Stereotypes: Back Talk from an American Region,* ed. Dwight B. Billings, Gurney Norman, and Katherine Ledford, with a foreword by Ronald D. Eller (Lexington, Ky., 1999), 161-73.

47. Kai T. Erikson, *Everything in Its Path: Destruction of Community in the Buffalo Creek Flood* (New York, 1976); Gerald M. Stern, *The Buffalo Disaster* (New York, 1977).

48. Don J. Goode, "A Study of Values and Attitudes in a Textbook Controversy in Kanawha County, West Virginia: An Overt Act of Opposition to Schools" (Ph.D. diss., Michigan State University, 1984), 89-125; Catherine Ann Candor, "A History of the Kanawha County Textbook Controversy, April 1974–April 1975" (Ph.D. diss., Virginia Polytechnic Institute, 1978), passim; Goode's and Candor's dissertations are held in Marshall University Archives. For a description of his activities as a parish minister before the textbook controversy see James Lewis, *West Virginia Pilgrim* (New York, 1976).

49. Interview with Giardina. Candor, in "A History of the Kanawha Textbook Controversy," 126, 132, 137, 143, 208-211, describes how outside, right-wing groups like the Heritage Foundation, Citizens for Decency through Law and Order got on the textbook bandwagon.

50. Interview with Denise Giardina; Charles C. Geisler, *Who Owns Appalachia? Landownership and Its Impact* (Lexington, Ky., 1983).

51. Denise Giardina, "A Coal-Field Victory," *The Progressive* 53 (March 1989), 14-15.

52. Interview with Giardina.

53. Nicholas Mills, "A Victory for Miner's Rights," *Nation* 242 (February 15, 1986), 175-78; "Labor Draws the Line," *Commonweal* 112 (September 6, 1985), 452-53; "The Coalfield Heavyweight Who's Going the Distance," *Business Week,* (October 21, 1985), 123, 126, 128. Richard A. Couto's piece "The Memory of Miners

and the Conscience of Capital: Coal Miners' Strikes as Free Spaces," in *Fighting Back in Appalachia: Traditions of Resistance and Change* (Philadelphia, 1993), 165-94, provides an excellent overview of events leading up to the Massey and Pittston strikes as well as insightful analysis of the miners' perspectives of the actual strikes. The most recent and best overall account of the Pittston strike is James R. Green's "Tying the Knot of Solidarity: The Pittston Strike of 1989-1990," in *The United Mine Workers of America: A Model of Industrial Solidarity?,* ed. John H.M. Laslett (University Park, Pa., 1996), 513-44.

54. Interview with Giardina.

55. Ibid.; Denise Giardina, "Union-Busting Rooted in History," *Charleston Gazette,* June 19, 1985.

56. *New York Times,* December 23, 1989; Couto, "The Memory Of Miners," 173-75.

57. Denise Giardina, "Moving Mountains," *Southern Exposure* 17 (summer 1989), 44.

58. Interview with Giardina.

59. Unless otherwise indicated, material pertaining to Giardina's activities during the Pittston Strike has been obtained from Interview with Giardina. To get a feeling for the elan and solidarity of the miners and their supporters during the strike, see Jim Sessions and Fran Ansley, "Singing across Dark Spaces: The Union/Community Takeover of Pittston's Moss 3 Plant," in *Fighting Back in Appalachia,* 195-223.

60. Giardina, "Moving Mountains," 45; Giardina, "Solidarity in Appalachia," *Nation* 249 (July 3, 1989), 14.

61 Giardina, "Moving Mountains," 45.

62. Denise Giardina, "Strike Zone: The 'Appalachian Intifada' Rages On," *The Village Voice* 7 (August 29, 1989), 31-36.

63. Interview with Giardina.

64. Denise Giardina, "Appalachian Mirror," *New York Times,* October 31, 1992.

65. Kent C. Ryden, *Mapping the Invisible Landscape* (Iowa City, 1993), 38.

66. Wendell Berry, *What Are People For?* (San Francisco, 1990), 85; Jim Wayne Miller, "Coming to Supper, Talking to the Children: Southern Appalachian Writers and Their Communities," *Appalachian Heritage* (spring 1994), 18-26.

67. William E. Lightfoot, "Regional Folklorists," in *Handbook of American Folklore* (Bloomington, 1983), 186-87.

68. Interview with Giardina.

69. Ibid.; Denise Giardina, "BlackGold: How Kentucky Citizens Forced the State to Tax Unmined Coal," *Southern Exposure* 18, no. 3 (fall 1990), 58-59; Giardina, "Malicious Medicine," *Southern Exposure* 19, no. 3 (fall 1991), 62-63.

70. Interviews with West, May 22, 1992.

71. Don West to Dear Friend, Cabin Creek, West Virginia, November 22, 1991, West Papers.

72. Richard Marius, "Don West's Sermon on the Mount," *Appalachian Journal* 10, no. 4 (summer 1983), 361-65.

73. Interviews with West, May 22, 1992.

Chapter Three: Coal Mining in the Novel, the Short Story, and Genre Fiction

1. M.M. Bakhtin, *The Dialogic Imagination: Four Essays* (Austin, 1992), 3-40; Gary Saul Morson and Caryl Emerson, *Mikhail Bakhtin: Creation of a Prosaics* (Stanford, 1990), 271-365; David Lodge, *After Bakhtin: Essays on Fiction and Criticism* (New York, 1990), 25-26.

2. Most creative efforts in portraying mining people tend to be monological rather than dialogical in their emphasis. Bakhtin explores the nature of the dialogical process in fiction most fully in *The Dialogic Imagination* and *Problems of Dostoevsky's Poetics* (Minneapolis, 1993). See also: Tzvetan Todorov, *Mikhail Bakhtin: The Dialogical Principle* (Minneapolis, 1998), 94-12; Morson and Emerson, *Mikhail Bakhtin: Creation of a Prosaics,* 231-68, 306-65; Brian McHale, *Postmodernist Fiction* (New York, 1987), 162-75; David Lodge, *After Bakhtin,* 87-99; Katerina Clark and Michael Holquist, *Mikhail Bakhtin* (Cambridge, Mass., 1984), 197-211, 238-52.

3. Morson and Emerson, *Mikhail Bakhtin: Creation of a Prosaics,* 263-65.

4. Bakhtin, *Problems of Dostoevsky's Poetics,* 68.

5. The following bibliographies have been used in finding coal mining novels: F. Newfeld, Daniel J.H. Leab, and Dorothy Swanson, *American Working Class History: A Representative Bibliography* (New York, 1983), 214-24; Fay M. Blake, *The Strike in the American Novel* (Metuchen, N.J., 1972); Walter Fuller Taylor, *The Economic Novel in America* (Chapel Hill, 1942); Walter Rideout, *The Radical Novel in the United States: 1900-1954* (Cambridge, 1965); Stephane Elise Booth, "The American Coal Mining Novel: A Century of Development," *Illinois Historical Journal* 81, no. 2 (summer 1988), 125-40; Robert F. Munn, "The Coal Novel in America: A Bibliography," *Bulletin of Bibliography* 38, no. 3 (July-September 1981), 105-109; Evelyn Hovanec, "Reader's Guide to Coal Mining Fiction and Selected Prose Narratives," *Bulletin of Bibliography* 43, no. 3 (September 1986), 159-71; Virginia Prestridge, *The Worker in American Fiction: An Annotated Bibliography* (Champaign, 1954). There are no "Dime Novels" included in this chapter primarily because of the excellent chapter, "The Molly Maguires and the Detectives," in Michael Denning's *Mechanic Accents: Dime Novels and Working-Class Culture in America* (New York, 1987), 118-48. Denning writes that in these novels strikes were always won and Pennsylvania mining patches were "wild and barren places," 141.

6. The ten nineteenth-century novels included are: Frank Lee Benedict, *Miss Van Kortland* (New York, 1870); Mary A Roe, *Free, Yet Forging Their Own Chains* (New York, 1876); Author Unknown, *The White Slaves of Monopolies: or John Fitz Patrick, the Miner, Soldier and Workingman's Friend* (Harrisburg, Pa., 1884); Patrick Justin McMahon, *Philip; or, The Mollie's Secret: A Tale of the Coal Regions* (Philadelphia, 1891); Dan Beard, *Moonblight and Six Feet of Romance* (New York, 1892); Harry Prentice, *The Slate-Picker: A Story of a Boy's Life in the Coal Mines* (New York, 1892); Rev. R.F. Bishop, *Camerton Slope: A Story of Mining Life* (New York, 1893); Henry Edward Rood, *The Company Doctor: An American Story* (New York, 1895); John Fox Jr., *A Mountain Europa* (New York, 1915 [first pub. 1887]); M.E. Thornton, *My "Budie" and I* (New York, 1899).

7. Rood, *Company Doctor,* 11; *The White Slaves of Monopolies,* 291; Roe, *Free Yet Forging,* 308; Bishop, *Camerton Slope,* 119; Rood, *Company Doctor,* 37; Beard, *Moonblight,* 19-20.

8. Roe, *Free Yet Forging,* 9-37, 222-23; Thornton, *My "Budie" and I,* 110; Bishop, *Camerton Slope,* passim. Blake, *The Strike in the American Novel;* See David Corbin's *Life, Work and Rebellion in the Coal Fields* (Urbana, 1981), 212-215, for ways in which the courts were arrayed against the miners.

9. McMahon, *Philip,* 6-8, 254-56; Roe, *Free Yet Forging,* 91; Rood, *The Company Doctor,* 34, 68-69, 126; Bishop, *Camerton Slope,* 212;

10. Rood, *Company Doctor,* 223.

11. McMahon, *Philip,* 242.

12. Thornton, *My "Budie" and I,* 23-24, 32-39, 58-60, 61.

13. The ten novels written during this era are: William V. Lawrence, *Under Which Master or the Story of the Long Strike at Coverdale: A Romance of Labor* (New York, 1901); William F. Gibbons, *Those Black Diamond Men* (New York, 1902); Matt Stan Kemp, *Boss Tom* (New York, 1904); Grace MacGowan Cooke, *The Grapple* (Boston, 1905); Arthur Newell, *A Knight of the Toilers* (Philadelphia, 1905); John F. Carter, *The Destroyers* (New York, 1907); Will W. Whalen, *The Lily of the Coal Fields* (Boston, 1910); Charles Carroll Swafford, *The Silent Conflict: A Story of Industrial Warfare* (Boston, 1916); Sherwood Anderson, *Marching Men,* ed. Ray Lewis White (1917; reprint, Cleveland, 1972); Upton Sinclair, *King Coal* (New York, 1917); Upton Sinclair, *The Coal War: A Sequel to "King Coal",* with an introduction by John Graham (Boulder, 1976). This sequel was written shortly after the appearance of *King Coal* but not published until 1976.

14. Francis Hackett, "The American Workingmen," in *The Achievement of Sherwood Anderson: Essays in Criticism,* ed. Ray Lewis White (Chapel Hill, 1966), 26-29. Hackett believes that although the novel is "fragmentary and rhetorical," its importance lies in the way it pushes the working class into the mainstream of American fiction. Irving Howe, *Sherwood Anderson* (Stanford, 1951), 83-85, is fearful of the use of a charismatic leader and also of the historical implications of the marching men movement, which falls apart because "Anderson hadn't the faintest notion of what to do with it." On the other hand, David D. Anderson, *Sherwood Anderson: An Interpretation* (New York, 1967), 24-27, does not fear the overtones of fascism suggested by Howe but instead views the novel as contrived in its attempt to show how groups responded to the dehumanizing aspects of the new materialism.

15. Booth, "The American Coal Mining Novel," 129.

16. Sinclair, *The Coal War,* 22-26.

17. Graham, introduction to *The Coal War,* by Upton Sinclair, lxxxix-lxxxvii.

18. Harris, *Upton Sinclair,* 153-54.

19. Graham, introduction to *The Coal War,* lxxix-xcii.

20. Sinclair, *King Coal,* 57; *The Coal War,* 330-31.

21. Eric Homberger believes that since Sinclair philosophically agreed with the right wing of the Socialist Party, Hal Warner's role throughout the novel is to tone down the action of the miners; Homberger, *Americans Writers and Radical Politics, 1900-39* (New York, 1986), 75.

22. Sinclair, *The Coal War,* 255-56; *King Coal,* 304.

23. Rideout, *Radical Novel,* 37-38.

24. Sinclair, *The Coal War,* 370-72

25. The novels written during this era are: George Brydges Rodney, *Jim Lofton: American* (New York, 1920); D. Thomas Curtin, *The Tyranny of Power* (Boston, 1923); Arthur Train, *The Needle's Eye* (New York, 1924); Mary E. Waller, *Deep in the Hearts of Men* (Boston, 1925); Jack Bethea, *Bed Rock* (New York, 1924) and *The Deep Seam* (New York, 1926); H.E. Danford, *The West Virginian* (New York, 1926); Will W. Whalen, *The Girl from Mine Run* (St. Louis, 1927) and *Strike* (Orrtanna, Adams Co., Pa., 1928); Agnes Smedley, *Daughter of Earth* (1929; reprint, Old Westbury, New York, 1976).

26. Waller, *Deep in the Hearts of Men,* 317.

27. Whalen, *Girl from Mine Run,* 164.

28. Shelley Fisher Fiskin suggests in her book *From Fact to Fiction* (New York, 1985) that there is a long history in American literature of journalistic facts finding their way into fiction.

29. For the stereotypical ways in which Appalachia has been portrayed see: Henry D. Shapiro, *Appalachia on Our Mind: The Southern Mountains and Mountaineers in the American Consciousness, 1870-1929* (Chapel Hill, 1978), passim; Whisnant, *All That Is Native and Fine,* passim; Batteau, *The Invention of Appalachia,* passim; Darlene Wilson, "The Felicitous Convergence of Mythmaking and Capital Accumulation: John Fox Jr. and the Formation of an (Other) Almost-White American Underclass," *Journal of Appalachian Studies* 1, no. 1 (1995), 5-44; Darlene Wilson, "A Judicious Combination of Incident and Psychology: John Fox Jr. and the Southern Mountaineer Motif," in *Confronting Appalachian Stereotypes: Back Talk from an American Region,* ed. Dwight B. Billings, Gurney Norman, and Katherine Ledford, with a foreword by Ronald D. Eller (Lexington, Ky., 1999), 98-118.

30. Train, *The Needle's Eye,* 316.

31. Smedley, *Daughter of Earth,* 96, 110.

32. Whalen, *Girl from Mine Run,* 60.

33. Emile Zola also compares miners to African Americans; Zola, *Germinal* (Baltimore, 1963), 74.

34. Depression-era novels are: Rollo Walter Brown, *The Firemakers: A Novel of Environment* (New York, 1931); Scott Nearing, *Free Born: An Unpublishable Novel* (New York, 1932); Jack Conroy, *The Disinherited* (1933; reprint with an introduction by Daniel Aaron, New York, 1963); Waldo Frank, *The Death and Birth of David Markand* (New York, 1934); Lauren Gilfillan [Harriet Woodbridge Gilfillan], *I Went to Pit College* (New York, 1934); Tillie Olsen, *Yonnodio from the Thirties* (1934; reprint, New York, 1975); Thomas Rowan, *Black Earth* (New York, 1935); Tom Tippett, *Horse Shoe Bottoms* (New York, 1935); McAlister Coleman and Stephen Raushenbush, *Red Neck* (New York, 1936); Alice Sligh Turnbull, *Remember the End* (1938; reprint, New York, 1967); John Dos Passos, *Adventures of a Young Man* (New York, 1939); Charles Edward Roudabush, *Mary of the Anthracite* (New York, 1939).

35. Blake, *The Strike in the American Novel,* 117-49.

36. Gilfillan, *I Went to Pit College,* 189-90.

37. Conroy, *The Disinherited,* 12; Conroy's "Tales from Monkey Nest," in *The Weed King and Other Stories* (West Port, Conn., 1985), 77-167, does not add to the coal camp experiences he describes in *The Disinherited.*

38. Olsen, *Yonnondio,* 13-14; Constance Coiner, *Better Red: The Writing and Resistance of Tillie Olsen and Muridel Le Sueur* (New York, 1955), 191; Christopher Wilson, "Recollecting *Yonnondio: from the Thirties,*" in *The Power of Culture: Critical Essays in American History,* ed. Richard Whitman Fox and T.J. Jackson Lears (Chicago, 1993), 56. Both Coiner and Wilson analyze Olsen's symbolic use of the mine as a way of suggesting the exploitative nature of capitalism.

39. Dos Passos, *Adventures of a Young Man,* 211.

40. Zona Gale, "A College Girl in the Pennsylvania Mines," *New York Herald Tribune,* March 4, 1934.

41. Paula Rabinowitz, *Labor and Desire: Women's Revolutionary Fiction in Depressed America* (Chapel Hill, 1953), 150.

42. Gilfillan, *I Went to Pit College,* 269.

43. William Bittner, *The Novels of Waldo Frank* (Philadelphia, 1955), 146-48. For a favorable review by another novelist on the Left see Edward Dahalberg, "Waldo Frank and the Left," *New Masses* 23 (April 1935), 22-23. Leane Zugsmith, *The Summer Soldier* (New York, 1938), fictionalizes the story of a group of men and women who go to Chew County, Kentucky, to investigate a lynching. The novel's overall structure, characters, and plot are a composite recreation of the work of the Dreiser and Frank Committees in Harlan Country six years earlier.

44. Dos Passos, *The Adventures of a Young Man,* 240, 266-67; John P. Diggins, *Up from Communism: Conservative Odysseys in American Intellectual History* (New York, 1975), 75-117. In the last "Camera Eye," *The Big Money* (New York, 1960), 462-63, Dos Passos incorporates his Harlan county experiences into his *USA* trilogy.

45. Barbara Foley, *Radical Representations: Politics and Form in U.S. Proletarian Fiction 1929-41* (Durham, 1993), 395.

46. Altenbaugh, *Education for Struggle,* 118; For a taste of Tippett's writing about the American labor movement, see *When Southern Labor Stirs* (New York, 1931).

47. Tippett, *Horse Shoe Bottoms,* 72, 67.

48. Ibid., 271, 287.

49. The novels of the 1940s and 1950s are: James Still, *River of Earth* (1940; reprint with a foreword by Dean Cadle, Lexington, Ky., 1978); Still, *The Run for the Elbertas* (Lexington, Ky., 1980); Sara Atherton, *Mark's Own* (New York, 1941); Irene D. Smith, *The Right to Live* (New York, 1941); William Bradsford Huie, *Mud on the Stars* (1942; reprint, New York, 1955); Francis Wallace, *Explosion* (New York, 1943); Ruth McKenney, *Jake Home* (New York, 1943); Jessie Stuart, "Vacation in Hell," *Voices from the Hills: Selected Readings in Southern Appalachia,* ed. Robert J. Higgs and Ambrose N. Manning (New York, 1975), 220-35; James M. Cain, *The Butterfly* (1946; reprint, New York, 1979); Fielding Burke [Oliver Tilford Dragan], *Sons of the Stranger* (New York, 1947); Dorothy Salisbury Davis, *The Clay Hand* (New York, 1950); Ben Ames Williams, *Own Glen* (Boston, 1950); Myra Page, *With Sun in Our Blood* (New

York, 1950), the most recent edition of which is *Daughter of the Hills,* introduction by Alice Kessler Harris and Paul Lauter (New York, 1977); William Furr, *Tomorrow Achieved* (Kansas City, 1946); John Burgan, *The Long Discovery* (New York, 1950); Henry George III, *Blood and Coal* (Philadelphia, 1950); Margaret Graham [G.L. MacDonald], *Swing Shift* (New York, 1951); Cyril Harris, *The Trouble at Hungerfords* (Boston, 1953); Taylor Caldwell, *Tender Victory* (New York, 1956); Stanley and Jeanette Bolton, *Black Blood in Kentucky* (New York, 1957); Lars Lawrence [Philip Stevenson], *Morning Noon and Night* (New York, 1954), *Out of the Dust* (New York, 1956), *Old Father Antic* (London, 1961), *The Hoax* (London, 1961); Albert Idell, *Stephen Hayne* (New York, 1951).

50. Cain, *The Butterfly,* v-xvi.

51. Joyce Carol Oates, for one, is unimpressed by Cain's defense of his subject matter as a product of his artistic imagination. "Cain never manages to become an artist; there is something sleazy, something eerily vulgar and disappointing in his work," Oates writes in "Man under Sentence of Death: the Novels of James M. Cain," in *Tough Guy Writers of the Thirties,* ed. David Madden (New York, 1979), 110.

52. McKenney, *Jake Home,* 29, 39; Atherton, *Mark's Own,* 161, 166-67; Idell, *Stephen Hayne,* 324, 404; Graham, *Swing Shift,* 14.

53. Although the importance of baseball in coal towns is included in such novels as Giardina's *Storming Heaven,* the collective *mentalité* of the importance of baseball in mining communities still awaits its scholar.

54. H.R. Stoneback, "Rivers of Earth and Troublesome Creek: The Agrarianism of James Still," *Kenyon Review* 10, no. 3 (autumn 1990), 3-26; Dean Cadle, "Man on Troublesome," *Yale Review* 57 (December 1967); Cadle, "Pattern of a Writer: Attitudes of James Still," *Appalachian Journal* 15, no. 2 (winter 1988), 104-43; Edward Fred Wing, "James Still: An Inquiry into the Intrinsic Value of the Works of a Regional Writer" (Ph.D. diss., Colorado State College, 1969).

55. Deborah S. Rosenfelt, afterword to *Daughter of the Hills,* by Myra Page, 247-48.

56. Foley, *Radical Representations,* 395.

57. Page, *Daughter of the Hills,* 240, 242-43.

58 Frederick R. Karl, *American Fictions: 1940-80* (New York, 1985), 358.

59. Marie Chay, *Pilgrim's Pride* (New York, 1961); Conrad Richter, *A Simple Honorable Man* (New York, 1962); Clarence Lewis and Ester Kellner, *Cry to the Hills* (New York, 1966); Robert Coover, *The Origins of the Brunists* (New York, 1966); David Grubb, *Fools Parade* (New York, 1969).

60. Howard Fast, *Power* (New York, 1962); J.E. Wood, *Danger in the Dark* (New York, 1965); Michael A. Musmanno, *Black Fury* (New York, 1966).

61. Musmanno discusses his activities on behalf of this legislation in the afterword to *Black Fury,* 371-91.

62. The novels of the 1970s are: James Lee Burke, *To the Bright and Shining Sun* (New York, 1970); Michael Quigley, *April is the Cruelest Month* (New York, 1971); Davis Grubb, *The Barefoot Man* (New York, 1971); Charleton Ogburn, *Winespring Mountain* (New York, 1973); James Sherburne, *Stand Like Men* (Boston, 1973); Gene Marvin, *Vestige of Valor* (New York, 1973); John Rolfe Gardiner, *Great Dream from*

Heaven (New York, 1974); Charlie Ward, *Silk Stocking Row* (Parsons, W.Va., 1975); John Sayles, *Union Dues* (Boston, 1977); John Knowles, *A Vein of Riches* (Boston, 1978); Michael Novak, *The Guns of Lattimer* (New York, 1978).

63. Charleton Ogburn, *Winespring Mountain* (New York, 1973), 190.

64. Jackson I. Cope's *Robert Coover's Fictions* (Baltimore, 1986) provides an introduction to Coover's work but has little analysis of *The Origin of the Brunists.*

65. Frederick R. Karl writes, in *American Fictions,* 365-66, that Coover patterned his main character on Italian philosopher Giordano Bruno, who argued that our personal perceptions influence everything we know. Not surprisingly, Bruno was burned at the stake in 1600 during the Inquisition.

66. Karl, *American Fictions,* 366.

67. Coover, *Origin of the Brunists,* 164.

68. Sherburne, *Stand Like Men,* 179-80, 137. When the Dreiser committee arrived in Harlan County, they discovered that among the most fervent supporters of the National Miners Union were several holiness ministers, including Finley Donaldson. Less than three months later, after the Communist Party had sent Donaldson and other local NMU supporters to New York for training, the group returned and issued a public statement denouncing both the union and the party for their atheism and their close ties to the Soviet Union. Donaldson later claimed that his accusations influenced over a thousand miners to leave the union. Hevener, *Which Side Are You On?,* 68-69, 80.

69. Sayles, *Union Dues,* 226, 161.

70. The novels of the 1970s and 1980s by Jayne Ann Phillips, Richard Curry, Breece D'J Pancake, Cathryn Hankla, Lee Smith, Mary Lee Settle, and Denise Giardina will be cited when discussed. The other novels and collections of short fiction are: Harry Caudill, *The Mountain, the Miner and the Lord* (Lexington, Ky., 1980); John Yount, *Hardcastle* (New York, 1980); Gerald Tomlinson, *On a Black Field* (New York, 1980); Robert Louis Nathan, *Coal Mine No. 7* (New York, 1980); Col. Ed Eads, *The Bloody Harlanite* (Marietta, Ga., 1980); Sophia Yarnall, *The Clark Inheritance* (New York, 1981); Tom Hillstrom, *Coal* (New York, 1984); Jan Kubicki, *Breaker Boys* (Boston, 1986); Jess Carr, *Intruder in the Wind* (Radford, Va., 1987); Catherine Gourley, *The Courtship of Joanna* (St. Paul, 1988); John Douglas, *Blind Spring Rambler* (New York, 1988); Ed Campbell, *Between Heaven and Hell* (Chalk Hill, Pa., 1990); Ellis Wynne Roberts, *Flames and Embers of Coal* (Washington, D.C., 1990); Sue Halsey, *Hannah's Dream* (New York, 1990); Frank C. Strunk, *Jordan's Wager* (New York, 1991) and *Jordan's Showdown* (New York, 1993); John O'Hara, *Gibbsville, Pa: The Classic Stories,* ed. Matthew Bruccoli (New York, 1992); K.C. Constantine, *The Man Who Liked Slow Tomatoes* (Boston, 1993) and *Always a Body to Trade* (Boston, 1993); William Diehl, *Primal Fear* (New York, 1994) and the sequel, *Show of Evil* (New York, 1996).

71. Diehl, *Primal Fear,* 134.

72. Jayne Anne Phillips, *Black Tickets* (New York, 1975); Breece D'J Pancake, *The Stories of Breece D'J Pancake* (Boston, 1983); Richard Curry, *The Wars of Heaven* (Boston, 1990).

73. In Phillips's first book of short fiction, *Black Tickets,* only a single story, "Country," thematically touches on coal mining. Curry's "Old Fires" and "Believer's Flood," in *The Wars of Heaven,* and Pancake's "Hollow," in *The Stories of Breece D'J Pancake,* are the only stories in their collections with mining themes. Avery F. Gaskins argues in "Middle-Class Townie: Jayne Anne Phillips and the Appalachian Experience," *Appalachian Journal* (spring 1992), 308-316, that Phillips has interpreted Appalachia from essentially a middle-class view, which, he believes, is a welcome critical perspective. It is likely, however, that she has had the same kind of contact with mining culture as the character Mitch in her novel *Machine Dreams* (New York, 1984), 314, who has only come into contact with them in local bars. As with so many young, socially conscience Appalachians, strip mining is the issue that has interested her. See Thomas E. Douglas, "Interview: Jayne Anne Phillips," *Appalachian Journal* (winter 1994), 182-316. Richard Curry, like Phillips, feels unbound to a specific place or subject matter, but he believes that there are "broad issues that writers from a region might share, like the coal miner story." Thomas E. Douglas, "Interview with Richard Curry," *Appalachian Journal* (summer 1993), 377. Finally, for an interesting analysis of the ways in which Breece D'J Pancake's alienation might have influenced his writing, see Ellesa Clay High, "A Lost Generation: The Appalachia of Breece D'J Pancake," *Appalachian Journal* (fall 1985), 34-40.

74. Cathryn Hankla, *A Blue Moon in Poorwater* (New York, 1988), 247-48.

75. Lee Smith, *Oral History* (New York, 1984), 234, 233.

76. Dorothy Combs Hill, *Lee Smith* (New York, 1992), 103-119; Pat Arnow, "Lee Smith: An Interview," *Now and Then* 6, no. 2 (summer 1989), 24-27.

77. Lee Smith, *Fair and Tender Ladies* (New York, 1988), 139, 159, 162.

78. Margaret Atwood, "In Search of *Alias Grace:* On Writing Canadian Historical Fiction," *The American Historical Review* 103, no.5 (December 1998), 1504.

79. Mary Lee Settle, *The Scapegoat,* introduction by Roger Shattuck (New York, 1980); Settle, *The Killing Ground* (New York, 1982); Settle, "Recapturing the Past in Fiction," *New York Times Book Review* (February 12, 1984), 36.

80. Brian Rosenberg, *Mary Lee Settle's Beulah Quintet: The Price of Freedom* (Baton Rouge, 1991), 131.

81. Nancy Carol Joyner, "Mary Lee Settle's Connections: Class and Clothes in the Beulah Quintet," in *Women Writers of the Contemporary South,* ed. Peggy Whitman Preshaw (Jackson, Miss., 1984), 169.

82. Rosenberg, *Mary Lee Settle's Beulah Quintet,* 101.

83. Settle based much of Mother Jones's dialogue on stenographic transcripts she discovered while researching the West Virginia mine wars for *The Scapegoat.* Rosenberg, *Mary Lee Settle's Beulah Quintet,* 109.

84. Settle, *The Scapegoat,* 298, 216, 217.

85. Richard Sennett and Jonathan Cobb, *The Hidden Injuries of Class* (New York, 1973), passim.

86. Settle, *The Scapegoat,* 302.

87. Ibid., 302. What Bakhtin sees in Dostoevsky's main characters is also found to some extent in several of Settle's. "They all acutely sense their own inner

unfinalizability, their capacity to outgrow, as it were, from within and to render untrue any externalizing and finalizing definition of them. As long as a person is alive he lives by the fact that he is not yet finalized, that he has not yet uttered his ultimate word." Bakhtin, *Problems of Dostoevsky's Poetics,* 59.

88. Settle, *The Killing Ground,* 305.

89. Ibid., 271-78, 374.

90. Rosenberg, *Mary Lee Settle's Beulah Quintet,* 131.

91. Settle, *The Killing Ground,* 384.

92. Mary Lee Settle, *Choices* (New York, 1995), 12.

93. Ibid., 74.

94. Settle, *The Killing Ground,* 384.

95. See, for example, Thomas E. Douglas, "Interview with Denise Giardina," *Appalachian Journal* (summer 1993), 384-93; Laurie Lindberg, "Lleyellyn and Giardina, Two Novels about Coal Mining," *Journal of Appalachian Studies* 1 (1989), 133-40. Lon Savage, in *Thunder in the Mountains: The West Virginia Mine War 1920-21* (Pittsburgh, 1990), and Corbin, in *Life, Work and Rebellion in Coal Fields,* 176-252, offer detailed accounts of the mine wars in West Virginia. Former West Virginia Attorney General (1925-33) Howard B. Lee, in *Bloodletting in Appalachia* (Morgantown, 1969), offers a more partisan perspective in defending the role of the state government. Dubofsky and Van Tyne's *John L. Lewis,* 76-78, also provides a brief synthesis.

96. Corbin, *Life, Work and Rebellion in the Coal Fields,* 195-224, discusses the roles of Sheriff Sid Hatfield and Ed Chambers, his former police officer and a UMWA member, in the Matewan Massacre and their subsequent murder on the steps of the Welch County courthouse on August 1, 1921. According to Corbin, 210, their murder triggered the armed march by miners on Logan, West Virginia, in the summer of 1921.

97. Giardina, *Storming Heaven* (New York, 1987), 209, 169. The disagreement between Rachel and Dillon can only be fully understood through their discourses, which frame their relationship. If less complex it is nonetheless similar to those found in most of Dostoevsky's major works. In each case the idea or conflict is "inter-individual and inter-subjective—the realm of its existence is not individual consciousness but dialogic communion *between* consciousnesses." Bakhtin, *Problems of Dostoevsky's Poetics,* 88.

98. Denise Giardina, *The Unquiet Earth* (New York, 1992), 222.

99. Ibid., 217.

100. Elaine Showalter, "Feminist Criticism in the Wilderness," in *The New Feminist Criticism,* ed. Elaine Showalter (New York, 1985), 259-60.

101. Foley, *Radical Representations,* 237-46.

102. Dorothy E. Smith, *The Everyday World as Problematic: A Feminist Sociology* (Boston, 1987), 107-08.

103. Tonette Bond Inge, ed., *Southern Women Writers: The New Generation* (Tuscaloosa, 1990), 5-6.

104. Settle, "Recapturing the Past," 36.

105. George Lukacs, *The Historical Novel* (Boston, 1963), 42.

106. Atwood, "In Search of *Alias Grace,*" 1516.

107. Jim Wayne Miller, "Nostalgia for the Future," *The Kentucky Review* 8, no. 2 (summer 1988), 31.

Chapter Four: Stage and Screen

1. Robert Richardson, *Literature and Film* (Bloomington, 1969), 97; Charles Eidsvik, *Cineliteracy: Film among the Arts* (New York, 1978), 162.

2. This feeling can be compared to the ways in which 1930s audiences responded to gangster films. See Robert Warshow, "The Gangster as Tragic Hero," in *Things in the Driver's Seat: Readings in Popular Culture,* ed. Harry Russell Huebel (Chicago, 1972), 97-102.

3. *American Film Institute Catalog, Feature Films, 1911-1920* (New York, 1988), 111.

4. Susan Sontag, *Styles of Radical Will* (New York, 1969), 112.

5. Tom Zaniello, *Working Stiffs, Union Maids, Reds and Riffraff* (Ithaca, 1996), 97-102.

6. Although African American miners appear less frequently than immigrant miners in most of the plays, *Bloodstream* has a predominantly black cast. African American miners also appear in Leo Pride's plays as tokens of a heterogeneous workforce. Only in *Fortune's Hired Man* does Pride provide any insight into an African American character, who, in this instance, happens to work on the farm of a deeply racist miner. And finally, although the Biggs family is important in Robert Schenkkan's *The Kentucky Cycle,* in the modern era most of the males either are on the wrong side of the law or appear to have questionable ethics. In short, only occasionally does an African American miner rise above the stereotypical in these mining dramas. Like their ethnic counterparts, they are an incomplete presence on stage in their "otherness."

7. I appreciate Billy Edd Wheeler's assistance in locating "Slatefall," which is published in *A Guide to Oral Interpretation: Solo and Group Performance* 2nd ed., ed. Louise M. Scrivner and Dan Robinette (Indianapolis, 1980), 226-42. Other sources used to uncover coal mining plays were: *The Oxford Companion to American Theater,* 2nd ed., ed. Gerald Bordman (New York, 1992); Michael Goldstein, *The Political Stage: American Drama and Theater of the Great Depression* (New York, 1974); *McGraw-Hill Encyclopedia of World Drama,* 5 vols., ed. Stanley Hochman (New York, 1972); *The New York Times Theater Reviews 1920-1970,* 10 vols., with an introduction by Brooks Atkinson (New York, 1971); *Chicorel Theater Index to Plays in Anthologies, Periodicals, Discs And Tapes,* ed. Marietta Chicorel (New York, 1970); *An Index to One Act Plays,* compiled by Hannah Lagasa and Winifred ver Nooy (Boston, 1924); *Play Index,* 1138 vols. (New York, 1953).

8. Much like the Mother Jones production, an unpublished play by Geina Miller, "The Spirit of the Molly Maguires," has been performed annually at the Mauch Chunk Old Opera House in Jim Thorpe, Pennsylvania. *The Anthracite History Journal* 3, no. 1 (December 1996), 2.

9. Leo B. Pride, *The Haunted Coal Mine, One Act Plays for Stage and Study,*

5th ser., with preface by Elmer L. Rice (New York, 1929), 286; Frederick Schlick, *Bloodstream* (Boston, 1934), 8; S. Sylvan Simon, *Trouble in Tunnel Nine,* in *Thrillers! Seven New Non-Royalty Plays for Men and Boys,* compiled by S. Sylvan Simon (New York, 1943), 7, 5; Pride, *Fortune's Hired Man* in *The Shadow of the Mine, and Other Plays of the Coal Fields* (New York, 1929), 141; *On the Way Home,* in *The Shadow of the Mine,* 84; E.J. Eustace, *The King of the Mountains, a Play in Five Acts* (1975) reprinted from the *Bulletin of the New York Public Library* 76 (New York, 1972), act 1, sc. 2, lines 159-63, p. 14; Jason Miller, *Nobody Hears a Broken Drum, a Play in Two Acts* (New York, 1970), act 1, p. 8.

10. Lee Pennington, *The Scotian Women* (Louisville 1984), act 1, p. 19; act 2, p. 35.

11. Albert Maltz, *Black Pit* (New York, 1935), v; Schenkkan, *Fire in the Hole,* part 2: 211.

12. Matt Williams, *Between Daylight and Boonville* (New York, 1979), act 2, p. 69.

13. Schenkkan, *The Kentucky Cycle,* 336-38.

14. Schenkkan, *Fire in the Hole,* part 2: 212, 230, 233, 264.

15. Gaventa, *Power and Powerlessness,* 175. It is possible that Schenkkan had the April 8, 1911, Banner mine disaster in mind when he wrote his play. For an analysis of this disaster see Robert David Ward and William Warren Rogers, *Convicts, Coal and the Banner Mine Tragedy* (Tuscaloosa, Ala., 1987).

16. Schenkkan, *Fire in the Hole,* part 2: 309.

17. Schenkkan does not intend for his plays to be interpreted out of sequence. In a concluding "Author's Note," 333-38, he states that *The Kentucky Cycle* transcends place and time. Jack Wright, "The Kentucky Cycle," *Ace Magazine* 6, no. 4 (July 1992), 8, quotes director Warren Shook's claim at the play's Los Angeles opening that "This could just as easily be called *The California Cycle.* It's not about hillbillies. It's a reflection of the state of the union." Others are not convinced, including Jack Wright ("The Kentucky Cycle," pp. 8-13, 37) and playwright Jo Carson, who spoofs both Schenkkan and Shook by claiming that she has begun writing just such a play, "Jo Carson's Los Angeles Cycle," *Now and Then* (April 1994), 12-13. See also Bobbie Ann Mason, "Recycling Kentucky," *The New Yorker* 36, no. 69 (Nov. 1, 1993), 50-62, and the essays by Finlay Donesky, Rodger Cunningham, Herbert Reid, and Gurney Norman in *Confronting Appalachian Stereotypes* (Lexington, 1999), 283-332.

18. Malcolm Goldstein, *The Political Stage,* 70-72. For the play's critical reception see Kenneth Eble, *Albert Maltz* (Boston, 1978), 31-32.

19. Jo Carson, *A Preacher with a Horse to Ride, a Play in Two Acts* (typescript copy of play provided by author April 1993), act 1, p. 32. The play has been published in *Alternate Roots: Plays from the Southern Theater,* ed. Kathie deNobriga and Valetta Anderson (Portsmouth, N.H., 1994), 267-334.

20. Carson, *A Preacher with a Horse to Ride,* act 2, p. 67-68.

21. Paula Cizmar, *The Death of a Miner: A Drama* (New York, 1982), p. 12.

22. Ibid., pp. 17, 61-62.

23. Ibid., p. 39. Faced with a daily barrage of sexual harassment, Mary Alice and Winona speculate that in the future most promotions will inevitably go to women rather than men because the men have more trouble handling the pressures of mining.

Mary Alice is more explicit in explaining how these pressures affect male sexuality, pp. 40-41, "Yeah . . . miners who are getting up in the world end up having trouble getting it up."

24. Ibid., p. 17.

25. Ibid., p. 107.

26. Olga Carlisle and Rose Styron, "Arthur Miller," *Writers at Work: The Paris Review Interviews,* 3rd ser., ed. George Plimpton (New York, 1967), 213.

27. Robert Rosenstone, *Visions of the Past: The Challenge of Film to Our Idea of History* (Cambridge, 1995), 31-32.

28. Steven Mintz and Randy Roberts, *Hollywood's America: United States History through Its Films* (New York, 1993), 27.

29. All nineteen films are feature length, but fragments are all that are available for some. The following sources have been used in identifying, viewing, and reading about the films analyzed in this chapter: *The American Film Institute Catalog of Motion Pictures Produced in the United States, Feature Films* 6 vols., ed. Kenneth W. Munden (New York, 1971); J.W. Williamson, *Southern Mountaineers in Silent Films: Plot Synopses of Movies about Moonshining, Feuding and Other Mountain Topics* (Jefferson, N.C., 1994); and *Hillbillyland: What the Movies Did to the Mountains and What the Mountains Did to the Movies* (Chapel Hill, 1995); Zaniello, *Working Stiffs, Union Maids, Reds and Riffraff; Video Hound's Golden Movie Retriever* (Detroit, 1994); and especially the generous assistance of Rosemary Haynes at the Library of Congress Motion Picture, Broadcasting and Recorded Sound Division, who directed me to the microfilm copyright file on feature films.

30. The Library of Congress Film Division has only three reels of this film.

31. Other films touching on coal mining include *Dynamite Allen* (1921), a tiresome melodrama involving murder, kidnapping, and mistaken identity in predictable ways in a mining setting. *The Man Who Dared* (1933) follows the improving fortunes of an immigrant miner from Bradiwood, Illinois, through his election as mayor of Chicago in the early twentieth century. *Bolero* (1934) barely touches on the mining scene as Raoul De Baere (George Raft) leaves his work underground to become a dancer. *State Police* (1938) is a 1930s gangster movie in which miners and police join together in an unusual alliance against racketeers who are trying to control the Pennsylvania coalfields. In *Jeepers Creepers* (1939) there are good and bad miners; the bad ones work as strip miners for an unscrupulous coal baron. Finally, a 1943 film, *Black Diamonds,* dramatizes the efforts of a crusading journalist who poses as a miner to expose unsafe working conditions in his hometown mine.

32. The following films involve efforts either to preserve or gain control of valuable coal deposits: *The Heart of the Hills* (1914), *Heart o' the Hills* (1919), *In Old Kentucky* (1919), *Hill Billy* (1921), *Human Hearts* (1922), and the 1936 version of *Trail of the Lonesome Pine.*

33. *The Miner's Daughter* (1908), *The Strike at the Mine* (1912), *The Black Wall* (1912), *The Blind Miner* (1912), *Fire at the Mine* (1912), *Her Final Choice* (1913), and *The Secret of the Mine* (1913) place explosions, cave-ins, and trapped miners at the center of the action.

34. *The Molly Maguires; Or, Labor Wars in the Coal Mines* (1908), *The Strike at the Mines* (1911), *The Secret of the Mine* (1913), *A Throw of the Dice* (1914), *The Sons of Toil* (1915), *Woman's Way* (1916), and *Threads of Fate* (1917).

35. In *Who's Cheating?* (1925), the main character goes into his father's coal mine to realize his manhood. In *Buried Alive in a Coal Mine* (1913), a young man does the same to recoup a family fortune. Matters of the heart rather than the pocketbook are at stake in *Her Final Choice* (1913). One of two suitors to the film's heroine proves his worth and wins her hand by acting courageously after a mine explosion.

36. Joanne Barkan, "Class Warfare on the Big Screen," *Democratic Left* 15 (Nov.-Dec. 1987), 23-24.

37. JanMohamed, in "The Economy of Manichean Allegory," *The Post-Colonial Studies Reader* 18, writes that "Genuine and thorough comprehension of otherness is possible only if the self can somehow negate or at least severely bracket the values, assumptions and ideology of his culture."

38. Marat Moore, "Where the Rubber Meets the Road, John Sayles Talks about His Coal Mining Movie *Matewan,*" *Now and Then* 5 (spring 1988), 5. John Alexander Williams, "John Sayles Plays the Preacher," *Appalachian Journal* (summer 1988), 347.

39. John Sayles, *Thinking in Pictures: The Making of the Film* Matewan (Boston, 1987), 8.

40. Barkan, "Class Warfare on the Big Screen," 24.

41. Sayles, *Thinking in Pictures,* 155.

42. Homer H. Hickam Jr., *October Sky* (New York, 1999), 382.

Chapter Five: Coal Mining Fiction for the Young

1. C.S. Lewis, "On Three Ways of Writing for Children," in *Only Connect: Readings on Children's Literature,* ed. Sheila Egoff, G.T. Stubbs, and L.F. Ashely (New York, 1980), 208.

2. Paul Hazard, *Books for Children and Men* (Boston, 1960), 1-2.

3. Rebecca J. Lukens, *A Critical Handbook of Children's Literature,* 4th ed. (Blenview, Ill., 1990), 99.

4. Ibid.; James Steel Smith, *A Critical Approach to Children's Literature* (New York, 1967), 15-20; Margaret R. Marshall, *An Introduction to the World of Children's Books* (Guilford, United Kingdom, 1982), 25-27; Charlotte S. Huck, *Children's Literature,* 3rd ed. (New York, 1976), 6-7.

5. Diana Wynne Jones, "The Heroic Ideal—A Personal Odyssey," *The Lion and the Unicorn* 13, no. 1 (June 1989), 133.

6. Peter Hunt, *An Introduction to Children's Literature* (New York, 1994), 169.

7. Kenneth L. Donelson and Alleen P. Nilsen, *Literature for Today's Young Adults* (Glenview, Ill., 1980), 5.

8. In addition to the bibliographical sources listed for adult fiction in chapter three, I relied on George Brosi's knowledge of Appalachian literature as well as his periodic advertisements for books in *Appalachian Mountain Books.* Eugene Povirk of SouthPaw Books in Conway, Massachusetts, also conducted searches for me as did

the now-defunct Trans Allegheny Books in Charleston, West Virginia. Since many of the books for young children are short and have no page numbers, citations will only be used for books written for older children and young adults.

9. Appalachian scholar George Brosi takes exception to Dionetti's confusion about work in a coal mine, noting that breaker boys usually did not work in the mines and that those who did work underground, "just like cave explorers, did not experience either winter cold or summer heat!" "Booklist and Notes," *Appalachian Heritage* (fall 1992), 76.

10. Roberta Herrin, "Appalachian Books for All Children," *Now and Then* 4, no. 1 (spring 1982), 34-35, believes that Rylant's interpretation of Appalachia is often more stereotypical than accurately descriptive.

11. Although didacticism is associated primarily with eighteenth- and nineteenth-century children's literature, a number of recent critics suggest that it is alive and thriving in contemporary works. Donelson and Nilsen, *Literature for Today's Young Adults,* 17-21; Huck, *Children's Literature,* 8-9, 396; John Rowe Townsend, "Didacticism's Modern Dress," in *Only Connect: Readings on Children's Literature,* ed. Sheila Egoff, G.T. Stubbs, and L.F. Ashely (New York, 1980), 55-58, 62.

12. Sheila Egoff, "Inside and Out: A Canadian's View of Traits and Trends in Contemporary Children's Literature," in *A Track to Unknown Water,* ed. Stella Less (Metuchen, N.J., 1987), 343-48.

13. Burton Egbert Stevenson, *Tommy Remington's Battle* (New York, 1901), 4; Nan Hayden Agle and Ellen Wilson, *Three Boys and a Mine,* illustrated by Marian Honigman (New York, 1954), 39; Lois Lenski, *Coal Camp Girl* (New York, 1959), 7; Annabel and Edgar Johnson, *The Bearcat* (New York, 1960), 19-20; Scott O'Dell, *Journey to Jericho,* illustrated by Leonard Weisgard (Boston, 1969), 2; Dareen Rappaport, *Trouble at the Mines,* illustrated by Joan Sandin (New York, 1987), 7

14. Johnson and Johnson, *The Bearcat,* 56.

15. Cynthia Rylant, *A Blue-Eyed Daisy* (New York, 1985), 3; Catherine A. Welch, *Danger at the Breaker ,* illustrated by Andrea Shine (Minneapolis, 1992), 9, 48.

16. Nicholas Tucker, *The Child and the Book: A Psychological and Literary Exploration* (Cambridge, 1981), 55, 61, 65.

17. Lenski, *Coal Camp Girl,* 170; O'Dell, *Journey to Jericho,* 19-20; Francis Rolt-Wheeler, *The Boy with the U.S. Miners* (Boston, 1922), 50, 40-43.

18. Agle, *Three Boys and a Mine,* 29; Stevenson, *Tommy Remington's Battle,* 11; Rappaport, *Trouble at the Mines,* 26; O'Dell, *Journey to Jericho,* 16.

19. Sheila Egoff, "Precepts, Pleasures, and Portents: Changing Emphasis in Children's Literature," in *Only Connect: Readings on Children's Literature,* ed. Sheila Egoff, G.T. Stubbs, and L.F. Ashely (New York, 1980), 431.

20. Smith, *A Critical Approach to Children's Literature,* 21.

21. Ibid., 52.

22. Ibid., 21. Carol Nackenoff suggests in *The Fictional Republic: Horatio Alger and American Political Discourse* (New York, 1994), 71, 91, that when Alger thought of mining it was gold mining in the West.

23. Hugh Agee, "Adolescent Initiation: A Thematic Study in the Secondary

School," in *Literature in Adolescents: Selection and Use,* ed. Richard A. Meade and Robert C. Small (Columbia, 1973), 135. British critic David Rees is quoted in *The Oxford Companion to Children's Literature,* ed. Humphrey Carpenter and Mari Prichard (New York, 1991), 162, as suggesting that the issues that most frequently concern adolescents are those relating to "discovering qualities and limitations; acquiring skills; and with the question: who am I? What is my place in the world? Can I function adequately and maturely?"

24. Kirk Munroe, *Dirick Sterling: A Story of the Mines* (New York, 1888), 93.

25. Jay Parini, *The Patch Boys* (New York, 1986), 12.

26. James Forman, *A Ballad for Hogskin Hill* (New York, 1979), 16. Other novels that use strip mining issues to move their narratives while paying little attention to deep mining except as a means of evoking the past are Virginia Hamilton's *M.C. Higgins, the Great* (New York, 1974) and Jenny Davis's *Good-Bye and Keep Cold* (New York, 1989).

27. Forman, *A Ballad for Hogskin Hill,* 12, 58-59.

28. Parini, *The Patch Boys,* 65-66.

29. N.A. Perez, *Breaker* (Boston, 1988), 173, 200.

30. Phyllis Reynolds Naylor, *Wrestle the Mountain* (Chicago, 1971), 49, 73.

Chapter Six: Coal Mining and the Poetic Imagination

1. Daniel Hoffman, "Poetry: Schools of Dissidents," in *Harvard Guide to Contemporary American Writing,* ed. Daniel Hoffman (Cambridge, 1979), 497; Dana Giola, *Can Poetry Matter? Essays on Poetry and American Culture* (St. Paul, 1992), 10.

2. Giola, *Can Poetry Matter?,* 1-6.

3. Bertolt Brecht, "A Worker Reads History," in *Selected Poems,* trans. H.R. Hays (New York, 1947), 109.

4. W.H. Auden, "Making, Knowing and Judging," *The Dyer's Hand and Other Essays* (New York, 1948), 50-51, describes the two approaches he uses in reading a poem: "The first is technical: here is a verbal contraption. 'How does it work?' The second is, in the broadest sense, moral: 'What kind of a guy inhabits this poem? What is his notion of the good life or the good place? What is his notion of the Evil One? What does he conceal from the reader? What does he conceal even from himself?'" Auden's second approach has most often been used in analyzing the poems in this chapter.

5. In selecting appropriate coal mining poems and poets I have been tremendously assisted by the encyclopedic range of knowledge and amazing generosity of the late poet, dramatist, and novelist Jim Wayne Miller. Also helpful were the following: Rita Quillen, "Modern and Contemporary Mountain Poetry," *Appalachian Journal* (fall 1985), 51-65; Karen Blomain, ed., *Coalseam: Poems from the Anthracite Region,* with a foreword by Frank MacShane (Scranton, 1993), 110-113; Peter Oresick and Nicholas Coles, ed., *Working Classics: Poems on Industrial Life* (Urbana, 1990) passim.

6. William Cullen Bryant, "A Meditation on Rhode Island Coal," *The Treasury of American Poetry,* ed. Nancy Sullivan (New York, 1978), 62-64.

7. Wallace, *St. Clair,* 233.

8. Ibid., 232; Samuel H. Daddow, *Trevaro and Other Occasional Poems* (Pottsville, Pa., 1853), 149.

9. Daddow, *Trevaro,* 110-111; 116-17.

10. Audre Lorde, "Coal," in *Norton Anthology of Literature by Women* (New York, 1985), 2250; Suzanne Matson, "Love in the Coal Mine," *Working Classics,* 160; Irene McKinney, "Six O'Clock Mine Report," *Six O'Clock Mine Report* (Pittsburgh, 1989), 13; Louis Untermeyer, "Caliban in the Coal Mines," *Modern American Poetry,* ed. Louis Untermeyer (New York, 1958), 373.

11. Jay Parini, "Working the Face," *Another Country* (New York, 1982), 18; Louise McNeil, "The Company," *Elderberry Flood* (Charleston, W.Va., 1979), 90; John Beecher, "Run of the Mine," *Collected Poems 1924-1974* (New York, 1974), 12; Mike Yarrow, "Laid Off Miner," *Appalachian Journal* (winter 1988), 165-66; Simon Head, "The New, Ruthless Economy," *The New York Review of Books* 43 (February 26, 1996), 47-52. Virtually all of these poets have devoted poems or portions of poems to the destructive impact that coal mining, above and below ground, has had upon the environment.

12. Robert Wrigley, "Diary of the Strike," *The Sinking of Clay City* (Port Townsend, Wash., 1979), 12, is one of the few poets or novelists to have written about the Herrin Massacre of June 22, 1922. Around the nation this killing of scab workers confirmed the old image of miners as brutes. Wrigley tries to describe the atmosphere of hatred and suffering brought to this mining community by the company's use of replacement workers. Jenny Lind Cawood, "Sundown Song—Harlan County," *Black Diamonds in the Sun* (Radford, Va., 1991), 40.

13. Billy Edd Wheeler, "Dreams of My Mountain Past and Present," *Songs of a Woods Colt* (New York, 1969), 83; Beecher, "Like Judas, Wasn't It?" *Collected Poems 1924-74,* 23-27; Patricia Shirley, "God Bless John L. Lewis," "Harmony," "Trust the Old Ways," and "The Devil Take John L Lewis," *Mary Pearl Kline* (Big Timber, Mont., 1990), 66-69, 68; Roy Lee Harmon, "John L. Lewis," *Unto the Hills* (Beckley, W.Va., 1957), 9; McNeill, "John L.," *Elderberry Flood,* 101.

14. Richard Hague, "Watching Bison at the State Preserve, Noble County, Ohio," *Ripening* (Columbus, Ohio, 1984), 12; Hague, "Sacks: A Folk Declension," *Mill Smoke Marrow* (Huron, Ohio, 1991), 28-29; Mary Joe Coleman, "Floyd Coleman, My Grandfather" and "Noah Totten," *Take One Blood Red Rose* (Cambridge, Mass., 1978), n.p.; George Ella Lyon, "Salvation," *Mountain* (Hartford, 1983), 18; Don Johnson, "Taking the Greyhound from Coaltown," *The Importance of Visible Scars* (Ocean Bluff, Mass., 1984), 13; Richard B. Patterson, "Black Lung Marriage," *Appalachian Heritage* (winter 1990), 63.

15. Lillie B. Chaffin, "Appalachian Deaths and Resurrections," *8th Day 13th Moon* (Pikeville, Ky., 1974), 3-4; Muriel Dressler, "What'll I Do," *Appalachia* (Charleston, W.Va., 1977), 31; Harvey Elliot, "Numbers," *Working Classics,* 70-71; Lee Pennington, "Dark Smell," in *Poems from the Hills,* ed. William Plumley (Charleston, W.Va., 1971), 57.

16. Shirley, "Depression," *Mary Pearl Kline,* 66; Louise McNeill, "Overheard

on a Bus," *Hill Daughter* (Pittsburgh, 1991), 94; Anthony Petrosky, "A Pennsylvania Family," *Working Classics,* 196-97; Ann Cobb, "The Commitment," *Appalachian Heritage* (winter 1978), 3; Jim Wayne Miller, "Ballad of Thomas Ratliff," *The More Things Change the More They Stay the Same* (Frankfort, Ky., 1971), n.p. Jim Wayne Miller argues in "Coal and Communism," *The More Things Change,* that just as those who oppose strip mining in present-day Kentucky are often branded as radicals, songwriter and midwife Aunt Molly Jackson confronted similar labels in the 1920s and 1930s while battling for union recognition:

> And the operators passed the word she was
> a "Rooshian Red."
> When she heard the charges, this is what
> she said:
> "No Rooshian ever put a notion in my head!
> I think of them starvin babies cryin,
> Their stomachs swelling, mortifying,
> I fed them warm bean soup and rocked by
> the light of a coal-oil lamp,
> I was fifty-two years old and past
> Before I ever heard of a Communist,
> I got my ideas livin all my life in the coal-
> mine camps.

17. Arline Thorne, "Mining the Seam," *Mining the Seam* (St. Albans, W.Va., 1992); James Ballowe, "C Remembers Grandparents," *The Coal Miners* (Peoria, Ill., 1979), 58; Kip Knott, "Inheriting Sunday Creek," *The Weight of Smoke* (Columbus, Ohio, 1991), 23-24; Anthony Petrosky, *Jurgis Petraskas* (Baton Rouge, 1983), 3.

18. Scotty Lee Hamilton, "Pappa's Home," *Appalachian Heritage* (spring 1977), 53; Mike Yarrow, "Laid Off Miner," *Appalachian Journal,* 164-65; Ernest Kroll, "Slate Fall," *Appalachian Journal* (autumn 1982), 41; Wheeler, "Cooger Long," *Songs of a Woods Colt,* 12-13.

19. Russell Marano, *Poems from a Mountain Ghetto* (Webster Springs, W.Va., 1979), passim.

20. Wheeler, *Songs of a Woods Colt,* 16-17; Barbara Smith, "Century #1, Portrait of a Coaltown," in *Old Wounds, New Words: Poems from the Appalachian Poetry Project,* ed. Bob Henry Baber, George Ella Lyon, and Gurney Norman (Ashland, Ky., 1994), 141; Joseph W. Caldwell, "Section Boss," *Sabbatical on Winifrede Hollow* (St. Albans, W.Va., 1993), 14; Stanley Plumly, "Porches," *In the Outer Dark* (Baton Rouge, 1970), 18.

21. "Red Caps" are miners still undergoing training.

22. P.J. Laska, "Lucille McDowell," "The Widow Horvath on Coal Run Then and Now," "Burley Belcher's Warning," "Ancestral," and "Extra Munction," *The Day the Eighties Began* (Bedford, N.H., 1991), 29, 30, 35, 36, 38-39; Laska, "The Coal Field Passage," "Red Dirt Afternoon," "Epitaph for a Coal Camp," and "The Coal

Poets," *Wages and Dreams* (Morgantown, W.Va., 1980), n.p.; Laska, "Song of Terry," *Mucked* (Williamson W.Va., 1978), n.p.; Laska, "Song of the Old Layland Mine," *Songs and Dances* (Prince, W.Va., 1977), 12-13.

23. All of the Don West poems are in *A Land of Plenty: A Don West Reader* (Los Angeles, 1982).

24. James B. Goode, *Up from the Mines* (Ashland, Ky., 1993), 14.

25. Ibid., 11-13.

26. The Goode poems are in either *Up from the Mines* or *Poets of Darkness* (Jackson, Miss., 1981), passim.

27. Frank MacShane, foreword to *Coalseam,* ed. Karen Blomain, 11.

28. Karen Blomain, introduction to *Coalseam,* 17.

29. The following appear in *Coalseam:* Thomas Kielty Blomain, "So the Coal Was Gone," 108-09; Karen Blomain, "Mango," "The Miner's Wife Leaves Home," and "The Dancers," 97-98, 85-86, 47-48; Bim Angst, "Sickness," 101-02; Vincent D. Balitas, "Paynes Patch," 35-43; Anthony Petrosky, "Father and Mother," 64-73.

30. Harry Humes, "My Mother at Evening," "The Photograph," "Robbing the Pillars," "At the Counting House of Buck Run Mine," and "Walking the Anthracite," *Coalseam,* 28-29, 87, 98-99, 50, 56.

31. Terrence Des Pres, *Praises & Dispraises* (New York, 1988), xiv-xv.

32. Kenneth Burke, *Attitudes towards History* (Los Altos, Calif., 1959), 53.

33. Wallace Stevens, *The Necessary Angel: Essays on Reality and the Imagination* (New York, 1951), 36.

34. Frantz Fanon, *Black Skin, White Masks* (New York, 1967), 140.

Chapter Seven: Voices from within the Mining Community

1. W.S. Applegate, "Tales from the Mines," *United Mine Workers Journal* (August 16, 1900), 3. (Journal cited hereafter as *UMWJ.*)

2. Dan Kelliher, "The Author's Fate," *UMWJ* (March 3, 1904), 6.

3. James F. Murphy, *The Proletarian Moment: The Controversy over Leftism in Literature* (Urbana, 1991), 108.

4. George Korson, *Coal Dust on the Fiddle: Songs and Stories of the Bituminous Industry* (Philadelphia, 1943), 20-21; Douglas Wixson, *Worker-Writer in America: Jack Conroy and the Tradition of Midwestern Literary Radicalism, 1889-1990* (Urbana, 1994), 36; Henry George Weiss, "Give Us Poems for Workers," *New Masses* 4 (July 1929), 22.

5. "A Poetical Labor Leader," *UMWJ* (June 9, 1904), 2.

6. Jim Wayne Miller, "Nostalgia for the Future," *The Kentucky Review* 8, no. 2 (summer 1988), 29-30.

7. Wixson, *Worker-Writer in America,* 37-38.

8. Cary Nelson, *Repression and Recovery: Modern American Poetry and the Politics of Cultural Memory 1910-1945* (Madison, 1989), 124.

9. In using contributors to *UMWJ, The Progressive Miner,* and *The Socialist Labor Star,* I have selected those who appear to be directly associated with the coal mining community—miners, family members, etc.—rather than outsiders with no

connection to the profession. Occasionally, I used an unsigned and unidentified contribution that reflects the outlook of mining people and is presumably written by someone closely associated with the industry. Neither scientific, systematic, nor foolproof, this method is an impressionistic attempt, to paraphrase George Orwell, to analyze voices from inside the whale. On a related matter, Wixson's claim in *Worker-Writers in America,* 38, that contributors to the *UMWJ* and other union publications were never able to bridge "the space between oral and written discourse" may well be true, but the traditional nature of the discourse in no way detracts from the intensity of the feelings expressed. A more serious problem is that most who contributed to these union publications were undoubtedly circumspect in their willingness to criticize the union or its leadership; even had they been willing to do so, it is unlikely that their contributions would have been accepted by the journal. As a result, the contributions examined in this chapter offer an interesting if impressionistic view of how those either within or closely associated with the mining community viewed their lives and work. The political honesty concerning the union and its leadership found in Marat Moore's splendid collection of oral interviews, *Women in the Mines: Stories of Life and Work* (Boston, 1996), is either lacking or filtered in the *UMWJ* poems I have used, though numerous other issues and concerns are not. Finally, from a slightly different perspective, Robert W. Weir suggests in *Beyond Labor's Veil: The Culture of the Knights of Labor* (University Park, Pa., 1996), 152-53, that the inclusion of poetry in nineteenth-century working-class journals "owes more to the need for the labor press to compete with the popular press than to artistic expressiveness." As in other chapters throughout the book, the message rather than the medium has been most closely scrutinized.

10. Virginia Barton Le Roy, "The Strike at Rushton," *UMWJ* (January 13, 1910), 8.

11. Unidentified Contributor, "In the Anthracite," *UMWJ* (September 11, 1902), 3; Tom James, "In West Virginia," *UMWJ* (January 9, 1902), 3; J.J. Sullivan, "Non Persona Grata," *UMWJ* (May 30, 1895), 6; Isaac Hanna, "The Company Store," *UMWJ* (May 23, 1895), 8; D.E. Griffith, "Nisi Dominus Trustra," *UMWJ* (September 18, 1902), 3; Unidentified Contributor, "The Progressive Miners of American Our Only Salvation," *The Progressive Miner* (December 23, 1932), 3; M.A. Skaggs, "Fifty Years and How," *UMWJ* (August 1, 1940), 21.

12. T.E. Ashman, "Agreed to Disagree," *UMWJ* (April 14, 1904), 7; D.E. Griffith, "The Hungry Mine Mule," *UMWJ* (November 12, 1908), 3; Oakely Revels, "A Coal Thief," *UMWJ* (February 1, 1943), 18; Betsy E. Summers, "A Funny Slice of Life," *United Mine Workers Journal: UMWA Members and Families Tell It to the World,* no. 9 (November 1991), 20-21. (Hereafter cited as *UWMJ: Tell It to the World.*)

13. Dall Lee, "The Audacious Coal Miner," *UMWJ* (December 1, 1944), 23; W.E. Motes, "Soldiers on the Home Front," *UMWJ* (December 15, 1943), 21; A Jasonville, Indiana, Miner, "That Little Lump of Coal," *The Progressive Miner* (September 30, 1932), 4.

14. A Fallen Brother, "The Blackleg's Lament," *UMWJ* (October 8, 1891), 3; Joe Shields, "In Memory of Two Fellow Workmen Killed at Jasonville, Ind.," *UMWJ* (December 15, 1927), 18.

15. John Brophy, *A Miner's Life* (Madison, 1964), 209, believed mining to be a hopeless profession primarily because of the lack of any regulations on its operation.

16. J. Alex Killingsworth, "Rockefeller Rule in Colorado," *UMWJ* (April 22, 1915), 10; A Retired Miner, "Open-Shop Employers' Creed," *UMWJ* (June 1, 1928), 15.

17. C.F. Quinn, "A Woman's Influence," *UMWJ* (July 22, 1915), 8; Daniel J. Mundy, "To Old Coal Miners," *UMWJ* (May 1, 1923), 17.

18. Unidentified Contributor, "Plea for Peace," *UMWJ* (October 30, 1902), 3; Fred Mooney, *Struggle in the Coal Fields: the Autobiography of Fred Mooney,* ed. J.W. Hess (Morgantown, 1967), 38; Unidentified Contributor, "Ellsworth, Pa.," *UMWJ* (March 3, 1904), 6.

19. Wm. R. Johns, "The Oppression at Colorado," *UMWJ* (July 28, 1904), 1; Eugene H. Robertson, "An Old Timers Experience," *UMWJ* (November 15, 1969), 15; Frank Westwood, "The Mine Workers Sought Day," *UMWJ* (April 1, 1937), 18; Armando Folio, "To Be Loyal to the Union," *UMWJ* (November 15, 1942), 22; E.M.B., "Cheer and Smile," *The Progressive Miner* (March 15, 1935), 2.

20. Mary E. Forbes, "What Does a Miner Read?" *UMWJ* (September 15, 1945), 23; Elizabeth A. Paulig, "Seen in W.Va.," *UMWJ* (November 15, 1945), 23; Breazeal Napier, "The Red-Blooded Union Man," *UMWJ* (September 15, 1946), 15.

21. David Corbin, *Life, Work, and Rebellion in the Coal Fields* (Urbana, 1981), 64, 75-76.

22. Ronald Lewis, *Black Coal Miners in America: Race, Class and Community Conflict* (Lexington, 1987), 101-139, 148-156; Lewis, "Coal Miners and the Social Equality Wedge in Alabama, 1880-1908," in *The United Mine Workers of America: A Model of Industrial Solidarity?* ed. John H.M. Laslett (University Park, Pa., 1996) 297-319; Joe William Trotter Jr., *Coal, Class and Color: Blacks in Southern West Virginia, 1915-32* (Urbana, 1990), 52-54, 102-29.

23. Stanley Kimmel, *The Kingdom of Smoke* (New York, 1932), 15.

24. "Huber Joe," "Of Mines and Men," *UMWJ* (December 1, 1954), 15.

25. W.E. Holland, "Safety First," *UMWJ* (April 16, 1914), 5; Raymond Leonard, "Safety First," *UMWJ* (July 1, 1952), 15. For an analysis of the safety concerns of miners during the hand-loading era see Keath Dix, *Work Relations in the Coal Industry: The Hand-Loading Era, 1880-1930* (Morgantown, 1977).

26. Ruby Lee Mitchell, "Coal Miner," *UMWJ* (July 15, 1953), 15; L.L. Jenkins, "The Miners," *UMWJ* (March 15, 1967), 23; Kenneth Linville, "Courage Within," *UMWJ* (May 1, 1952), 15.

27. Marsha Mast, "A Special Breed of Miner," *UMWJ: Tell It to the World,* 15; Funson Edwards, "Mining Folks," *UMWJ* (February 15, 1951), 15.

28. Raymond Leonard, "On the Run," *UMWJ* (August 1, 1955), 15; John Ermel, "Knocks," *UMWJ* (November 15, 1970), 22; Louis Nougaret, "The Other Shift," *UMWJ* (May 1, 1972), 31; John Maslyar, "A Miner's Day," *UMWJ* (January 15, 1965), 23.

29. Bob Fowler, "Safety Slips," *UMWJ* (August 15, 1953), 15; John Ermel, "A Coal Miner's Wake," *UMWJ* (February 15, 1972), 23; William J. Meyers, "The Little Dust Pump," *UMWJ: Tell It to the World,* 14; Violet Grisham, "Coal Miner's Daugh-

ter," *UMWJ* (February 15, 1972), 19; Anthony Guidon, "A Miner—Tough and Tender," *UMWJ* (June 1, 1948), 15

30. M.A. Thompson, "No Saint the Miner, but Every Inch a Man, *UMWJ* (January 1, 1946), 23; Olive Thomas, "To a Coal Miner," *UMWJ* (December 1, 1957), 23; Unidentified Contributor, "The Coal Miner—The Rare Breed," *UMWJ* (May 1978), 12.

31. Carol A.B. Giesen, *Coal Miners' Wives: Portraits of Endurance* (Lexington, Ky., 1995), 8-9.

32. Kathy Shutty, "Hoot Owl Blues," *UMWJ* (January 1-15, 1976), 17.

33. A Miner's Wife, "A Tale of Woe," *UMWJ* (March 18, 1897), 4; A member of Local Union 6132, Newfield, Pa., "The Old Days," *UMWJ* (May 1, 1958), 23.

34. Thomas Barrett, "Life of the Miner Man's Wife," *UMWJ* (August 1, 1940), 20; Francis Marley Bell, "At the Mine's Door," *UMWJ* (May 15, 1947), 23; For confirmation of these feelings, see Giesen, *Coal Miners' Wives,* 18.

35. Columbus Ratliff, "Remember?" *UMWJ* (January 15, 1955), 15; Dolly Shultz Young, "Chappie," *UWMJ: Tell It to the World,* 23; Brenda Sheets, "Daddy's Dinner Bucket," *United Mine Workers Journal: Rank-and-File Voices,* no 12 (December 1984), 18 (hereafter *Rank-and-File Voices*); Jane Colgan, "To L.A.M.," *UMWJ* (March 1, 1972), 27.

36. Giesen, *Coal Miners' Wives,* 89-112.

37. Frances Mizerak, "A Coal Miner," *UMWJ* (November 1, 1956), 23; Sandy Stiltner Coleman, "Coal Miner's Daughter," *UMWJ* (May 16-31, 1976), 21.

38. Unidentified Contributor, "An Old Timer," *UMWJ* (January 1, 1971), 31; Terri Lynne Brown, "Coal Miners Contract," *UMWJ* (May 1-15, 1974), 13; Ruby Thompson, "Children of the Mines," *UMWJ* (April 1, 1937), 19; Frances Mizerak, "A Coal Miner," *UMWJ* (November 1, 1956), 23; Jean Pettry, "Memories," *UMWJ* (July 1, 1965), 15.

39. For the ways in which mine tragedies have been described and commemorated in ballads, see James Taylor Adams, *Death in the Dark: A Collection of Factual Ballads of American Mine Disasters* (Big Laurel, Va., 1941).

40. Mrs. Freelin Dalton, "The Men of Consol No. 9," *UMWJ* (October 1, 1969), 23. A number of hidden variables may have tempered the responses of the bereaved, including fear of losing housing and burial payments or the pressure of having other loved ones still working for the company involved in the disaster.

41. John H. Richards, "Remember the Miner, Too," *UMWJ* (December 22, 1904), 5; Alex Reese, "Safety Last," *UMWJ* (May 1, 1963), 15; Tom Barrett, "My Union," *UMWJ* (August 1, 1940), 20; George R. Moore, "Black Damp Explosion," *UMWJ* (November 6, 1913), 2; James Sinnott, "The Monongah Disaster," *UMWJ* (January 9, 1908), 4.

42. Carrie Comper, "Why?" *UMWJ* (April 1, 1950), 15; Garland Vaiers, "Explosion on Cabin Creek," *UMWJ* (December 1, 1951), 15.

43. Ed Rantovich, "Town Towers," *UMWJ* (August 1, 1961), 15; T.J. Murphy, "Tribute to John L. Lewis and the Coal Miners," *UMWJ* (August 15, 1948), 15; K.C. Crist, "Miner's First Psalm," *UMWJ* (September 15, 1949), 15; Mary Blackburn,

"The Miner's Rights," *UMWJ* (February 1, 1959), 23; J.T. Jones, "The Miner," *UMWJ* (March 1, 1942), 19; Reba K. Hughes, "A Lump of Coal," *UMWJ* (March 1, 1960), 23; Raymond Leonard, "Coal Miner's Final Exams," *UMWJ* (September 15, 1950), 15; Mrs. James Fair, "A Miner's Fate," *UMWJ* (January 1, 1945), 18; Mrs. C.D. McDonald, "To the Brave," *UMWJ* (May 15, 1947), 23; The Golden Miner, "The Road to Number Three," *UMWJ* (May 30, 1901), 6; Bud Chapman, "A Miner's Goodbye," *UMWJ* (February 15, 1948), 15; John Ermel, "Pick Miner's Heaven," *UMWJ* (March 1, 1972), 27.

44. W.E. Jones, "The Old Miner," *UMWJ* (December 1, 1949), 15; John A. Poyle, "Our Beloved Pensioners," *Rank-and-File Voices,* 25. Whether it was because of the aftermath of turmoil in the union or the nature of his personality, Arnold Miller's presidency (1972-77) is one of the least praised by journal contributors.

45. Oscar Langford, "Mother Jones," *UMWJ* (July 17, 1902), 3; William R. Johns, "Mitchell Day," *UMWJ* (November 20, 1902), 7; By a Miner, "Captain John's Gun Boat," *The Progressive Miner* (May 12, 1933), 2. For an analysis of Lewis during these years, see chapters 19 and 20 of Dubofsky and Van Tine's *John L. Lewis.*

46. Hulan Belcher, "Mothers and Sons," *UMWJ* (April 1, 1943), 18; W.E. Motes, "Soldiers on the Home Front," *UMWJ* (December 15, 1943), 21; M.L. Martin, "Coal Went to War," *UMWJ* (December 1, 1945), 21.

47. "Tamp N. Barr," "Do You Remember?" *UMWJ* (August 15, 1949), 15; Edward Falkowski, "The Mine That Is Gone," *UMWJ* (December 15, 1948), 15; Rose Buckley, "Coal Miners," *UMWJ: Tell It to the World,* 16.

48. Marye "Dusty" Rhodes, "Faded Dream," *UMWJ* (July 1, 1962), 23; Len Shetline, "Coaltown," *UMWJ* (August 1, 1963), 23; Michael Whetstine, "Day after Day," *Rank-and-File Voices,* 14.

49. Ed Falkowski, "Anthracite Laurel," *UMWJ* (December 1, 1927), 16; Robert Klem, "The Layoff at Jonesville," *UMWJ* (March 1, 1956), 15; William B. Gamblin, "Does It Really Rain Acid?" *UMWJ: Tell it to the World,* 29.

50. Joseph W. Brown, "Me and Old Uncle Bill," *UMWJ* (May 1, 1957), 15; The Missouri Serpant [*sic*], "Beneath the Sod," *UMWJ* (January 22, 1903), 14; Francis Maloney, "All in a Day's Work," *UMWJ* (January 1, 1952), 15; J.L. Fitts, "The Lovers," *Socialist Labor Star* 3, no. 23 (November 6, 1914), 3; W.H.T., "Holly Grove," *Socialist Labor Star* 2, no. 29 (December 12, 1913), 1; Grace Shilling White, "The Coal Miner's Widow," *UMWJ* (February 15, 1955), 15.

51. Jock Wilson, *The Dark and the Damp* (New York, 1951), 219-220, 254-55; John Minnich Wilson, *Black Diamonds* (New York, 1947), 77.

52. Ed Falkowski, "Coal Town," *New Masses* (August 1928), 7; Falkowski, "A Miner's Good Morning," *New Masses* (July 1928), 17; Kimmel, *Kingdom of Smoke,* 69.

53. I.T. Krebs, "The Underground Slave," *UMWJ* (April 5, 1900), 7; D.R, an untitled poem, *UMWJ* (July 12, 1917), 6; C.W. Perry, "Don't Curse the Miner," *UMWJ* (January 1, 1931), 15; Carl Hill, "The Miner's Life," *UMWJ* (July 15, 1944), 23; Mrs. Paul Cheuvront, "In 30 and 40 and Now in the Coal Mines," *UMWJ* (April 15, 1972), 28.

54. C.J. Meade, "The Coal Miner," *UMWJ* (March 1, 1949), 15; Earl B. Ditmars,

"The Miner," *UMWJ* (July 1, 1949), 15; Steve Miller, "To the Coal Miner," *UMWJ* (July 1, 1960), 23.

55. Giesen, *Coal Miners' Wives,* 112.

56. E. Anthony Rotundo, *American Manhood: Transformations in Masculinity from the Revolution to the Modern Era* (New York, 1993), 10-30, 167-93, 227-32, 234-36, 268-69; Melissa Dabakis, "Douglas Tilden's Mechanics Fountain: Labor and the 'Crisis of Masculinity' in the 1890s," *American Quarterly* 47, no. 2 (June 1995), 204-230; Michael Kimmel, *Manhood in America* (New York, 1996), 261-328.

57. Kimmel, *Manhood in America,* 5.

58. M.A. Thompson, "No Saint the Miner, but Every Inch a Man," *UMWJ* (January 1, 1946), 23.

59. Scot, "The Miner's Lament," *UMWJ* (November 26, 1896), 8; Tom James, "In West Virginia," *UMWJ* (January 9, 1902), 3; Harry Rager, "The Coal Miner," *UMWJ* (February 15, 1944), 23.

60. M.K. Stokes, "One Dollar a Day," *UMWJ* (May 15, 1972), 27; Raymond H. Leonard, "To John L. Lewis," *UMWJ* (April 15, 1950), 15; James S. Boyle, "Sheppard at the Lever," *UMWJ* (February 26, 1903), 7; C.W. Thomas, "Ode to a Miner," *UMWJ* (October 15, 1945), 23; M.A. Thompson, "No Saint the Miner, but Every Inch a Man," *UMWJ* (January 1, 1946), 23. Although Meade Arble never considered a coal mining career, and his wife, Garda, detested virtually everything about living in a mining community, she firmly believed that her husband was a better man for having worked as a miner. Meade Arble, *Long Tunnel* (New York, 1976), 225.

61. D.E. Griffith, "The Old Miner's Complaint," *UMWJ* (September 2, 1909), 7; Dennis E. Prichett, "Old King Coal," *UMWJ* (January 1980), 4; Reba K. Hughes, "The Coal Miner," *UMWJ* (April 1, 1959), 23; Michael J. Smajda, "A Miner's Glory," *UMWJ* (January 15, 1972), 27.

62. Sandy Stiltner Coleman, "Coal Miner's Daughter," *UMWJ* (May 16-31, 1976), 21; Raymond Leonard, "Coal Train," *UMWJ* (September 1, 1951), 15; Claude Hunter, "Last Shift," *UMWJ* (January 1, 1953), 15; Dennis E. Prichett, "Old King Coal," *UMWJ* (January 1980), 4; L.L. Jenkins, "The Miners," *UMWJ* (March 15, 1967), 23.

63. Hulan Belcher, "Mothers and Sons," *UMWJ* (April 1, 1943), 18; Maude Kearney Browning, "The Miner's Son," *UMWJ* (December 1, 1943), 23; Funson Edwards, "Mining Folk," *UMWJ* (February 15, 1951), 15; Ted Verbitsky, "Shenandoah: Anthracite Mine Town," *UMWJ* (August 1, 1949), 15; Raymond Leonard, "Coal Miner Retired," *UMWJ* (September 15, 1943), 15; Eugene H. Robertson, "Old-Timer," *UMWJ* (May 1, 1961), 23; Walter Farmer Roop, "When We Retire," *UMWJ* (January 15, 1952), 15.

64. Barbara Angle, "Any Man: Kate's Story," *Rank-and-File Voices,* 7-11; Angle, *Rinker* (Washington, D.C., 1979); Angle, *Those That Mattered* (New York, 1994). Two novels by the miner/writers G.C. Jones, *Growing up Hard in Harlan County* (Lexington, Ky., 1985), and Jack B. Reese, *Grubbing the Bowels of the Earth,* verify the outlooks of various *UMWJ* contributors in this chapter but differ little. On the other hand, although the following offer interesting insights into the coal mining life, none

do so from the purely imaginative perspectives of the other works examined, and thus they are excluded from the discussion: Joseph Husband, *A Year in a Coal-Mine* (Boston, 1911); Fred Mooney, *Struggle in the Coal Fields: the Autobiography of Fred Mooney* (Morgantown, 1967); John Brophy, *A Miner's Life* (Madison, 1964); Jock Wilson, *The Dark and the Damp* (New York, 1951); Meade Arble, *The Long Tunnel;* Loretta Lynn with George Vecsey, *Loretta Lynn: A Miner's Daughter* (New York, 1976); Eric McKeever, *Tales of the Mine Country* (Ormond Beach, Fla., 1992); Wesley W. Phipps, *Coal Miner's Son* (South Charleston, W.Va., 1985); R. Glenn Ray, "Portal to Portal: My Experience Mining Coal in Ohio," *Appalachian Journal* (fall 1993), 24-49. The following are all sensitive oral histories of mining people but are not the creations of mining people themselves, and they are similarly excluded: George Vecsey, *One Sunset a Week: the Story of a Coal Miner* (New York, 1974); John Bodnar, *Anthracite People: Families, Unions and Work* (Harrisburg, 1983); Matt Witt, *In Our Blood* (New Market, Tenn., 1979); Walter L. Dinteman, *Anthracite Ghosts* (Scranton, 1995); Carol A.B. Giesen, *Coal Miners' Wives;* Marat Moore, *Women in the Mines;* Thomas Dublin, *When the Mines Closed: Stories of Struggles in Hard Times* (Ithaca, 1998).

65. Angle, *Rinker,* 15, 17.

66. Ibid., 23.

67. Ibid., 1.

68. Cowley, *Exile's Return,* 41-42.

69. Angle, *Rinker,* 46, 67, 74.

70. Angle, *Those That Mattered,* 222-223, 207. Many of the women interviewed by Marat Moore for *Women in the Mines* verify Portia's experiences.

71. Angle, *Those That Mattered,* 228, 297.

72. Angle, "Any Man: Kate's Story," 11; Angle, *Those That Mattered,* 306.

73. Angle, *Those That Mattered,* 142, 12, 59.

74. Ibid., 214, 289.

Conclusion

1. Paulo Freire, *Pedagogy of the Oppressed,* trans. Myra Bergman Ramos (New York, 1999), 90-91.

2. Tzvetan Todorov, *The Fantastic: A Structural Approach to a Literary Genre* (Ithaca, 1975), 24-40.

3. Harry Levin, *The Power of Blackness: Hawthorne, Poe, Melville* (New York, 1958), 3-35, 217-37.

4. Tom Engelhardt, *The End of Victory Culture: Cold War America and the Disillusioning of a Generation* (New York, 1995), 19, 155-171.

5. Roger Cunningham, "The View from the Castle: Reflections on the *Kentucky Cycle* Phenomenon," in *Confronting Appalachian Stereotypes: Back Talk from an American Region,* ed. Dwight B. Billings, Gurney Norman, and Katherine Ledford (Lexington, Ky., 1999), 300-312.

6. Julia Kristeva, *Strangers to Ourselves* (New York, 1991), 17-18.

7. Leon Fink, *In Search of the Working Class* (Chicago, 1994), 203.

8. Dorothy E. Smith, *The Everyday World as Problematic: A Feminist Sociology* (Boston, 1987), 112.

9. Spivak, "Can the Subaltern Speak?" in *Colonial Discourse and Post-Colonial Theory*, ed. Patrick Williams and Laura Chrisman (New York, 1994), 69.

10. Gary Saul Morson and Caryl Emerson, *Mikhail Bakhtin: Creation of a Prosaics* (Stanford, 1990), 427-28.

11. Robert N. Wilson, *The Writer as Social Seer* (Chapel Hill, 1979), 20.

12. Nelson, *Repression and Recovery*, 124-25.

13. Frantz Fanon, *Black Skin, White Masks: The Experiences of a Black Man in a White World* (New York, 1967), 232.

14. Howard Nemerov, *Figures of Thought: Speculations on the Meaning of Poetry and Other Essays* (Boston, 1978), 70.

15. Rose Buckley, "Coal Miners," *UMWJ: Tell it to the World*, 16.

16. Homer Hickam, *The Coalwood Way* (New York, 2000), 97.

Index